PERMISSIONLESS INNOVATION

Permissionless Innovation
The Continuing Case for Comprehensive Technological Freedom

Revised and Expanded Edition

BY ADAM THIERER

MERCATUS CENTER
George Mason University

Arlington, Virginia

ABOUT THE MERCATUS CENTER AT GEORGE MASON UNIVERSITY

The Mercatus Center at George Mason University is the world's premier university source for market-oriented ideas—bridging the gap between academic ideas and real-world problems.

A university-based research center, Mercatus advances knowledge about how markets work to improve people's lives by training graduate students, conducting research, and applying economics to offer solutions to society's most pressing problems.

Our mission is to generate knowledge and understanding of the institutions that affect the freedom to prosper and to find sustainable solutions that overcome the barriers preventing individuals from living free, prosperous, and peaceful lives.

Founded in 1980, the Mercatus Center is located on George Mason University's Arlington and Fairfax campuses.

Mercatus Center at George Mason University
3434 Washington Blvd., 4th Floor
Arlington, VA 22201
www.mercatus.org
703-993-4930

Cover and interior designs by Joanna Andreasson
Editing and typesetting by EEI Communications
Index by Connie Binder

Library of Congress Cataloging-in-Publication Data
Names: Thierer, Adam D., author.
Title: Permissionless innovation : the continuing case for comprehensive technological freedom / Adam Thierer.
Description: Revised and expanded edition. | Arlington, Virginia : Mercatus Center at George Mason University, [2016]
Identifiers: LCCN 2016009785 (print) | LCCN 2016011132 (ebook) | ISBN 9781942951247 (pbk.) | ISBN 9781942951254 (Kindle e-book)
Subjects: LCSH: Technology and state. | Research--Government policy. | Freedom of information. | Technology and law.
Classification: LCC T14 .T443 2016 (print) | LCC T14 (ebook) | DDC 338.9/26--dc23
LC record available at http://lccn.loc.gov/2016009785

CONTENTS

"Innovation Opportunity" Essays

"What matters is the successful striving for what at each moment seems unattainable. It is not the fruits of past success but the living in and for the future in which human intelligence proves itself."

—F. A. Hayek, *The Constitution of Liberty* (1960)

WHICH POLICY VISION WILL GOVERN THE FUTURE?

The central fault line in innovation policy debates today can be thought of as the "permission question."[1] The permission question asks, *Must the creators of new technologies seek the blessing of public officials before they develop and deploy their innovations?* How that question is answered depends on the disposition one adopts toward new inventions and risk-taking more generally.[2] Two conflicting attitudes are evident.

One disposition is known as the "precautionary principle." Generally speaking, it refers to the belief that new innovations should be curtailed or disallowed until their developers can prove that they will not cause any harm to individuals, groups, specific entities, cultural norms, or various existing laws, norms, or traditions.

The other vision can be labeled "permissionless innovation." It refers to the notion that experimentation with new technologies and business models should generally be permitted by default. Unless a compelling case can be made that a new invention will bring serious harm to society, innovation should be allowed to continue unabated and problems, if any develop, can be addressed later.

In this book, I will show how precautionary principle thinking is increasingly creeping into modern technology policy discussions, explain why that is dangerous and must be rejected, and argue that policymakers should instead unapologetically embrace and defend the permissionless innovation vision—not just for the Internet but also for all new classes of networked technologies and platforms.

My argument in favor of permissionless innovation can be summarized as follows:

- *If public policy is guided at every turn by fear of hypothetical worst-case scenarios and the precautionary mindset, then innovation becomes less likely.* Social learning and economic opportunities become far less likely under a policy regime guided by precautionary principle regulatory schemes. In practical terms this means fewer services, lower-quality goods, higher prices, diminished economic growth, and a decline in the overall standard of living. Put simply, living in constant fear of worst-case scenarios—and premising public policy on them—means that best-case scenarios will never come about. When public policy is shaped by precautionary principle reasoning, it poses a serious threat to technological progress, economic entrepreneurialism, social adaptation, and long-run prosperity.

- *Wisdom is born of experience, including experiences that involve risk and the possibility of occasional mistakes and failures.* Patience and a general openness to permissionless innovation represent the wise disposition toward new technologies not only because permissionless innovation provides breathing space for future entrepreneurialism and invention, but also because it provides an opportunity to see how societal attitudes toward new technologies evolve. As the old adage goes, "nothing ventured, nothing gained." More often than not, citizens have found ways to adapt to technological change by employing a variety of coping mechanisms, new norms, or creative fixes.

- *Not every wise ethical principle, social norm, or industry best practice automatically makes wise public policy prescriptions.* If we hope to preserve a free and open society, we must not convert every ethical directive or societal norm—no matter how sensible—into a legal directive. Attempting to do so means the scope of human freedom and innovation will shrink precipitously.

- **The best solutions to complex social problems are almost always organic and "bottom-up" in nature.** Education and empowerment, social pressure, societal norms, voluntary self-regulation, and targeted enforcement of existing legal norms (especially through the common law) are almost always superior to "top-down," command-and-control regulatory edicts and bureaucratic schemes of a "Mother, May I?" (i.e., permissioned) nature.

- For the preceding reasons, **when it comes to technology policy, permissionless innovation should, as a general rule, trump precautionary principle thinking.** To the maximum extent possible, the default position toward new forms of technological innovation should be "innovation allowed." The burden of proof rests on those who favor precautionary regulation to explain why ongoing experimentation with new ways of doing things should be prevented preemptively.

We are today witnessing the clash of these conflicting worldviews in a fairly vivid way in many current debates, not just about the Internet and information technology policy, but about other emerging technologies and developments.[3] "[E]ven as consumers move faster toward building digital lives," notes technology policy expert and consultant Larry Downes, "lawmakers are increasingly if spastically putting on the brakes, embracing pro-innovation policies only when it's convenient."[4]

Indeed, in many new sectors, policymakers are smothering technologies with precautionary controls that artificially limit life-enriching innovations. In recent years, for example, taxicab commissions across the nation have tried to stop Uber, Lyft, and other ride-sharing services from offering better transportation options to consumers.[5] Similarly, the state of New York has threatened the home rental company Airbnb, demanding data from all users who have rented out their apartments or homes in New York City.[6] In 2013, the Food and Drug Administration (FDA) ordered 23andMe to stop marketing health information in its at-home $99 genetic analysis kit and only allowed limited testing information to be accessible to consumers after it was allowed back on the market.[7]

But many other new innovations are also at risk. Federal and state officials are already exploring how to regulate the "Internet of Things,"[8] wearable devices, smart cars,[9] commercial drones,[10] Bitcoin,[11] 3-D printing,[12] robotics,[13] advanced medical devices,[14] and many other new technologies that have barely made it out of the cradle. This revised and expanded edition of *Permissionless Innovation* includes more detailed case studies about those "innovation opportunities." These new sectors and technologies, I argue, risk being endangered by precautionary principle thinking. By contrast, a liberal dose of permissionless innovation thinking can help spur the next great industrial revolution by unlocking amazing opportunities in these and other arenas, boosting long-term growth and prosperity in the process.

In extolling these innovation opportunities, I will argue that it is essential to allow them to evolve in a relatively unabated fashion. A few caveats are in order, however.

First, "permissionless innovation" is not an absolutist position that denies any role for government. Rather, it is an aspirational goal that stresses the benefit of pushing "innovation allowed" as the best default position to begin debates about technology policy. The burden of proof should be on those who favor preemptive, precautionary controls to explain why ongoing trial-and-error experimentation with new technologies or business models must be disallowed. There may indeed be times when a dose of precautionary policy is necessary, but a rigorous benefit-cost analysis must be conducted in each case to illustrate why the freedom to experiment and innovate should be curtailed.

Second, contrary to what some critics will claim, advocacy of permissionless innovation as the optimal policy default is not about

"protecting corporate profits" or assisting any particular technology, industry sector, or set of innovators. Rather, the push for permissionless innovation is premised on the belief that

- individuals as both citizens and consumers should continue to enjoy the myriad benefits that accompany an open
  information ecosystem and technological landscape;

- the general freedom to experiment with new and better
  ways of doing things is essential for powering the next
  great wave of industrial innovation and rejuvenating our
  dynamic, high-growth economy; and

- preserving social and economic freedom more generally
  should be preferred over the central-planning mentality
  and methods that throughout history have stifled human
  progress and prosperity.

Of course, even if I can convince you that this represents the
most sensible approach to crafting technology policy, nagging
questions remain about the risks associated with many new innovations. In his recent book on technological criticism, *A Dangerous
Master: How to Keep Technology from Slipping beyond Our Control*,
bioethicist Wendell Wallach insists, "The promoters of new technologies need to speak directly to the disquiet over the trajectory
of emerging fields of research. They should not ignore, avoid, or
superficially dampen criticism to protect scientific research."[15]

I take this charge seriously, as should others who herald the
benefits of permissionless innovation as the optimal default for
technology policy. We must be willing to take on the hard questions raised by critics and then also offer constructive strategies
for dealing with a world of turbulent technological change. I will
outline some of those practical solutions throughout this book, but
I should also note that much of what follows has been adapted and
condensed from my recent law review articles, filings to federal
agencies, editorials, and blog posts. Most of those essays are listed
in the appendix on page 135, and readers should consult them for
a fuller exploration of the issues discussed here.[16]

My colleagues and I at the Mercatus Center at George Mason University will continue to be active on these and other emerging technology policy issues where the clash between permissionless innovation and precautionary principle thinking is likely to be on display.[17]

ABOUT THE NEW EDITION

This expanded second edition of *Permissionless Innovation* includes a variety of changes as well as several all new sections. The bulk of the new sections are found in chapter III, which features an in-depth exploration of how the United States and Europe have taken starkly different approaches to innovation policy over the past two decades and explores what that has meant for digital innovation on both sides of the Atlantic. That section leads into a lengthy new discussion of "global innovation arbitrage," or the ways in which innovators are now able to move around the globe in search of more hospitable regulatory environments.

Importantly, that chapter also now includes a much deeper exploration of modern tech critics and their rationales for "permissioning" technological innovation. Chapter II also now includes a new section responding to the primary question I received in discussions of the previous edition: When, exactly, does it make sense to exercise some precaution and regulate technology preemptively?

Another new section, found in chapter V, explores concerns about the various economic disruptions associated with new technologies, including rising worries about the impact of robotics and automated systems on existing sectors or professions.

Finally, this edition includes an expanded section in chapter VI containing policy recommendations and expanded case studies of major technological innovations, including commercial drones, driverless cars, 3-D printing, virtual reality, the "Internet of Things," advanced medical technologies, and more. And the text includes a wide variety of other tweaks and improvements.

CHAPTER I
WHY PERMISSIONLESS INNOVATION MATTERS

A. FROM SCARCITY TO ABUNDANCE

Until just recently, humans lived in a state of extreme information poverty.[1] Our ancestors were starved for informational inputs and were largely at the mercy of the handful of information producers and distributors that existed in each era.[2]

The rise of the Internet and the modern information economy changed all that.[3]

We are now blessed to live in a world of unprecedented information abundance and diversity. We enjoy a wealth of ubiquitous, instantly accessible information and media in which we can access and consume whatever content we want, wherever, whenever, and however we want it. Better yet, we have access to communications networks and media platforms that give all men, women, and children the ability to be publishers and express themselves to the entire planet.

But we ain't seen nothin' yet. We stand on the cusp of the next great industrial revolution and developments that could vastly enhance the welfare of people across the planet. "Inventions previously seen only in science fiction, such as artificial intelligence, connected devices and 3D printing, will enable us to connect and invent in ways we never have before," notes a recent World

Economic Forum report on the amazing technological revolutions that could lie ahead.[4]

Yet those technological advancements will happen only if we preserve the fundamental value that has thus far powered the information age revolution: "permissionless innovation," which refers to the general freedom to experiment and learn through ongoing trial-and-error experimentation.[5] Just as permissionless innovation powered the Internet and the modern digital revolution, it can bring dynamism to the rest of the economy as well. There is no reason this ethos should be restricted to today's information sector.

Unfortunately, while many Internet pundits and advocates often extol the permissionless innovation model for the information sector, they ignore its applicability outside that context. That is unfortunate, but we can and should expand the horizons of permissionless innovation in the physical world, too. We need the same revolutionary approach to new technologies and sectors, whether based on bits (the information economy) or atoms (the industrial economy).

The various case studies outlined in this book will show how the need to seek regulatory permission can harm innovation in the physical world, not just the virtual one. The costs of this forgone innovation are high. Policymakers should not impose prophylactic restrictions on the use of new technologies without clear evidence of actual, not merely hypothesized, harm.[6] More often than not, humans adapt to new technologies and find creative ways to assimilate even the most disruptive innovations into their lives.

Certainly, complex challenges exist—e.g., concerns related to safety, security, privacy, economic disruption—as they always do with new inventions.[7] But there are good reasons to be bullish about the future and to believe that we will adapt to it over time. A world of permissionless innovation will make us healthier, happier, and more prosperous—if we let it.

B. WHAT IS PERMISSIONLESS INNOVATION?

Even though the many benefits associated with the rise of the commercial Internet and modern digital technologies are only roughly two decades old, we have already come to take these developments for granted. We expect new and more powerful computers, tablets, and smartphones every year. We expect better and faster broadband. We expect more online content, services, and networking platforms. And so on.

Amazingly, each year we get all this and more, most of which we could not have anticipated even a short time ago. Even as we enjoy this technological cornucopia we sometimes forget that, not that long ago, information scarcity and limited consumer choice were the norm. We should pause and ask ourselves, How is it that in the span of just a few decades we have witnessed the greatest explosion in information availability and human connectedness that the world has ever known?

The answer comes down to two words: permissionless innovation.

Vint Cerf, one of the fathers of the Internet, credits permissionless innovation for the economic benefits that the net has generated.[8] As an open platform, the Internet allows entrepreneurs to try new business models and offer new services without seeking the approval of regulators beforehand.

But permissionless innovation means much more than that. It refers to the tinkering and continuous exploration that takes place at multiple levels—from professional designers to amateur coders; from large content companies to dorm-room bloggers; from nationwide communications and broadband infrastructure providers to small community network-builders. *Permissionless innovation is about the creativity of the human mind to run wild in its inherent curiosity and inventiveness.* In other words, permissionless innovation is about freedom. Permissionless innovation, notes Larry Downes, "advances policies that encourage private experimentation and investment, such as exempting emerging technologies, whenever possible, from restrictions and taxes accreted over long periods of time to resolve forgotten problems generated by earlier innovations."[9]

Some scholars and policymakers speak of innovation policy as if it is simply a Goldilocks-like formula that entails tweaking various policy dials to get innovation *just right*.[10] In reality, what innovation policy comes down to is a question of values and attitudes.

Cultural attitudes, social norms, and political pronouncements profoundly influence opportunities for entrepreneurialism, innovation, and long-term growth.[11] For progress and prosperity to be possible, a sociopolitical system must respect what economic historian Deirdre McCloskey refers to as the "bourgeois virtues" that incentivize invention and propel an economy forward.[12] "A big change in the common opinion about markets and innovation," she has argued, "caused the Industrial Revolution, and then the modern world. . . . The result was modern economic growth."[13] That was true for the Industrial Revolution as well as the information revolution. And it will be just as true for the next great technological revolution—again, if we let it.[14]

There are limits to how much policymakers can influence these cultural attitudes and values, of course. Nonetheless, to the extent they hope to foster the positive factors that give rise to expanded entrepreneurial opportunities, policymakers should appreciate how growth-oriented innovation policy begins with a specific disposition toward technological change.[15] As the economic historian Joel Mokyr notes, "[T]echnological progress requires above all tolerance toward the unfamiliar and the eccentric."[16]

For innovation and growth to blossom, entrepreneurs need a clear green light from policymakers that signals a general acceptance of risk-taking—especially risk-taking that challenges existing business models and traditional ways of doing things.[17] That's permissionless innovation in a nutshell, and if there was one thing policymakers could do to help advance long-term economic growth, it is to first commit themselves to advancing this ethic and making it the lodestar for all their future policy pronouncements and decisions.[18]

And they will have to constantly nurture this policy environment because, as Mokyr concludes, technological innovation and economic progress must be viewed as "a fragile and vulnerable plant, whose flourishing is not only dependent on the appropriate surroundings and climate, but whose life is almost always short. It is highly sensitive to the social and economic environment and can easily be arrested by relatively small external changes."[19]

INNOVATION OPPORTUNITY: "Big Data" and the Data-Driven Economy

Kenneth Cukier and Viktor Mayer-Schönberger, authors of *Big Data: A Revolution That Will Transform How We Live, Work, and Think*, define big data as "the vast quantity of information now available thanks to the Internet, and which can be manipulated in ways never before possible."[20]

Many of the information services and digital technologies that we already enjoy and take for granted today came about not necessarily because of some initial grand design, but rather through innovative thinking after the fact about how preexisting data sets might be used in interesting new ways.[21] That's the power of big data.

Data collection and data sets are used to tailor new and better digital services to us and also to target ads to our interests, which helps keep online content and service cheap or free.[22] Data-driven innovations are all around in services such as language translation tools, mobile traffic services, digital mapping technologies, spam and fraud detection tools, instant spell-checkers, and more. The economic benefits associated with data-driven innovation are profound[23] but can be hard to measure and are likely being underestimated as a result.[24]

The White House and the Federal Trade Commission (FTC) have acknowledged these realities.[25] "The growth in mobile and social networking services in particular is striking, and is funded, in part, by the growth of targeted advertising that relies on use of consumer data," notes the FTC.[26] This growth is equally true for the "app economy," which relies heavily on data collection and advertising.[27] The sharing economy also depends on data collection.[28] But big data also powers many other life-enriching, even life-saving, services and applications.[29]

Of course, "big data" raises a variety of big privacy and security concerns, leading to calls for new regulations. Various privacy advocates have pushed these efforts, fearing that, without new rules, we will forever lose control of our data or, worse yet, be subjected to new forms of economic or social discrimination. Although there are serious privacy-related harms associated with personal-data collection and use, they are mostly confined to health and financial information, which are far more sensitive in nature. However, we already have privacy rules covering those classes of information.

But if new laws or regulations preemptively curtail data collection based on such fears, innovative services, devices, and applications might be lost in the future. There are great benefits associated with data-driven innovation and lawmakers should be careful when seeking to curtail commercial data collection and use or else they could kill the goose that lays the Internet's golden eggs.[30] New data restrictions could raise direct costs for consumers, discourage new marketplace competition, and undermine America's global competitive advantage in this space.[31]

The harms that are sometimes alleged about commercial data collection and use are almost never substantiated.[32] No one is being excluded from the information economy or denied new services because of these practices. To the contrary, data collection means all consumers enjoy a fuller range of goods and services, usually at a very low price. Finally, the critics often also ignore the extent to which people adapt to new information technologies and practices over time.

The better way to deal with concerns about big data is through stepped-up consumer education efforts to teach children and adults alike to think critically about their online interactions and how to safeguard information. Companies and organizations should also be encouraged to improve data stewardship, engage in "privacy by design" and "security by design" (see chapter VI), and keep their users better informed about their data practices.

But heavy-handed regulatory approaches to data collection and use will likely derail the many benefits a data-driven economy brings us.

C. HOW PERMISSIONLESS INNOVATION POWERED THE INFORMATION REVOLUTION

Although permissionless innovation fueled the success of the Internet and much of the modern tech economy in recent years, before the early 1990s, commercial use of the Internet was prohibited. A 1982 Massachusetts Institute of Technology (MIT) handbook for the use of ARPAnet, the progenitor of what would become the Internet, warned students:

> It is considered illegal to use the ARPAnet for anything which is not in direct support of government business. . . . Sending electronic mail over the ARPAnet for commercial profit or political purposes is both anti-social and illegal.

> By sending such messages, you can offend many people, and it is possible to get MIT in serious trouble with the government agencies which manage the ARPAnet.[33]

During the time when the Internet remained a noncommercial platform, it served mostly as a closed communications club reserved for academics, a handful of technologists and engineers, and assorted government bureaucrats. Undoubtedly, the restrictions on commercial use of the Internet were thought to have served the best of intentions. But public policies should never be judged by intentions but rather by their actual real-world results.[34] In this case, those who imposed restrictions on commercial use of the Internet probably were simply unable to imagine the enormous benefits that would be generated by allowing it to become an open platform for social and commercial innovation.

Regardless, the opportunity costs of those prohibitions were enormous. "Opportunity cost" refers to the forgone benefits associated with any choice or action.[35] When we think about technological innovation, it is vital to keep the concept of opportunity cost in mind. Every action—especially political and regulatory action—has consequences. The 19th-century French economic philosopher Frédéric Bastiat explained the importance of considering the many unforeseen, second-order effects of economic change and policy.[36] Many pundits and policy analysts pay attention to only the first-order effects—what Bastiat called "the seen"—and ignore the subsequent and often "unseen" effects.

When commercial uses of an important resource or technology are arbitrarily prohibited or curtailed, the opportunity costs of such exclusion may not always be immediately evident. Nonetheless, those unseen effects are very real and have profound consequences for individuals, the economy, and society.

In the case of the Internet, a huge opportunity cost was associated with the initial limitations on its use and its commercial development. Only when this mistake was corrected in the early 1990s through the commercial opening of the net did the true opportunity costs of the original restrictions become evident.

As soon as the net was commercialized, social and economic activity online exploded in previously unimaginable ways. New innovations like email, listservs, and web browsers quickly gained widespread adoption. Websites—personal, corporate, and otherwise—multiplied rapidly. E-commerce took off. Sophisticated search engines emerged. And then blogs, social networks, smartphones, tablets, mobile applications, and various other digital devices and services developed so rapidly that it became hard to keep track of them all.[37]

These innovations were able to flourish because our default position for the digital economy was "innovation allowed" or permissionless innovation. No one had to ask anyone for the right to develop these new technologies and platforms.

This explosion of innovation did not happen by accident. Policy attitudes fostered these developments. Specifically, beginning in the early 1990s, a bipartisan group of policymakers gave innovators the green light to let their minds run wild and experiment with an endless array of exciting new devices and services. US policymakers signaled that permissionless innovation would be the norm for the Internet and digital technology in America through a series of decisions and policy statements.

In the mid-1990s, the Clinton administration decided to allow open commercialization of what was previously just the domain of government agencies and university researchers.[38] Shortly thereafter, Congress passed and President Bill Clinton signed the Telecommunications Act of 1996, which notably avoided regulating the Internet like analog-era communications and media technologies.

Importantly, the Telecom Act included an obscure provision known as "Section 230," which immunized online intermediaries from onerous liability for the content and communications that traveled over their networks. The immunities granted by Section 230 let online speech and commerce flow freely, without the constant threat of legal action or onerous liability looming overhead for digital platforms.[39] Today's vibrant Internet ecosystem likely would not exist without Section 230.[40] Another important legislative development occurred in 1998, when Congress enacted the Internet Tax Freedom Act, which blocked all levels of government in the United States from imposing discriminatory taxes on the Internet.

An equally important policy development took place in 1997, when the Clinton administration released *The Framework for Global Electronic Commerce*. The *Framework* outlined the US government's approach toward the Internet and the emerging digital economy.[41] The *Framework* was a succinct and bold market-oriented vision for cyberspace governance that recommended reliance on civil society, contractual negotiations, voluntary agreements, and ongoing marketplace experiments to solve information-age problems.[42] Specifically, it said that "the private sector should lead [and] the Internet should develop as a market driven arena not a regulated industry."[43] "[G]overnments should encourage industry self-regulation and private sector leadership where possible" and "avoid undue restrictions on electronic commerce."[44] The document added that "parties should be able to enter into legitimate agreements to buy and sell products and services across the Internet with minimal government involvement or intervention."[45] "Where governmental involvement is needed, its aim should be to support and enforce a predictable, minimalist, consistent and simple legal environment for commerce."[46]

The permissionless innovation policy disposition that was enshrined in *The Framework for Global Electronic Commerce* let a rising generation of creative minds freely explore this new frontier for commerce and communications.[47] As Federal Trade Commission Commissioner Maureen K. Ohlhausen has observed, "[T]he success of the Internet has in large part been driven by the freedom to experiment with different business models, the best of which have survived and thrived, even in the face of initial unfamiliarity and unease about the impact on consumers and competitors."[48] It is proof positive that policy attitudes toward change and progress matter deeply and can have a profound influence on an economy's innovative potential.

D. TOWARD THE NEXT GREAT TECHNOLOGICAL REVOLUTION

But the story of permissionless innovation isn't over, nor is the Internet the only or last great platform for commercial and social innovation.

We stand on the cusp of the next great technological revolution.[49] Many of the underlying drivers of the digital revolution—massive increases in processing power, exploding storage capacity, steady miniaturization of computing, ubiquitous communications and networking capabilities, the digitization of all data, and more—are beginning to have a profound impact beyond the confines of cyberspace.[50] As venture capitalist Marc Andreessen explained in a widely read 2011 essay about how "software is eating the world":

> More and more major businesses and industries are being run on software and delivered as online services—from movies to agriculture to national defense. Many of the winners are Silicon Valley–style entrepreneurial technology companies that are invading and overturning established industry structures. Over the next 10 years, I expect many more industries to be disrupted by software, with new world-beating Silicon Valley companies doing the disruption in more cases than not.
>
> Why is this happening now? Six decades into the computer revolution, four decades since the invention of the microprocessor, and two decades into the rise of the modern Internet, all of the technology required to transform industries through software finally works and can be widely delivered at global scale.[51]

What this means is that "meatspace"—the world of atoms and physical things—is primed for the same sort of revolution that the world of bits—the information economy—has undergone over the past two decades. The world of kinetic, ambient, automated computing and networking that has made our digital products and virtual services better, faster, and more ubiquitous is now ready to spread to the physical world.[52] "The past ten years have been about discovering new ways to create, invent, and work together on the Web," noted Chris Anderson in his 2012 book *Makers*. "The next ten years will be about applying those lessons to the real world."[53]

In other words, we are witnessing what Internet innovator Sam Altman, president of Y Combinator, calls the "softwarization of hardware," which he describes as

> an age in which new products—actual, physical electronics products—will go from idea to store shelves in a matter of months. A future in which warehouses and distribution centers cease to exist, because factories produce finished goods from raw materials on demand, and they never stop moving through the supply chain. Only it turns out all of this is possible today. The "hardware renaissance" that began in Silicon Valley in just the last five years, born of rapid prototyping technologies, has become something much larger and more important. It has been a sea change in every stage of producing physical objects, from idea to manufacturing to selling at retail.[54]

When all of our everyday technologies have embedded microchips, sensors, and antennas, the promise of an "always-on" and fully customizable world will truly be upon us. Of course, it is easy to see why this "Internet of Things" or world of "machine-to-machine communications" might spook some people. But these developments will also lead to rapid advances in robotics, autonomous systems, artificial intelligence, and additive manufacturing.

INNOVATION OPPORTUNITY: The "Internet of Things"

The so-called Internet of Things (IoT) is emerging and it promises to usher in profound changes that will rival the first wave of Internet innovation.[55] The IoT, also called the "Internet of Everything,"[56] is sometimes viewed as being synonymous with "smart" systems, such as "smart homes," "smart buildings," "smart health," "smart grids," "smart mobility," and so on.[57] As microchips and sensors are increasingly embedded into almost all "smart devices" we own and come into contact with, a truly "seamless web" of connectivity will finally exist.[58]

The promise of the IoT, as described by *New York Times* reporter Steve Lohr, is that "billions of digital devices, from smartphones to sensors in homes, cars and machines of all kinds, will communicate with each other to automate tasks and make life better."[59] According to various projections, an estimated 35 to 40 billion networked devices will be in use by 2019.[60]

The benefits associated with these developments will be enormous. McKinsey Global Institute estimates a total potential economic impact of $3.9 trillion to $11.1 trillion a year by 2025,[61] and the consultancy IDC estimates that this market will grow at a compound annual growth rate of 7.9 percent between now and 2020, to reach $8.9 trillion.[62] Cisco analysts estimate that the IoT will create $14.4 trillion in net profit between 2013 and 2022, which amounts to an increase in global corporate profits by roughly 21 percent.[63] The biggest impacts will be in health care, energy, transportation, and retail services.

Of course, as with every major technological revolution, these advances will be hugely disruptive—for both the economy and social norms. Safety, security, and privacy concerns have already been raised,[64] and the Federal Trade Commission has already conducted a workshop investigating the privacy and security implications of the IoT and issued a major report recommending a variety of privacy and security "best practices" for the IoT.[65] Some critics are already forecasting the equivalent of a privacy apocalypse with the rise of these technologies and have called for preemptive controls.[66]

If policymakers want to foster the growth of the IoT and get this next technological revolution off to a fast start, they will need to resist the temptation to base policy on worst-case thinking about these technologies.[67] Instead, they should embrace permissionless innovation, just as they did before for the Internet itself.[68]

Constructive solutions exist to the privacy and security concerns about IoT technologies.[69] Common-law remedies including privacy torts and existing targeted rules (such as "Peeping Tom" laws) can address privacy and security harms as they develop. When safety issues arise, a massive body of federal health and safety rules already exists to address them, and lawsuits are likely to fly at the first sign of any product defects. The FTC will also continue to police "unfair and deceptive" practices. The agency has already been very active in overseeing tech companies and holding them to the privacy and security promises they make to their consumers. The FTC and other policymakers have also sensibly recommended better privacy and security "by design" efforts for the IoT, although those best practices should not be mandated.

More privacy-enhancing tools—especially robust encryption technologies—can also help secure IoT devices, and government officials would be wise to promote these tools instead of restricting them. Finally, governments and other organizations can also help educate the public about the potential dangers of new IoT technologies, including potentially inappropriate uses.

But policymakers should avoid mandating these things in a top-down, heavy-handed fashion. A patient "wait-and-see" approach is the prudent policy disposition toward the Internet of Things if we hope to realize its maximum potential.

As is noted throughout this book, our first reaction to highly disruptive new innovations such as these is often one of fear and trepidation. We assume the worst for a variety of reasons, and there are many reasons that pessimism and worst-case scenarios often dominate discussions about new technologies and business practices.

It is therefore unsurprising that today's unfolding world of ambient computing, ubiquitous sensors, robots, private drones, and intelligent devices is conjuring dystopian sci-fi scenarios of the machines taking over our lives and economy. Equally fear-inducing are the concerns about those technologies related to safety, security, and especially privacy. As will be discussed in more detail in the next chapter, those fears already animate countless books and articles being published today. But this is where the permission question comes into play for all these emerging technologies. "The remaining question," notes my Mercatus Center colleague Eli Dourado, "is whether we will welcome them or try to smother them with regulations and arguments over the transitional gains. The best way to ensure a more prosperous future is to eagerly embrace and support the new technologies. . . . But they may be coming whether we want them or not, so we need to start thinking about how we'll assimilate them into our lives."[70]

Consider the field of medicine and the potential for digital technology to help revolutionize the medical profession, thus improving patient care. Unfortunately, America's healthcare sector is already so heavily regulated that many leading technology companies and investors shy away from investing in new innovations in this space.[71] In particular, the FDA's complex and costly review process for new drugs and devices makes it extremely difficult for new innovators to get their life-enriching medical services to market quickly.[72] "Due to 'regulatory uncertainty' . . . [and] the complete and utter capriciousness and unpredictability in the FDA review process of new medical products," notes Dr. Joseph V. Gulfo, "venture capitalists are becoming less inclined to fund very early stage companies."[73]

Indeed, leading venture capitalists avoid investments in advanced medical technology companies because of the costs associated with years of delay and potential long-run disapproval. "If it says 'FDA approval needed' in the business plan, I myself scream in fear and run away," says Tim Chang, managing director at Mayfield Fund, a venture capital firm. Chang has never backed a company that needed to go through the FDA's review process.[74] Even major tech companies like Google, which could potentially absorb the significant costs associated with FDA review, still don't want any part of it. "Generally, health is just so heavily regulated. It's just a painful business to be in," says Sergey Brin, one of Google's founders. "I think the regulatory burden in the U.S. is so high that . . . it would dissuade a lot of entrepreneurs."[75]

If the FDA's highly precautionary approach to innovative opportunities doesn't adapt to accommodate new marketplace realities, American citizens will lose access to many life-enriching and even life-saving drugs and devices. It's another reason why the fight for permissionless innovation is so essential.

Of course, we cannot accurately predict how all these new technologies will be used in the future.[76] Nor can we forecast the chances that any particular innovation will even pan out.[77] Nevertheless, our experience with the Internet and modern information technology should give us hope that—if innovation and entrepreneurship are allowed to proceed without regulators placing heavy-handed precautionary hurdles in the way—the many new technologies discussed throughout this book will have the chance to usher in amazing, life-enriching changes. For that reason, as *Wall Street Journal* columnist L. Gordon Crovitz has argued, "the freedom to innovate without asking permission should become the rule for all US industries, not the rare exception."[78]

CHAPTER II
SAVING PROGRESS FROM THE TECHNOCRATS

A. THOSE WHO FEAR THE FUTURE

Not everyone embraces permissionless innovation. Instead, many critics adopt a mindset that views the future as something that is to be feared, avoided, or at least carefully planned. This is known as the "stasis mentality" and it is, at its root, what motivates precautionary principle–based thinking and policymaking.

In her 1998 book, *The Future and Its Enemies*, Virginia Postrel contrasted the conflicting worldviews of "dynamism" and "stasis" and showed how the tensions between these two visions would affect the course of future human progress.[1] Postrel made the case for embracing dynamism—"a world of constant creation, discovery, and competition"—over the "regulated, engineered world" of the stasis mentality. She argued that we should "see technology as an expression of human creativity and the future as inviting" while also rejecting the idea "that progress requires a central blueprint." Dynamism sees progress as "a decentralized, evolutionary process" in which mistakes aren't viewed as permanent disasters but instead as "the correctable by-products of experimentation."[2] In sum, they are learning experiences.

Postrel notes that our dynamic modern world and the amazing technologies that drive it have united diverse forces in opposition to its continued, unfettered evolution:

[It] has united two types of stasists who would have
once been bitter enemies: reactionaries, whose central
value is stability, and technocrats, whose central value is
control. Reactionaries seek to reverse change, restoring
the literal or imagined past and holding it in place. . . .
Technocrats, for their part, promise to manage change,
centrally directing "progress" according to a predictable
plan. . . . They do not celebrate the primitive or traditional. Rather, they worry about the government's inability to control dynamism.[3]

Although there are differences at the margin, reactionaries (who
tend to be more politically and socially "conservative") and technocrats (who tend to identify as politically "progressive") are united
by their desire for greater control over the pace and shape of technological innovation. They both hope enlightened and wise public
officials can set us on a supposedly "better path," or return us to an
old path from which we have drifted.

Robert D. Atkinson presented another useful way of looking at this
divide in his 2004 book, *The Past and Future of America's Economy*:

This conflict between stability and progress, security and
prosperity, dynamism and stasis, has led to the creation
of a major political fault line in American politics. On
one side are those who welcome the future and look at
the New Economy as largely positive. On the other are
those who resist change and see only the risks of new
technologies and the New Economy. As a result, a political divide is emerging between *preservationists* who want
to hold onto the past and *modernizers* who recognize that
new times require new means.[4]

Similarly, Robert Graboyes, a colleague of mine at the Mercatus
Center, has framed debates over healthcare innovation in terms of a
clash between "fortress" versus "frontier" mindsets.[5] "The Fortress
is an institutional environment that aims to obviate risk and protect

established producers (insiders) against competition from newcomers (outsiders). The Frontier, in contrast, tolerates risk and allows outsiders to compete against established insiders," he writes.[6]

Like Postrel's "stasis versus dynamism" paradigm, both Atkinson's "preservationists versus modernizers" dichotomy and Graboyes's "fortress versus frontier" divide correctly identify the fundamental pessimism and conservatism that lies at the heart of the stasis mentality.[7] The best explanation for this risk-averse attitude is probably psychological. "We are a conservative species," notes Scott Berkun, author of *The Myths of Innovation*. "Conformity is deep in our biology."[8] This is what psychologists and economists refer to as "loss aversion," or the tendency for us to want to hold on to what we've already got instead of taking a risk on the unknown.

Permissionless innovation is undesirable to the stasis-minded because they do not believe we can preserve some of the things that have been regarded as making previous eras or generations great, such as a specific form of culture, a particular set of institutions or business models, or other norms or values. These critics lament the way modern progress is unfolding because many new technologies are so fundamentally disruptive and are quickly dislodging old standards and institutions.[9] For them, that which is familiar is more comforting than that which is unknown or uncertain.[10] That's the security blanket that the stasis or preservationist mentality provides: the certainty that *un*certainty should be discouraged or even disallowed.

Moreover, as Postrel also noted, concerns from both reactionaries and technocrats about "a future that is dynamic and inherently unstable" and that is full of "complex messiness"[11] will lead them to frequently employ fear tactics when debating new technologies and developments.[12] Indeed, both groups will "claim fear as an ally: fear of change, fear of the unknown, fear of comfortable routines thrown into confusion," Postrel says. "They promise to make the world safe and predictable, if only we will trust them to design the future, if only they can impose their uniform plans."[13] They want to replace this messiness and uncertainty "with the reassurance that some authority will make everything turn out right."[14]

Employing such fear tactics and a heavy dose of worst-case thinking, reactionaries will say we need to control innovation for the sake of order, security, tradition, institutions, and so on.[15] Technocrats will insist that greater control is needed in the name of justice, equality, privacy, and other assorted values. But the ends matter less than the means: increased control over the course of future developments is the glue that binds both worldviews together in opposition to permissionless innovation. What both groups share in common is how they seek to gain control over the future course of technological development. Their answer is the "precautionary principle" and it is the antithesis of permissionless innovation.

INNOVATION POLICY: THE CONFLICT OF VISIONS

PRECAUTIONARY PRINCIPLE	PERMISSIONLESS INNOVATION
"Stasis"	"Dynamism"
"Preservationists"	"Modernizers"
"Fortress"	"Frontier"
Progress should be carefully guided	Progress should free-wheeling
Fear of risk and uncertainty	Embrace of risk and uncertainty
Stability/safety first	Spontaneity first
Equilibrium	Experimentation
Centralized control	Decentralized control
Wisdom through better planning	Wisdom through trial and error
Anticipation and regulation	Adaptation and resiliency
Ex ante (preemptive) solutions	Ex post (responsive) solutions
"Better safe than sorry"	"Nothing ventured, nothing gained"

B. THE TECHNOCRAT'S TOOL: THE PRECAUTIONARY PRINCIPLE

Ironically, it is failure that makes permissionless innovation such a powerful driver of positive change and prosperity.[16] Many social and economic experiments fail in various ways. Likewise, many new technologies fail miserably. *That is a good thing.* We learn how to do things better—both more efficiently and more safely—by making mistakes and dealing with adversity. Challenges and failures also help individuals and organizations learn to cope with change and devise systems and solutions to accommodate technological disruptions.[17]

There's nothing sacrosanct or magical about technology, of course. Technology and technological processes are not an end but the means to achieve many different ends. Just as there is no one best way for a government to plan a society or economy, there is no one best way for humans to apply technology to a specific task or set of problems. What makes permissionless innovation so important is that this ongoing process of experimentation and failure helps bring us closer to ideal states and outcomes (more wealth, better health, etc.).

But we will never discover better ways of doing things unless the process of evolutionary, experimental change is allowed to continue. We need to keep trying and even *failing* in order to learn how we can move forward.[18] As playwright Samuel Beckett once counseled: "Ever tried. Ever failed. No matter. Try again. Fail again. Fail better."[19] Perhaps the clearest historical example of the logic of "failing better" comes from Thomas Edison, who once famously noted of his 10,000 failed lightbulb experiments, "I have not failed 10,000 times. I have not failed once. I have succeeded in proving that those 10,000 ways will not work. When I have eliminated the ways that will not work, I will find the way that will work."[20]

The value of failing better and learning from it was the core lesson stressed by the late political scientist Aaron Wildavsky in his life's work, especially his 1988 book, *Searching for Safety*. Wildavsky warned of the dangers of "trial *without* error" reasoning and contrasted it with the trial-and-error method of evaluating risk and seeking wise solutions to it. Wildavsky argued that real wisdom is born of experience and that we can learn how to be wealthier and healthier as individuals and a society only by first being willing to embrace uncertainty and even occasional failure:

The direct implication of trial without error is obvious: If you can do nothing without knowing first how it will turn out, you cannot do anything at all. An indirect implication of trial without error is that if trying new things is made more costly, there will be fewer departures from past practice; this very lack of change may itself be dangerous in forgoing chances to reduce existing hazards. . . . Existing hazards will continue to cause harm if we fail to reduce them by taking advantage of the opportunity to benefit from repeated trials.[21]

When this logic takes the form of public policy prescriptions, it is referred to as the "precautionary principle."[22] The precautionary principle generally holds that, because new ideas or technologies could pose some theoretical danger or risk in the future, public policies should control or limit the development of such innovations until their creators can prove that they won't cause any harms.[23] Advocates of the precautionary principle believe policymakers should regulate new technology "early and often" to "get ahead of it" by addressing social and economic concerns preemptively.[24] Stated differently, the precautionary principle holds that risk-taking innovators and their creations are "guilty until proven innocent"[25] and that it is "better to be safe than sorry" by regulating innovations before they are allowed into the wild.[26]

The problem with letting such precautionary thinking guide policy is that it poses a serious threat to technological progress, economic entrepreneurialism, social adaptation, and long-run prosperity.[27] If public policy is guided at every turn by the precautionary principle, technological innovation is impossible because of fear of the unknown;[28] hypothetical worst-case scenarios trump all other considerations.[29] But we lose something important when we regulate against imaginary problems.[30] Social learning and economic opportunities become far less likely, perhaps even impossible, under such a regime.[31] In practical terms, the precautionary principle results in fewer services, lower-quality goods, higher prices, diminished economic growth, and a decline in the overall standard of living.[32]

This is why, to the maximum extent possible, the default position toward technological experimentation should be "innovation allowed," or permissionless innovation.[33] If we hope to prosper both as individuals and as a society, we must defend the general freedom to experiment and learn through trial and error, and even to fail frequently while doing so.[34]

As will be noted in more detail below, preemptive and precautionary policy constraints should generally be reserved for circumstances in which immediate and extreme threats to human welfare exist. Stated differently, when it comes to new forms of technological innovation, we need to adopt an "*anti*–precautionary principle" mindset.[35]

Alas, fears of hypothetical worst-case scenarios often dominate discussions about new innovations. Chapter IV discusses some historical examples. But first, we consider why Chicken Little–ism continues to predominate so many discussions about modern technology policy.[36]

C. WHY DOES DOOMSAYING DOMINATE DISCUSSIONS ABOUT NEW TECHNOLOGIES?

One of the reasons that precautionary thinking often creeps into technology policy discussions is that, as already noted, our collective first reaction to new technologies is often one of deep pessimism and even dystopian dread.[37] We assume the worst for a variety of reasons.[38] In the extreme, the initial resistance to new technologies sometimes takes the form of a full-blown "technopanic," which refers to "intense public, political, and academic responses to the emergence or use of media or technologies, especially by the young."[39] Some new technologies were initially resisted and even regulated because they disrupted long-standing social norms, traditions, and institutions.

What drives this fear and the resulting panics? There are many explanations for why we see and hear so much fear and loathing in information technology policy debates today, and even some occasional technopanics.[40] Many general psychological explanations account for why human beings are predisposed toward pessimism and are risk-averse to new technologies and technological developments.[41] For a variety of reasons, humans suffer from this sort of "negativity bias" and are, consequently, poor judges of risks to themselves or those close to them.[42] Harvard University psychology professor Steven Pinker, author of *The Blank Slate: The Modern Denial of Human Nature*, notes,

> The mind is more comfortable in reckoning probabilities in terms of the relative frequency of remembered or imagined events. That can make recent and memorable events—a plane crash, a shark attack, an anthrax infection—loom larger in one's worry list than more frequent and boring events, such as the car crashes and ladder falls that get printed beneath the fold on page B14. And it can lead risk experts to speak one language and ordinary people to hear another.[43]

Clive Thompson, a contributor to *Wired* and the *New York Times Magazine*, also notes that "dystopian predictions are easy to generate" and "doomsaying is emotionally self-protective: if you complain that today's technology is wrecking the culture, you can tell yourself you're a gimlet-eyed critic who isn't hoodwinked by high-tech trends and silly, popular activities like social networking. You seem like someone who has a richer, deeper appreciation for the past and who stands above the triviality of today's life."[44]

Beyond these root-cause explanations, many other specific factors contribute to the rise of technopanics and lead us to fear new technological developments. Importantly, however, each of these particular explanations builds on previous insight: innate pessimism and survival instincts combined with poor comparative risk-analysis skills lead many people to engage in, or at least buy into, technopanics.

- **Generational differences:** Generational differences often motivate pessimistic attitudes about the impact of technology on culture and society. Parents and policymakers who dread the changes to cultural or privacy-related norms ushered in by new technologies often forget that, as children, they, too, heard similar complaints from their elders about the gadgets and content of their generation. Yet these cycles of "juvenoia"—or "exaggerated anxiety about the influence of social change on children and youth"—repeat endlessly and drive panics from one generation to the next.[45]

- **Hyper-nostalgia:** As already noted, many stasis-minded critics just can't seem to let go of the past.[46] They are too invested in it or wedded to something about it. They engage in forms of hyper-nostalgia and ask us to imagine there existed some earlier time that was more unique and valuable than the unfolding present or unpredictable future.[47] Such critics are guilty of both "rosy retrospection bias," or "the tendency to remember past events as being more positive than they actually were,"[48] and a general "pessimistic bias," or "a tendency to overestimate the severity of economic problems and underestimate the (recent) past, present, and future performance of the economy."[49] These critics fear how technological change challenges the old order, traditional values, settled norms, traditional business models, and existing institutions—even as the standard of living generally improves with each passing generation. We see this at work, for example, in debates about privacy when critics yearn for the supposed solitude of the past, or in copyright debates when critics bemoan the loss of record stores and traditional methods of experiencing music. More generally, nostalgic reasoning is often heard in debates about economic disruption and the loss of certain professions or business models.

- **Bad news sells:** Many media outlets and sensationalist authors sometimes use fear-based tactics to gain influence or sell books. Fearmongering and prophecies of doom are always effective media tactics; alarmism helps break through all the noise and get these messages heard. "Curmudgeons, doomsayers, utopians and declinists all have an easier time getting our attention than opinion leaders who want to celebrate slow and steady improvement," notes science policy author Steven Johnson.[50]

- **The role of special interests:** Many groups and institutions exaggerate fears and agitate for action because they benefit from it either directly by getting more resources from government, the public, or other benefactors, or indirectly from the glow of publicity that their alarmism generates. Many companies also overhype various online concerns and then also overplay the benefits of their particular tool as a silver-bullet solution to online pornography, privacy, or cybersecurity concerns. Again, bad news sells and, in this case, it sells products and services to fearful citizens. More generally, the countless incumbent companies and special interest groups that lobby government today often exploit fears about new technologies to defend older technologies that they produce or favor. "The past, in general, is over-represented in Washington," notes Rep. Jim Cooper (D-TN). "The future has no lobbyists."[51]

- **Elitist attitudes:** Academic skeptics and cultural critics often possess elitist attitudes about the technologies, platforms, or new types of media content that the masses or youth adopt before they do. These elitist views are often premised on the "juvenoia" and hyper-nostalgic thinking described above. Some researchers also have an incentive to perpetuate fear because alarmist research grabs attention and attracts more funding.

- **"Third-person-effect hypothesis":** When some people encounter perspectives or preferences at odds with their own, they are more likely to be concerned about the impact of those things on others throughout society and to call on government to take action to correct or counter those perspectives or preferences. Psychologists refer to this as the "third-person-effect hypothesis" and it explains many technopanics and resulting calls for government intervention, especially as they relate to media policy and free speech issues.[52]

Most technopanics blow over in time, but they can do real harm in the short term. Technopanics can encourage policymakers to adopt far-reaching controls on information flows and innovation opportunities more generally. This is especially likely to occur when what some label "moral entrepreneurs" or "fear entrepreneurs" take advantage of a state of fear to demand that "something must be done" about problems that are either imaginary or will be solved over time.[53]

Continuously elevated states of fear or panic can lead to dangerous tensions throughout society. For example, the past decade witnessed a "stranger danger" panic about hypothetical online boogeymen, leading to overblown suspicions about sexual predators online and even the general presence of males near children.[54] Similarly, excessive panic over cybersecurity matters can lead to paranoia about the potential danger of visiting certain websites or using certain digital tools that are, generally speaking, safe and beneficial to the masses.[55]

The final reason that these fear tactics are dangerous is that they lead to a "risk mismatch." That is, fear-based tactics and inflated threat scenarios can lead to situations where individuals and society ignore quite serious risks because they are overshadowed by unnecessary panics over nonproblems.

D. WHEN DOES PRECAUTION MAKE SENSE?

But aren't there times when a certain degree of precautionary policymaking makes good sense? Indeed, there are, and it is important to not dismiss every argument in favor of precautionary principle–based policymaking, even though it should not be the default policy rule in debates over technological innovation.

The challenge of determining when precautionary policies make sense comes down to weighing the (often limited) evidence about any given technology and its impact and then deciding whether the potential downsides of unrestricted use are so potentially catastrophic that trial-and-error experimentation simply cannot be allowed to continue. There certainly are some circumstances when such a precautionary rule might make sense. Governments restrict the possession of uranium and bazookas, to name just two obvious examples.

Generally speaking, permissionless innovation should remain the norm in the vast majority of cases, but there will be some scenarios where the threat of *tangible, immediate, irreversible, catastrophic* harm associated with new innovations could require at least a light version of the precautionary principle to be applied.[56] In these cases, we might be better suited to think about when an "anti-catastrophe principle" is needed, which narrows the scope of the precautionary principle and focuses it more appropriately on the most unambiguously worst-case scenarios that meet those criteria.[57]

PRECAUTION MIGHT MAKE SENSE WHEN HARM IS ...	PRECAUTION GENERALLY DOESN'T MAKE SENSE FOR ASSERTED HARMS THAT ARE ...
Highly probable	Highly improbable
Tangible (physical)	Intangible (psychic)
Immediate	Distant / unclear timeline
Irreversible	Reversible / changeable
Catastrophic	Mundane / trivial

But most cases don't fall into this category. Instead, we generally allow innovators and consumers to freely experiment with technologies, and even engage in risky behaviors, unless a compelling case can be made that precautionary regulation is absolutely necessary.[58] How is the determination made regarding when precaution makes sense? This is where the role of benefit-cost analysis (BCA) and regulatory impact analysis is essential to getting policy right.[59] BCA represents an effort to formally identify the tradeoffs associated with regulatory proposals and, to the maximum extent feasible, quantify those benefits and costs.[60] BCA generally cautions against preemptive, precautionary regulation unless all other options have been exhausted—thus allowing trial-and-error experimentation and "learning by doing" to continue. (The mechanics of BCA are discussed in more detail in chapter VI.)

This is not the end of the evaluation, however. Policymakers also need to consider the complexities associated with traditional regulatory remedies in a world where technological control is increasingly challenging and quite costly. It is not feasible to throw unlimited resources at every problem, because society's resources are finite.[61] We must balance risk probabilities and carefully weigh the likelihood that any given intervention has a chance of creating positive change in a cost-effective fashion.[62] And it is also essential to take into account the potential unintended consequences and long-term costs of any given solution because, as Harvard law professor Cass Sunstein notes, "it makes no sense to take steps to avert catastrophe if those very steps would create catastrophic risks of their own."[63] "The precautionary principle rests upon an illusion that actions have no consequences beyond their intended ends," observes Frank B. Cross of the University of Texas. But "there is no such thing as a risk-free lunch. Efforts to eliminate any given risk will create some new risks," he says.[64]

Oftentimes, after working through all these considerations about whether to regulate new technologies or technological processes, the best solution will be to do nothing because, as noted throughout this book, we should never underestimate the amazing ingenuity and resiliency of humans to find creative solutions to the problems posed by technological change.[65] (Chapter IV discusses the importance of individual and social adaptation and resiliency in greater detail.) Other times we might find that, while some solutions are needed to address the potential risks associated with new technologies, nonregulatory alternatives are also available and should be given a chance before top-down precautionary regulations are imposed. (Chapter VI considers those alternative solutions in more detail.)

Finally, it is again essential to reiterate that we are talking here about the dangers of precautionary thinking as a *public policy* prerogative—that is, precautionary regulations that are mandated and enforced by government officials. By contrast, precautionary steps may be far more wise when undertaken in a more decentralized manner by individuals, families, businesses, groups, and other organizations. In other words, as I have noted elsewhere in much longer articles on the topic, "there is a different choice architecture at work when risk is managed in a localized manner as opposed to a society-wide fashion," and risk-mitigation strategies that might make a great deal of sense for individuals, households, or organizations, might not be nearly as effective if imposed on the entire population as a legal or regulatory directive.[66]

Finally, at times, more morally significant issues may exist that demand an even more exhaustive exploration of the impact of technological change on humanity. Perhaps the most notable examples arise in the field of advance medical treatments and biotechnology. Genetic experimentation and human cloning, for example, raise profound questions about altering human nature or abilities as well as the relationship between generations.[67]

The case for policy prudence in these matters is easier to make because we are quite literally talking about the future of what it means to be human.[68] Controversies have raged for decades over the question of when life begins and how it should end. But these debates will be greatly magnified and extended in coming years to include equally thorny philosophical questions.[69] Should parents be allowed to use advanced genetic technologies to select the specific attributes they desire in their children? Or should parents at least be able to take advantage of genetic screening and genome modification technologies that ensure their children won't suffer from specific diseases or ailments once born?

Outside the realm of technologically enhanced procreation, profound questions are already being raised about the sort of technological enhancements adults might make to their own bodies. How much of the human body can be replaced with robotic or bionic technologies before we cease to be human and become cyborgs?[70]

And another example, "biohacking"—efforts by average citizens working together to enhance various human capabilities, typically by experimenting on their own bodies[71]—could become more prevalent in coming years.[72] Collaborative forums, such as Biohack.Me, already exist where individuals can share information and collaborate on various projects of this sort.[73] Advocates of such amateur biohacking sometimes refer to themselves as "grinders," which Ben Popper of the *Verge* defines as "homebrew biohackers [who are] obsessed with the idea of human enhancement [and] who are looking for new ways to put machines into their bodies."[74]

These technologies and capabilities will raise thorny ethical and legal issues as they advance. Ethically, they will raise questions concerning what it means to be human and the limits of what people should be allowed to do to their own bodies. In the field of law, they will challenge existing health and safety regulations imposed by the FDA and other government bodies.

Again, most innovation policy debates—including most of the technologies discussed throughout this book—do not involve such morally weighty questions. In the abstract, of course, philosophers might argue that *every* debate about technological innovation has an impact on the future of humanity and "what it means to be human." But few have much of a direct influence on that question, and even fewer involve the sort of potentially immediate, irreversible, or catastrophic outcomes that should concern policymakers.

In most cases, therefore, we should let trial-and-error experimentation continue because "experimentation is part and parcel of innovation" and the key to social learning and economic prosperity.[75] If we froze all forms of technological innovation in place while we sorted through every possible outcome, no progress would ever occur. "Experimentation matters," notes Harvard Business School professor Stefan H. Thomke, "because it fuels the discovery and creation of knowledge and thereby leads to the development and improvement of products, processes, systems, and organizations."[76]

Of course, ongoing experimentation with new technologies *always* entails certain risks and potential downsides, but the central argument of this book is that (a) the upsides of technological innovation almost always outweigh those downsides and that (b) humans have proved remarkably resilient in the face of uncertain, ever-changing futures.

In sum, when it comes to managing or coping with the risks associated with technological change, flexibility and patience is essential. One size most certainly does not fit all. And one-size-fits-all approaches to regulating technological risk are particularly misguided when the benefits associated with technological change are so profound. Indeed, "[t]echnology is widely considered the main source of economic progress"; therefore, nothing could be more important for raising long-term living standards than creating a policy environment conducive to ongoing technological change and the freedom to innovate.[77] The next chapter offers more evidence to back up that assertion and bolster the case for permissionless innovation as the optimal policy default.

CHAPTER III
WHY THIS CLASH OF VISIONS MATTERS

This chapter offers a fuller explanation of why the clash of visions between permissionless innovation and precautionary principle thinking really matters. In a nutshell, it comes down to the essential role technological innovation plays in advancing human prosperity.

We begin by examining traditional technological critics and their general complaints before turning to responses from historians, economists, political scientists, and others. The critics, as we will see, routinely ignore how essential technological innovation is to human flourishing and, more importantly, how well humans adapt to technological change when challenges develop. I'll also explain how the clash of these two visions plays out in the real world today and affects the standard of living of different countries.

A. A VERY BRIEF HISTORY OF TECHNOLOGICAL CRITICISM

There have always been critics who have worried about the effect technological change has on culture, the economy, and even humanity itself.[1] "For each new writer or thinker or government leader who has enthusiastically welcomed whatever changes technology might bring," observes the *Atlantic*'s James Fallows, "there has been a counterpart warning of its dangers."[2]

In his 2005 book, *Radical Evolution: The Promise and Peril of Enhancing Our Minds, Our Bodies—And What It Means to Be Human*, science writer Joel Garreau explains how debates about emerging technologies that might affect us are typically framed as "heaven" versus "hell" scenarios.[3] Those who espouse or embrace the "heaven" scenario believe that technology drives history relentlessly, and in almost every way for the better. Garreau describes the heaven crowd's belief that, going forward, "almost unimaginably good things are happening, including the conquering of disease and poverty, but also an increase in beauty, wisdom, love, truth, and peace."[4]

By contrast, those adopting the "hell" outlook believe that "technology is used for extreme evil, threatening humanity with extinction."[5] Garreau notes that what unifies the hell scenario theorists is the sense that in "wresting power from the gods and seeking to transcend the human condition," we end up instead creating a monster—or maybe many different monsters—that threatens our very existence. Garreau says this "Frankenstein Principle" can be seen in countless works of literature and technological criticism throughout history, and it is still very much with us today.[6]

In many ways, modern technological criticism can be traced back to Plato, who fretted about the impact writing would have on the traditions of oral teaching and storytelling.[7] In the past century, modern philosophers penned critiques of newer technological processes that brought Plato up to speed for the industrial era. For example, French philosopher Jacques Ellul *(The Technological Society)*, German historian Oswald Spengler *(Man and Technics)*, and American historian Lewis Mumford *(Technics and Civilization)* all took a dour view of technological innovation and our collective ability to adapt positively to it.[8] They decried the subjugation of humans to "technique" (Ellul)[9] or "technics" (Mumford)[10] and feared that technologies and technological processes would come to control us before we learned how to control them.

Neil Postman was probably the most well-known of the modern information technology critics and served as the bridge between the industrial era critics (like Ellul and Mumford) and today's many Internet age skeptics. Postman decried the rise of a "technopoly"—"the submission of all forms of cultural life to the sovereignty of technique and technology"—that would destroy "the vital sources of our humanity" and lead to "a culture without a moral foundation" by undermining "certain mental processes and social relations that make human life worth living."[11]

Other modern techno-critics have extended this line of thinking to computers, the Internet, digital networks, and the other emerging technologies discussed throughout this book. As the titles or subtitles of their recent tracts indicate, these critics worry about "What the Internet Is Doing to Our Brains,"[12] "How Today's Internet Is Killing Our Culture,"[13] "Being Human in the Age of the Electronic Mob,"[14] "Digital Barbarism,"[15] and "How to Keep Technology from Slipping beyond Our Control."[16]

Echoing the earlier critiques set forth by Ellul, Mumford, and Postman, "alienation through technique" is the overarching concern most modern tech pessimists rail against and claim they are saving us from. In their view, the ways in which technology enhances efficiency and productivity are sometimes viewed as a curse, and the subtle ways in which technological change alters language, learning, and relationships are treated as potential cultural catastrophes. "Freedom" in this pessimistic worldview is often cast in neo-Marxist terms, complete with not only those "alienation" concerns but also "false consciousness" theories (i.e., the idea that all the people using—and seemingly enjoying the benefits of—new technologies are really just pawns who are completely blind to the downsides). At their most pessimistic, many modern tech pessimists fall in line with Ellul's claim that "technique transforms everything it touches into a machine,"[17] and they hint that radical steps may be needed to curtail what they feel is the destructive impact of technology on the economy, culture, or humanity.[18] Some of them even seek to resuscitate and glorify Luddism and other antitechnology movements.[19]

Most notable in this regard is the scathing social criticism of the prolific techno-skeptic Evgeny Morozov, who goes so far as to argue that the very term "the Internet" is a meaningless construct.[20]

He engages in a sort of radical deconstructivism that suggests we are all somehow being fooled into thinking the Internet is as important or meaningful as most of us, quite rationally, believe it is. Morozov also rails against what he regards as the irrational exuberance of digital innovators, who supposedly believe technology can solve all the world's hard problems. He refers to this as "solutionism" and castigates all those who would engage in a "mindless pursuit of this silicon Eden" or "romantic and revolutionary" thinking about how new technology might improve our lives.[21]

The critiques set forth by the latest crop of critics have become even more specialized, zeroing in on emerging technologies such as robotics,[22] artificial intelligence,[23] sensors,[24] and the Internet of Things.[25] Again, the concerns range from social (e.g., privacy, safety, and security) to personal (e.g., impact on learning and concentration) to economic (e.g., fears about automation and job dislocation). And it is not unusual to also hear a fair share of end-of-world dystopian scenarios thrown around in many of their books and essays, including *Terminator*-inspired tales of killer robots destroying humanity.[26]

The critics often fail to devise a coherent political or regulatory agenda for countering what they see as an overreliance on technology. However, when they do come clean about their policy intentions, they are usually calling for quite radical policy interventions, often aimed at imposing sweeping political control over the future course of technological innovation.[27]

B. ANSWERING THE TECH CRITICS:
THE CASE FOR "RATIONAL OPTIMISM"

The problem with all these critics' arguments is that they overestimate the dangers of new innovations while ignoring, or at least greatly underplaying, the importance of technological innovation for economic and social progress.[28] And perhaps the most important shortcoming of these techno-critics, as I'll discuss in greater length in chapter IV, is that they consistently fail to appreciate how well humans adapt to technological change. In fact, they almost universally ignore how quickly we learn to cope with changes that—while challenging in the short term—ultimately come to be an accepted, and usually enriching, part of our lives.[29] Although they are rarely as direct about saying it as Morozov is, the work of some tech critics implies that all this modern innovation isn't necessary, or at least that there's just too much irrational exuberance about its potential.

It's easy for some modern technological critics to dismiss the wild-eyed enthusiasm of some creators because, at times, those innovators or others can overstate the potential of any given invention. When Pollyanna-ish pundits make sweeping claims about how any particular new technology will "change everything" or seemingly solve all the world's problems, the critics are right to call them out for such statements.

But that criticism can go too far and ignore the fact that, as James Surowiecki observes, "[i]n the delusions of entrepreneurs are the seeds of technological progress."[30] It is hard to believe, for example, that the world would really be a better place if it was completely devoid of the "romantic and revolutionary" thinking that Morozov and other critics deride. We need not always support the bullish enthusiasm of all modern entrepreneurs to nonetheless appreciate how their ongoing efforts to find solutions to hard problems can often yield very beneficial results—or even just powerful lessons following their failures.

This more practical disposition toward technological experimentation and change is what author Matt Ridley calls "rational optimism."[31] At a macro level, the rational optimist is generally bullish about the future and the prospects for humanity but is not naive about the challenges associated with technological change. At the micro level, the rational optimist seeks practical solutions to intractable problems through ongoing trial-and-error experimentation, but is not wedded to any one process or particular technology to get the job done.

This is the approach seen in the works of Herman Kahn,[32] Julian Simon,[33] F. A. Hayek,[34] Ithiel de Sola Pool,[35] and especially Aaron Wildavsky and Virginia Postrel, whose work was discussed earlier.

These "dynamist" thinkers express optimism about the role technology plays in advancing social and economic progress, but their optimism is always rooted in empiricism and rational inquiry, not blind faith in any particular viewpoint or ideology. Rational optimists don't hold an unthinking allegiance to technology as an autonomous force or savior to all of civilization's woes. Indeed, the blueprint that rational optimists offer is not utopian but *anti*-utopian: precisely because difficult problems defy easy solutions, we should look to devise a plurality of strategies to tackle them. New technological innovations might be among those strategies, but they are not the only ones we should rely on. Ongoing experimentation is the key to unlocking knowledge and prosperity.[36]

Importantly, rational optimists would never discourage the entrepreneurial dreaming and daring that so many modern tech critics deride. While Morozov and other critics might lambast those "romantic and revolutionary problem solvers," the truth is that the world is a better place because such people exist. Much of their entrepreneurial activity will yield socially beneficial results. Equally as important, however, is the fact that it will also produce many failures, but society will then learn from those mistakes and improve future experiments accordingly.

The goal is not to "save everything" with "the folly of technological solutionism," as Morozov worries. Rather, it is to seek to solve *some* problems through the application of practical knowledge to social and economic challenges through incessant experimentation with the new and different approaches to those problems.[37]

But rational optimists will not shy away from the fundamental truth that a symbiotic relationship exists between technological innovation and human flourishing. That connection, as noted next, is why the critics' complaints must be met with a full-throated response.

C. THE CONNECTION BETWEEN INNOVATION, ECONOMIC GROWTH, AND HUMAN FLOURISHING

Before we consider the profound benefits associated with innovation, we should try to define the term. Of course, defining "innovation" is notoriously difficult,[38] almost as challenging as settling on a good definition of "technology" itself.[39] The Organisation for Economic Co-operation and Development (OECD) rather dryly defines innovation as "the implementation of a new or significantly improved product (good or service), or process, a new marketing method, or a new organizational method in business practices, workplace organisation or external relations."[40] But, as is often the case with other attempted definitions of the term, the OECD caveats its definition by noting how "[t]his broad definition of an innovation encompasses a wide range of possible innovations" and that narrower and more nuanced definitions are available.[41]

W. Brian Arthur, author of *The Nature of Technology*, argues that the problem with trying to explore the concept of innovation directly is that "the idea is too diffuse, too nebulous, for that to be useful."[42] Despite that warning, he continues on to explain how

> [i]nnovation has two main themes. One is [a] constant finding or putting together of new solutions out of existing toolboxes of pieces and practices. The other is industries constantly combining their practices and processes with functionalities drawn from newly arriving toolboxes—new domains.... The result is new processes and arrangements, new ways of doing things, not just in one area of application but all across the economy.[43]

More concisely, in their book *Innovation Economics*, Robert D. Atkinson and Stephen J. Ezell define innovation as "the development and widespread adoption of new kinds of products, production processes, services, and business and organizational models."[44]

What these and most other definitions of innovation share in common, then, is a focus on new and better ways of doing things and, in particular, new ways of satisfying human wants and needs. Thus, even if its precise definition proves elusive, *what is most crucial about the process of innovation is that it serves as a means to an end: it helps drive progress and human flourishing.* "Innovation is more than the latest technology," notes Sofia Ranchordás, a resident fellow at Yale Law School, "it is a phenomenon that can result in the improvement of living conditions of people and strengthening of communities. Innovation can be technological and social, and the former might assist the latter to empower groups in ways we once thought unimaginable," she observes.[45]

The endless search for new and better ways of doing things drives human learning and, ultimately, prosperity in every sense—economic, social, and cultural. The pessimistic critics of technological progress and permissionless innovation have many laments, but they typically fail to consult the historical record to determine how much better off we are than our ancestors.[46] And that record is unambiguous, as Robert Bryce explains in his recent book, *Smaller Faster Lighter Denser Cheaper: How Innovation Keeps Proving the Catastrophists Wrong*:

> The pessimistic worldview ignores an undeniable truth: more people are living longer, healthier, freer, more peaceful, lives than at any time in human history... [T]he plain reality is that things are getting better, a lot better, for tens of millions of people around the world. Dozens of factors can be cited for the improving conditions of humankind. But the simplest explanation is that innovation is allowing us to do more with less.[47]

"Doing more with less" drives greater economic efficiency, expands the range of goods and services available, and generally lowers prices.[48] This raises our overall standard of living over the long term.[49]

Indeed, there exists widespread consensus among economic historians and scholars that, as the Cato Institute's Brink Lindsey asserts, "the long-term future of economic growth hinges ultimately on innovation."[50] Countless economic studies and historical surveys have documented the positive relationship between technological progress and economic growth. A 2010 white paper from the US Department of Commerce revealed that "[t]echnological innovation is linked to three-quarters of the Nation's post-WW II growth rate" and continued on to note that,

> [a]s it fuels economic growth, innovation also produces high-paying jobs. Recent studies by the Federal Reserve show that innovation in capital goods is the primary driver of increases in real wages. Without innovation, wages would be much lower. Additionally, across countries, 75% of differences in income can be explained by innovation-driven productivity differentials.[51]

These findings are reflected in many other major economic studies on the factors that drive economic growth. For example, two major economic surveys from 2003 and 2006 found that technological progress accounts for 30–34 percent of growth in Western countries.[52] And economists estimate that differences in technological adoption patterns account for 80 percent of the difference between rich and poor nations.[53]

Of course, just because the historical evidence linking innovation and long-term growth reveals an unambiguous and undeniable relationship, the short-term disruptions caused by technological change won't be any easier to swallow for some individuals, businesses, or public policymakers.

This is why attitudes toward innovation and entrepreneurship are so important. Progress-oriented policy requires a general openness to constant change and the "creative destruction" that Austrian-born economist Joseph Schumpeter famously spoke of in the 1940s, when he explained how cascading waves of continuous change, or what he described as the "perennial gales of creative destruction," were what spurred innovation and propelled an economy forward.[54] As my Mercatus Center colleague Jerry Ellig has explained it, in the Schumpeterian paradigm, "firms compete not on the margins of price and output, but by offering new products, new technologies, new sources of supply, and new forms of organization."[55]

The Schumpeterian paradigm and other "dynamic competition" models best capture the nature of competition and innovation in today's digital world.[56] The Schumpeterian model explains why some tech companies can gain scale so rapidly only to stumble and fall with equal velocity.[57] Digital Davids are constantly displacing cyber-Goliaths.[58] Social and economic risk takers and innovators are constantly shaking things up in the digital economy and bringing about equally seismic disruptions throughout our culture.[59] New disruptions flow from many unexpected quarters as innovators launch groundbreaking products and services while also devising new ways to construct cheaper and more efficient versions of existing technologies. The more this cycle repeats, the more likely economic growth becomes. But the Schumpeterian model also explains why technological innovation can be so gut-wrenching and generate so much opposition in the short term.

Indeed, it's amazing to think about all the once-mighty tech titans that ruled their respective sectors, only to be rapidly displaced by smaller start-ups a short time later.[60] For some, the velocity of their downfall was precipitous and fatal. Other times their decline and fall was gradual and incomplete as the shells of the old companies remain in existence even as their cores have been hollowed out. Consider a few examples:

- **IBM**: "Big Blue" was once synonymous with computing itself. IBM dominated the mainframe computer marketplace and kept antitrust officials in a 13-year tizzy. But both IBM and the government weren't paying attention to the personal computing revolution, which abruptly kicked IBM off its perch and utterly decimated its business and shareholder value throughout the 1980s. While it reinvented itself later and rebounded, it is a shadow of the company that once ruled the computing marketplace.

- **Kodak**: The postwar generation had "Kodak moments" and the film and camera giant's importance was significant enough that even singer Paul Simon begged, "Mama, don't take my Kodachrome away." But the combination of digital photography, online photo storage, and home printing would eventually wipe out Kodak's market dominance, even though the firm had seen much of the change coming. Its failure to adapt led the firm into bankruptcy in 2012.[61]

- **Sony**: For those coming of age in the early and mid-1980s, "Walkman" was synonymous with any portable music device. Sony had created a product that everyone wanted and all its competitors were forced to copy. A generation later, the device had lost much of its appeal—and whatever market dominance Sony once gained from it. By the late 1990s, digitized music and the rise of MP3 players meant that Apple and others would rapidly eat away at Sony's once-dominant position. Although the company rebounded and remains a major player in video games and other consumer electronics sectors, it is not the feared juggernaut it once was.

- **Atari**: For the first generation of video gamers, Atari was the name of the game. It dominated the home console market in the late 1970s. A few years later, it was "game over" for the company, primarily because of Nintendo's growing dominance of the console market in the late 1980s. While Nintendo would last longer and indeed is still with us, the firm faces vigorous competition from other platforms, including the unexpected rise of smartphones as a major gaming platform.

- **MySpace**: While Facebook dominates discussions about social networking today, it's already easy to forget that just a few years ago almost everyone expected MySpace to rule social networking for a long time to come. That concern over MySpace's hegemony peaked shortly after Rupert Murdoch and News Corp. bought the company in 2005 and led critics like Victor Keegan of the United Kingdom's *Guardian* newspaper to ask, "Will MySpace Ever Lose Its Monopoly?"[62] A short time later, however, MySpace lost its early lead and became a major liability for Murdoch—he paid $580 million for the company in 2005, but sold it for only $35 million in June 2011.[63]

- **Mobile phones**: The mobile phone handset and operating system (OS) marketplace has undergone continuous change over the past 15 years and is still evolving rapidly. When cellular telephone service first started taking off in the mid-1990s, handsets and mobile operating systems were essentially one in the same, and Nokia and Motorola dominated the sector with fairly rudimentary devices. The era of personal digital assistants—more commonly known as PDAs—dawned during this period, but mostly saw a series of overhyped devices, such as Apple's "Newton," that failed to catch on. In the early 2000s, however, a host of new companies and devices entered the market, many of which are still major players today, including LG, Sony, Samsung, Siemens, and HTC. Importantly, the sector began dividing into handsets versus OS. Leading mobile OS makers have included Microsoft, Palm, Symbian, BlackBerry (RIM), Apple, and Android (Google).

The sector continues to undergo constant change. Palm smartphones were wildly popular for a brief time and brought many innovations to the marketplace.[64] Palm underwent many ownership and management changes, however, and rapidly faded from the scene.[65] Similarly, RIM's BlackBerry was the dominant smartphone device for a time, but it has recently been decimated.[66] BlackBerry's roller-coaster ride has left it "trying to avoid the hall of fallen giants," in the words of an early 2012 *New York Times* headline.[67] Although the company once accounted for more than half of the American smartphone market, today its share has slipped into the single digits.[68]

Microsoft also had a huge lead in licensing its Windows Mobile OS to high-end smartphone handset makers until Apple and Android disrupted its business. It is hard to believe now, but just a few years ago the idea of Apple or Google being serious contenders in the smartphone business was greeted with derision, even scorn.

Famously, many commentators denigrated Apple's entry into the smartphone business because many industry analysts believed the market was mature.[69] Just a few years later, Nokia's profits and market share plummeted,[70] and Google purchased the struggling Motorola. Meanwhile, Palm is dead and Microsoft is struggling to win back market share lost to Apple and Google. "The violence with which new platforms have displaced incumbent mobile vendor fortunes continues to surprise," says wireless industry analyst Horace Dediu.[71]

In each of these cases, Schumpeterian change has brought us many new goods and services that have improved our overall standard of living. But precisely because disruption of this sort unsettles so many traditional businesses, sectors, and professions, the short-term opposition to change will always be vociferous.

Nonetheless, the vital lesson here is perfectly summarized by Daron Acemoglu and James A. Robinson, authors of *Why Nations Fail*, when they conclude: "Sustained economic growth requires innovation, and innovation cannot be decoupled from creative destruction, which replaces the old with the new in the economic realm and also destabilizes established power relations in politics."[72] When public policy discourages risk-taking and actively regulates to disallow permissionless innovation, the result is less entrepreneurialism, diminished competition, fewer consumer choices, and stagnated economic growth.[73] The following case study of Europe's declining global competitiveness in the digital marketplace over the past 20 years makes that abundantly clear.

D. THE REAL-WORLD IMPACT OF PERMISSIONLESS INNOVATION

Let's get even more concrete about how creative destruction plays out in the real world and how permissionless innovation affects the standard of living for different populations.[74] To do so, consider this question posed by James B. Stewart in a summer 2015 *New York Times* column: "Why hasn't Europe fostered the kind of innovation that has spawned hugely successful technology companies?"[75]

That question helps frame the importance of the debate between permissionless innovation and the precautionary principle.

Since the rise of the commercial Internet in the mid-1990s, the United States and the European Union have adopted starkly different visions toward the digital economy and innovation policy more generally.[76] This is particularly true as it relates to online advertising and the data collection practices that have powered digital commerce over the past two decades.[77] Beginning in 1995 with the adoption of its "Data Protection Directive," the European Union has instituted highly restrictive policies governing online data collection and use.[78] The EU's approach has been shaped by precautionary principle thinking at every turn, based largely on concerns about privacy and data security. Combined with "a deeply ingrained fear of failure that is a bigger impediment to entrepreneurship on the Continent than in other regions,"[79] this general aversion to change has greatly discouraged innovation in Europe.[80]

Indeed, attitudes toward risk and failure account for the significant differences in US and EU policy and help unlock the mystery of why American tech firms have grown so much faster and bigger than European firms.[81] German economist Petra Moser notes that Europeans are "trying to recreate Silicon Valley in places like Munich, so far with little success," because "[t]he institutional and cultural differences are still too great" and "[i]n Europe, stability is prized" above all else, she says.[82] In his recent *Times* essay on this transatlantic clash of visions, Stewart noted that

> [o]ften overlooked in the success of American start-ups is the even greater number of failures. "Fail fast, fail often" is a Silicon Valley mantra, and the freedom to innovate is inextricably linked to the freedom to fail. In Europe, failure carries a much greater stigma than it does in the United States.[83]

Moreover, he notes, "Europeans are also much less receptive to the kind of truly disruptive innovation represented by a Google or a Facebook."[84] What European regulators fail to appreciate is, as

Daniel Castro and Alan McQuinn of the Information Technology and Innovation Foundation observe, that "[i]nnovation is about risk, and if innovators fear they will be punished for every mistake . . . then they will be much less assertive in trying to develop the next new thing."[85] Meanwhile, the United States adopted a very different disposition that favored risk-taking and tolerated business failures and cultural disruptions. Disruptive technologies were embraced (or at least permitted) in the United States, resulting in the explosive growth of the Internet and America's information technology sectors (computing, software, Internet services, etc.) over the past two decades. Those sectors have ushered in a generation of innovations and innovators that are now household names across the world, including in Europe.

The result of the general freedom to experiment in this arena was not only an outpouring of innovation that was unprecedented in recent times but also a boost for US competitive advantage overall.[86]

For example, a recent Booz & Company report on the world's most innovative companies revealed that nine of the top 10 are based in the United States and that most of them are involved in computing.[87] Another recent survey revealed that the world's 15

2014: 10 MOST INNOVATIVE COMPANIES

2014 RANK	COMPANY	GEOGRAPHY	INDUSTRY
1	Apple	United States	Computing and electronics
2	Google	United States	Software and Internet
3	Amazon	United States	Software and Internet
4	Samsung	South Korea	Computing and electronics
5	Tesla Motors	United States	Automotive
6	3M	United States	Industrials
7	General Electric	United States	Industrials
8	Microsoft	United States	Software and Internet
9	IBM	United States	Computing and electronics
10	Procter & Gamble	United States	Consumer

Source: Barry Jaruzelski, "The Top Innovators and Spenders, 2013," Strategy&, accessed on October 15, 2014, http://www.strategyand.pwc.com/global/home/what-we-think/global-innovation-1000/top-innovators-spenders.

most valuable Internet companies (based on market capitaliza-tions) have a combined market value of nearly $2.5 trillion, but none of them are European while 11 of them are US firms.[88]

Meanwhile, the information technology market on either side of the Atlantic illustrates how investor money overwhelmingly flocks to US shores. The market capitalizations for America's major tech companies overwhelm European tech firms.[89]

The data on the overall size of the respective tech markets on either side of the Atlantic provide an even more dramatic contrast. As of 2015, the market value of Apple, Google, and Facebook *each* exceeded the *entire* value of the European market for tech "unicorns," or firms with a market value of over $1 billion. Airbnb's market value alone exceeds the value of all of Germany's billion-dollar technology companies combined.

Many European officials and business leaders are waking up to this grim reality and are wondering how to reverse this situation. Danish economist Jacob Kirkegaard of the Peterson Institute for International Economics notes that Europeans "all want a Silicon Valley. . . . But none of them can match the scale and focus on the new and truly innovative technologies you have in the United States. Europe and the rest of the world are playing catch-up, to the great frustration of policy makers there."[90]

Unsurprisingly, European officials are unhappy that American innovators enjoy competitive advantages in many digital sectors. As a result, some European policymakers are increasingly looking to force their more restrictive policies on US-based digital inno-vators.[91] The easier way to "level the playing field" between digital rivals on either side of the Atlantic would be for Europe to relax its restrictive, risk-averse policies, to give their innovators a better chance of learning from marketplace experimentation.[92] Of course, that would mean that European policymakers would need to be willing to embrace the possibility that many of those firms would fail, or to the extent they succeeded, that restrictive data collection policies and other regulations might need to be reformed.

Thus far, European officials have shown little willingness to embrace that option and are instead stepping up their efforts to

AMERICAN TECH GIANTS VS EUROPEAN "UNICORNS"

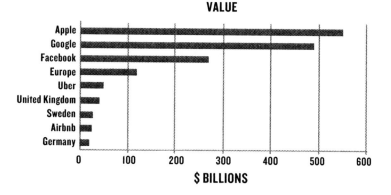

VALUE

Source: Manish Madhvani, et al., "European Unicorns: Do They Have Legs?" *GP Bullhound*, 2015, http://www.gpbullhound.com/wp-content/uploads/2015/06/GP-Bullhound-Research-Billion-Dollar-Companies-2015.pdf.

regulate technology companies, especially US-based firms.[93] In fact, within the so-called sharing economy, European governments have moved aggressively to limit or shut down ride-sharing provider Uber.[94] Following a major strike by French taxi drivers during summer 2015, France went so far as to arrest two Uber executives.[95] (Ironically, downloads of Uber's mobile app increased following the arrests.[96]) There's even talk in Europe of creating an EU-wide super-regulator, mostly to address concerns about US-based tech companies.[97]

Such moves are motivated by a fear of disruption and change. Whether it is economic or social norms, failure is often not an option in some European countries; public policies will protect industries, organizations, professions, or even just cultural norms that are threatened by technological change. The irony, however, is that the more aggressively European officials seek to avoid the possibility of various short-term failures, the more prone the continent is to potentially far more dangerous and systemic failures in the long term.[98] "The trouble with Europe's broad attack on U.S. tech companies is that it hurts Europe above all," observes Mike Elgan of *eWeek*. "Europe will never be able to regulate its way to tech competitiveness. It has to come from industry, not government." Elgan correctly argues that

Europe's problems with America's tech innovators "should be solved by European startups, innovation, [and] entrepreneurship not meddling EU commissions, politicians and judges."[99]

Whether European officials are willing to take steps to reverse this predicament remains to be seen. Regardless, the lesson for US policymakers should be clear: if they want to continue to produce world-leading technology innovators, they must avoid Europe's overly precautionary and highly risk-averse approach to policy. Permissionless innovation remains the better default policy position toward new entrepreneurs and technologies, no matter how disruptive they may be in the short term.

E. GLOBAL INNOVATION ARBITRAGE

As the preceding discussion indicates, when and where public policies or political attitudes are stacked against entrepreneurial opportunities, then innovation will be disincentivized and innovators will look to do business elsewhere. Thus, there's an even more practical reason why policymakers should take seriously the importance of permissionless innovation as a policy disposition: we increasingly live in a world where "global innovation arbitrage"[100] or "regulatory arbitrage for permissionless innovation" is a reality.[101] Just as capital now fluidly moves around the globe seeking out more hospitable regulatory treatment, the same is increasingly true for innovations. Innovators can, and increasingly will, move to those countries and continents that provide a legal and regulatory environment more hospitable to entrepreneurial activity.[102]

As noted, the United States essentially won the first round of the "Web Wars" and took a commanding lead in the battle for global digital supremacy in terms of Internet-enabled innovation. Again, this occurred because the United States got policy right.

Unfortunately, America's digital technology supremacy may be reversing itself with some new technological innovations. "As I watch our government go slow in promulgating rules holding back American innovation," noted Sen. Cory Booker (D-NJ) at a US

Senate Commerce Committee hearing in early 2015, we are "seeing technology exported from America and going other places."[103]

Consider what's been happening in such diverse fields as commercial drones, driverless cars, genetic testing, and the sharing economy as the global competition to attract innovation and investment on these fronts intensifies. In particular, consider how the United Kingdom has been taking steps on these fronts to attract innovators who are being shunned by US policymakers:

- **Drones**: US-based tech innovators such as Amazon and Google had been threatening to move their drone research offshore before the Federal Aviation Administration (FAA) finally started taking steps to liberalize its rules and open the skies for aerial innovation.[104] Amazon even sent the FAA a letter warning stating, "Without the ability to test outdoors in the United States soon, we will have no choice but to divert even more of our [drone] research and development resources abroad."[105] Meanwhile, other countries have been opening their skies to drone innovation.[106] Both the United Kingdom and Australia have been more welcoming to drone innovators.[107]

- **Driverless cars**: The United Kingdom is opening its doors—or roads, as the case may be—to autonomous vehicles, or "driverless car" technology.[108] The *New York Times* noted recently that "the country is positioning itself as a giant test track for global automakers," and that "[a] recent review of Britain's transport laws provided a green light for testing driverless cars on public roads—something often not allowed on the streets of other European countries. The country's policy makers also are completing industry guidelines to sidestep other potential roadblocks, like liability and insurance issues, that could still hamper carmakers' plans for autonomous cars."[109]

- **Genetic testing**: One of the more vivid recent examples of global innovation arbitrage involves 23andMe, which sells mail-order DNA-testing kits to allow people to learn more about their genetic history and their potential predisposition to various diseases. Unfortunately, the FDA is actively thwarting innovation on this front after ordering the company to halt sales in the United States.[110] The agency has recently taken steps to loosen regulation of 23andMe, although only for narrowly defined purposes.[111] On the other side of the Atlantic, UK officials seem to be welcoming the firm with open arms as the UK's Medicines and Healthcare Products Regulatory Agency said the company's test can be used there, albeit with caution.[112]

- **Sharing economy**: Sharing economy innovators are potentially at risk in the United States because of incessant bureaucratic meddling at the state and especially the local level.[113] If policymakers don't take steps to liberalize the layers of red tape that encumber new sharing economy start-ups, it is possible that some of these companies will start to look for opportunities offshore. The United Kingdom's Department for Business, Innovation & Skills recently published a white paper titled "Unlocking the Sharing Economy," which discusses how the British government intends to embrace the many innovations that could flow from this space.[114] The preface to the report opens with a telling passage from Matthew Hancock, a member of the UK Parliament and the Minister of State for Business, Enterprise, and Energy, in which he notes, "The UK is embracing new, disruptive business models and challenger businesses that increase competition and offer new products and experiences for consumers. Where other countries and cities are closing down consumer choice, and limiting people's freedom to make better use of their possessions, we are embracing it."[115]

That last line from Minister Hancock makes it clear that if other countries, including the United States, fail to create a more hospitable environment for innovation, then the United Kingdom and other countries will be all too happy to invite those companies to come set up operations there. The offshoring option is just as real in countless other sectors of the modern tech economy. Similar opportunities for such "global innovation arbitrage" exist for the Internet of Things and wearable tech, robotics, Bitcoin, and other advanced technologies. Moreover, this sort of jurisdictional competition for innovation can happen at multiple levels of government— cities, counties, states, countries, and continents.[116]

This reiterates why policy incentives matter so much. "America right now is the net exporter of technology and innovation in the globe, and we can't lose that advantage," notes Senator Booker. "[W]e should continue to be the global innovators on these areas."[117] But that will happen only if American policymakers are willing to embrace permissionless innovation for these new technologies.

INNOVATION OPPORTUNITY: Private Drones

Unmanned aircraft systems (UASs), or drones, are poised to become far more ubiquitous in coming decades.[118] Many hobbyists already use drones for a remarkable range of applications. As *New York Times* tech columnist Farhad Manjoo has noted, drone enthusiasts "see almost limitless potential for flying robots" and they see drones as "a platform—a new class of general-purpose computer, as important as the PC or the smartphone, that may be put to use in a wide variety of ways."[119] Drones could also have many important news-gathering uses for both professional media organizations and average citizens.[120]

The commercial benefits could also be profound. As Sen. Cory Booker (D-NJ) has argued, "[T]he potential possibilities for drone technology to alleviate burdens on our infrastructure, to empower commerce, innovation, jobs . . . to really open up unlimited opportunities in this country is pretty incredible to me."[121] A 2013 study from the Association for Unmanned Vehicle Systems International, which represents the industry, predicted $82.1 billion in economic impact between 2015 and 2025 from the integration of UASs into the nation's airspace.[122]

Drones are already positively transforming many sectors, including agricultural and weather monitoring, disaster response management, law enforcement (especially missing persons searches), and entertainment services (such as movie production). Major tech innovators, such as Google,[123] Amazon,[124] and Facebook,[125] are already actively experimenting with drone technologies to provide services to the public, but many smaller drone innovators exist (such as DJI, Parrot, and 3D Robotics). These manufacturers of commercial drones had revenue exceeding $600 million in 2014.[126]

Those numbers would likely be much larger if not for endless foot-dragging by federal regulators. Congress ordered the FAA to come up with a plan to integrate drones into domestic airspace by September 2015, but the agency missed the deadline and has continued to delay progress.[127] This is partially due to the fact that private drones have already raised many safety and privacy concerns.[128] The FAA invited comments in a proceeding about drone privacy,[129] and legislation limiting private or commercial drone use has already been introduced at the federal level[130] and in many states.[131] In early 2015, the White House issued a memorandum addressing such concerns and creating a multistakeholder process to develop best practices for drone privacy.[132]

Some drone regulation is likely inevitable, but preemptive controls could curtail many of the benefits that could flow from relatively unrestrictive experimentation with UASs.[133] Restrictions on news-gathering uses of private drones could also raise serious First Amendment concerns.[134]

It may be the case that existing laws and policies—property rights, nuisance laws, torts, "Peeping Tom" laws, etc.—could cover the most concerning privacy-infringing scenarios.[135] For safety issues, UAS operators could simply be held liable in court for damages that they cause, much as automobile drivers can be held liable for their damages. New legal standards for UAS-related controversies will evolve gradually through a body of common-law cases, as they have for many other technologies.[136]

Generally speaking, however, permissionless innovation should guide policy decisions for the nation's airspace.[137] New rules must leave ample space for future innovation opportunities so that, like the Internet, airspace can become a platform for commercial and social innovation.[138] Unfortunately, some companies have been exporting development of these technologies abroad owing to the uncertainty of the regulatory environment here in the United States.[139]

CHAPTER IV
HOW WE ADAPT TO TECHNOLOGICAL CHANGE

I n this chapter, we consider why the worst fears about new technologies usually do not come to pass. The reason is simple: humans have the uncanny ability to adapt to changes in their environment, bounce back from adversity, and learn to become wiser and more resilient over time.

This has important ramifications for the policy debate between the precautionary principle mindset and the notion of permissionless innovation. If adaptation is not just possible but even extremely likely, then there is even less reason to preemptively restrict social and economic experimentation with new technologies and technological processes.

A. FROM PANIC TO EVENTUAL ADAPTATION

As chapter III noted, when new inventions first come on the scene, the initial reaction from philosophers, scientists, and pundits is often fear and loathing about the potential ramifications of technological change for both the culture and the economy. "Armageddon has a long and distinguished history," Garreau notes. "Theories of progress are mirrored by theories of collapse."[1]

In his magisterial history of apocalyptic theories, *The Idea of Decline in Western History*, Arthur Herman documented how such "declinist" thinking—or what Garreau referred to as "hell" scenarios—have been a pervasive, reoccurring feature of most past academic writing and social commentary. The irony of much of this pessimistic declinist thinking, however, is that, "[i]n effect, the very things modern society does best—providing increasing economic affluence, equality of opportunity, and social and geographic mobility—are systematically deprecated and vilified by its direct beneficiaries," Herman says. "None of this is new or even remarkable."[2]

Indeed, despite the fact that the general real-world trend has been in the direction of steady improvements in human health, welfare, and convenience, the skeptics persist in thinking that impending doom lies just around the corner. Even if the sky didn't fall before as predicted, critics will always insist that *this time it's different!* And many people believe them.

Chapter II offered some explanations for this strange phenomenon. In a nutshell, this behavior is rooted in our innate tendency to be pessimistic as well as a desire for greater certainty about what the future holds.[3] By taking advantage of these tendencies, "the gloom-mongers have it easy," notes Dan Gardner in his book, *Future Babble: Why Expert Predictions Are Next to Worthless, and You Can Do Better*, because their predictions "*feel* right to us. And that conclusion is bolstered by our attraction to certainty."[4]

But just because those pessimistic predictions *feel* right, it doesn't mean they are right. Again, the historical record is unambiguous: ongoing technological innovation has done more to improve the human condition that any other factor.

Yet, not only do the techno-critics consistently fail to appreciate what the historical record has to say about innovation fueling progress and prosperity, those critics also pay little attention to just how effectively humans adapt to ongoing technological change. "The good news is that end-of-the-world predictions have been around for a very long time, and none of them has yet borne fruit," Garreau reminds us.[5] Why not? Let's return to his framework for the answer. After discussing the "Heaven" (optimistic) and "Hell" (skeptical or pessimistic) scenarios cast about by countless tech writers throughout history, Garreau outlines a third, and more pragmatic, "Prevail" option, which views history "as a remarkably effective paean to the power of humans to muddle through extraordinary circumstances."[6]

The "Prevail" or "muddling through" scenario offers the best explanation for how we learn to cope with technological disruption and prosper in the process. As Garreau explains it, under the Prevail scenario, "humans shape and adapt [technology] in entirely new directions."[7] He rightly notes, "Just because the problems are increasing doesn't mean solutions might not also be increasing to match them."[8] As John Seely Brown and Paul Duguid noted in their 2001 essay responding to "doom-and-gloom technofuturists":

> [T]echnological and social systems shape each other. The same is true on a larger scale. . . . Technology and society are constantly forming and reforming new dynamic equilibriums with far-reaching implications. The challenge . . . is to see beyond the hype and past the oversimplifications to the full import of these new sociotechnical formations.[9]

It is this process of "constantly forming and reforming new dynamic equilibriums" that is typically overlooked by technology critics. Or, to the extent the critics are willing to engage in a discussion on this matter at all, they often change the topic and instead stress the disruptions that happened along the way—i.e., the social or economic norms that were challenged by technological change.[10]

That technological change disrupts is, of course, a truism by its very nature.[11] Something is lost in the process. In terms of economics, it may be a job or a business that is lost, or perhaps even an entire profession or sector that disappears. It terms of culture, it may be a particular art form or medium of expression. And in terms of society more generally, technological change might fundamentally alter the ways we interact with each other and the world around us.

All this is undoubtedly true, but what of it? What can we learn from this? What were the mechanics of that adaptive process? As social norms, personal habits, and human relationships were disrupted, what helped us muddle through and find a way of coping with new technologies? Likewise, as existing markets and business models were disrupted, how were new ones formulated in response to the given technological disruption? Finally, how did legal norms and institutions adjust to those same changes?

Individual and societal acclimation to technological change is worthy of serious investigation if for no other reason than it has continuously happened! And what is most remarkable about this process is that we humans have again and again figured out how to assimilate new technologies into our lives despite how much those technologies disrupted our personal, social, economic, cultural, and legal norms.[12] We prevailed and prospered.

B. RESILIENCY AND ITS BENEFITS

Moreover, while technological change often brings sweeping and quite consequential change, there is great value in the very act of living through it.[13] A great deal of wisdom is born of experience, including experiences that involve risk and the possibility of occasional mistakes and failures while both developing new technologies and learning how to live with them. It is wise to continue to be open to new forms of innovation and technological change, not only because that openness provides breathing space for future entrepreneurialism and invention, but also because it provides an opportunity to see how societal attitudes toward new technologies evolve—and to learn from it.

When we do evaluate this process dispassionately, we find that citizen attitudes about most emerging technologies typically follow a familiar cycle: initial *resistance,* gradual *adaptation,* and then eventual *assimilation* of a new technology into society. More often than not, citizens have found ways to adapt to technological change by employing a variety of coping mechanisms, new norms, or other creative fixes.[14]

In other words—to use Garreau's phrasing—we "muddle through" and prevail. But the best word to describe this process is *resiliency.* Andrew Zolli and Ann Marie Healy, authors of *Resilience: Why Things Bounce Back,* define resilience as "the capacity of a system, enterprise, or a person to maintain its core purpose and integrity in the face of dramatically changed circumstances."[15] "To improve your resilience," they note, "is to enhance your ability to resist being pushed from your preferred valley, while expanding the range of alternatives that you can embrace if you need to. This is what researchers call preserving adaptive capacity—the ability to adapt to changed circumstances while fulfilling one's core purpose—and it's an essential skill in an age of unforeseeable disruption and volatility."[16]

Skeptics and critics will retort that just because humans have muddled through previous rounds of technological disruption and proved to be quite resilient, doesn't mean it was easy or that something worse might not happen next time around.[17] It's certainly true that this process of "muddling through" isn't always neat or pretty. But the fact that people and institutions learned to cope with past technological disruptions and become more resilient over time is worthy of serious investigation and respect. And, again, what we learned from living through that process was likely extremely valuable in its own right.

Consider how almost every digital service that we use today presents us with a series of tradeoffs. For example, email has allowed us to connect with a constantly growing universe of our fellow humans. Yet, spam clutters our mailboxes and the sheer volume of email we get sometimes overwhelms us. Likewise, in just the past few years, smartphones have transformed our lives in so many ways for the better in terms of not just personal convenience but also personal safety. On the other hand, smartphones have become more than a bit of nuisance in certain environments (theaters, restaurants, and other closed spaces). And they also put our safety at risk when we use them while driving automobiles.

But, again, we adjust to most of these new realities and then we find constructive solutions to the really hard problems—and that sometimes includes legal remedies to rectify serious harms. But as messy and uncomfortable as muddling through can be, we must always remain aware of what we gain in the process and ask ourselves what the cost of taking the alternative path would be.

Attempts to throw a wrench in the works and derail new innovations or delay various types of technological change are always going to be tempting, but such interventions will come at a potentially very steep cost: less entrepreneurialism, diminished competition, stagnant markets, higher prices, and fewer choices for consumers. As noted, if we spend all our time living in constant fear of worst-case scenarios—and premising public policy upon such fears—then many best-case scenarios will never come about.

C. OVERCOMING TECHNOPANICS: SOME CASE STUDIES

Let's consider a few case studies of how many new technologies were initially resisted because they disrupted long-standing social norms, traditions, and institutions, but then were quickly assimilated into our lives after a brief adjustment period:

- **The telegraph:** It may seem silly today, but one of the very earliest modern communications technologies—the telegraph—raised profound concerns as it became more widespread. An 1858 editorial by the *New York Times* declared that the telegraph was "superficial, sudden, unsifted, [and] too fast for the truth" and questioned, "What need is there for the scraps of news in ten minutes? How trivial and paltry is the telegraphic column?"[18] While the *Times* was willing to admit the device might be of some value, it wondered if there would be more widespread benefit: "That it will be of very great use cannot be questioned, but how will its uses add to the happiness of mankind? Has the land telegraph done any good? Has it banished any evil, mitigated any sorrow?"[19] While it certainly didn't banish all evils or sorrows from our lives, it seems clear that the telegraph helped profoundly reshape society for the better by providing near-instantaneous transmission of news and other communications to diverse populations.

- **The telephone:** Many modern media and communications technologies have challenged well-established norms and conventions, but few were as socially disruptive as the telephone. Writing in *Slate*, Keith Collins explains that "when the telephone was invented, people found the concept entirely bizarre. So much so that the first telephone book, published in 1878, had to provide instructions on how to begin and end calls. People were to say 'Ahoy' to answer the phone and 'That is all' before hanging up."[20] But people quickly adjusted to the new device. "Ultimately, the telephone proved too useful to abandon for the sake of social discomfort," notes Collins. "It was also something people could get used to in their own homes. They didn't have to overcome the awkwardness in public. . . . That was a barrier another device would have to deal with 100 years later."[21] Of course, when cell phones did come along 100 years later, people got over that "awkwardness," too. Today, mobile phones are viewed by most of us as indispensable devices.

- **Cameras / public photography:** The introduction and evolution of the camera and photography provides another useful example of social adaptation. The camera was viewed as a highly disruptive force when photography became more widespread in the late 1800s and the *New York Times* even protested the "Kodak fiends" who took pictures of others in public.[22] Advocates also took notice. Indeed, the most important essay ever written on privacy law, Samuel D. Warren and Louis D. Brandeis's famous 1890 *Harvard Law Review* essay on "The Right to Privacy," decried the spread of public photography and called for its regulation.[23] The authors lamented that "instantaneous photographs and newspaper enterprise have invaded the sacred precincts of private and domestic life" and claimed that "numerous mechanical devices threaten to make good the prediction that 'what is whispered in the closet shall be proclaimed from the house-tops.'"[24] But personal norms and cultural attitudes toward cameras and public photography evolved quite rapidly and they became ingrained in human experience. At the same time, social norms and etiquette evolved to address those who would use cameras in inappropriate, privacy-invasive ways.

- **Transistors:** The rise of the transistor in the 1940s and '50s paved the way for the microchip and modern computing revolutions. But the transistor also gave rise to concerns about miniaturized microphones that could be used to secretly "bug" people's private conversations. Lawmakers and early privacy advocates "cried foul, anticipating wide-spread abuse," and congressional hearings followed.[25] Panicky press reports quickly followed and famously included a cover story in the May 1966 issue of *Life* magazine (the most popular magazine at the time) that voiced concerns about the spread of "a vast array of inexpensive, easy-to-install snooping devices which can be bought over the counter with no questions asked."[26] But there was no wave of decentralized public bugging as predicted, and by the 1980s fears about transistors had subsided and the panic about widespread bugging had passed.

- **Caller ID:** Although caller identification tools are widely used today, they were the subject of a heated privacy debate in the 1990s.[27] The Electronic Privacy Information Center and other privacy advocates wanted the Federal Communications Commission (FCC) to block the reve-lation of telephone numbers by default, requiring users to opt in to allow their phone numbers to be displayed.[28] Today, caller ID is a routine feature in not just traditional phones but all smartphones.

- **RFID:** When radio-frequency identification (RFID) tech-nologies first came on the scene in the early years of the 21st century, a brief panic followed. Privacy advocates feared that the tracking technology would allow all our movements to be monitored in real time. In the extreme, RFID was likened to the biblical threat of the "mark of the beast."[29] Legislative bills to regulate privacy-related aspects of RFID technology were introduced in several states, although none passed.[30] Fears about RFID were greatly exaggerated and the panic largely passed within a few years.[31] Today, RFID technologies represent the foundation on which many other digital systems and Internet of Things technologies are being developed.[32]

- **Gmail:** When Google launched its Gmail service in 2004, it was greeted with hostility by many privacy advocates and some policymakers.[33] Rather than charging some users for more storage or special features, Google paid for the service by showing advertisements next to each email "contextually" targeted to keywords in that email. Some privacy advocates worried that Google was going to "read users' email" and pushed for restrictions on such algorithmic contextual targeting.[34] But users enthusiastically embraced Gmail and the service grew rapidly. By summer 2012, Google announced that 425 million people were actively using Gmail.[35] Users adapted their privacy expectations to accommodate this new service, which offered them clear benefits (free service, generous storage, and improved search functionality) in exchange for tolerating some targeted advertising.

- **Wireless location-based services:** In spring 2011, Apple and Google came under fire for retaining location data gleaned by iPhone- and Android-based smartphone devices.[36] But these "tracking" concerns were greatly overblown—almost all mobile devices must retain a certain amount of locational information to ensure various services work properly, and these data were not being shared with others.[37] Users who are highly sensitive about locational privacy can always turn off locational tracking or encrypt and constantly delete their data.[38] But most consumers now routinely use wireless location-based services, regardless of privacy concerns.

INNOVATION OPPORTUNITY: Wearable Technologies

Wearable technologies are networked devices that can collect data, track activities, and customize experiences to users' needs and desires. These devices typically rely on sensor technologies as well as existing wireless networking systems and protocols (Wi-Fi, Bluetooth, near field communication, and GPS) to facilitate those objectives.[39]

These technologies are a subset of the Internet of Things, but they deserve special attention because of their rapid growth and potential widespread societal impact.[40] BI Intelligence estimates that "the global wearables market will grow at a compound annual rate of 35% over the next five years, reaching 148 million units shipped annually in 2019, up from 33 million units shipped this year."[41]

Although rudimentary wearable technologies—such as calculator wristwatches, hearing aids, and Bluetooth-enabled communications headsets—have been on the market for many years, this market is now expanding quite rapidly.[42] Many wearable technologies are already on the market today and are used primarily for health and fitness purposes. The so-called "quantified self" movement refers to individuals who use digital logging tools to continuously track their daily activity and well-being. Popular examples of wearables include fitness tracking and feedback products like Jawbone and FitBit that allow individuals to continuously measure and share daily fitness activities to isolate and improve their outcomes.[43] Apple, Pebble, Samsung, and other companies are also offering "smart watches" that are, in essence, wearable smartphones strapped to one's wrist full time.

In the future, wearable devices and sensor-rich fabric[44] could be used for personal safety and convenience applications, whether at home or out and about in the world. Sophisticated wearable health devices will soon remind users to take medications or contact medical professionals as necessary and eventually help users track and even diagnose various conditions before advising a course of action.[45] For example, wearable technologies are already being used by many elderly individuals to ensure they can report medical emergencies to caregivers and family members. Medical Body Area Network sensors in professional health care are also set to take off and "will enable patient monitoring information such as temperature to be collected automatically from a wearable thermometer sensor."[46]

Other experiments with implantable "hearable" devices (that augment what we can hear and sense around us),[47] "smart" contact lenses and glasses,[48] and even tactile networked patches and fabrics[49] seek to cheaply and seamlessly monitor other health vitals like blood glucose levels, blood pressure, brain activity, and stress to improve preventative medicine and save billions in healthcare costs.[50]

In terms of personal convenience, wearables could be used in both homes and workplaces to tailor environmental experiences, such as automatically adjusting lighting, temperature, or entertainment as users move from one space to another. In this sense, these wearable devices and applications could eventually become "lifestyle remotes" that help consumers control or automate many other systems around them, regardless of whether they are in their home, office, or car.

Companies will also use wearables to tailor services to users who visit their establishments. Disney has created a "Magic Band" that can help visitors to their entertainment parks personalize their experience before they even arrive at the facilities.[51] And many other sectors and professions, including surgery and emergency medical care, retail and entertainment, and law enforcement and firefighting, are already being transformed by wearable technologies.[52]

As with other Internet of Things devices, wearable technologies will raise a variety of safety, security, and especially privacy concerns.[53] Again, a diverse array of strategies will be needed to address these concerns, including education and empowerment strategies aimed at helping citizens better protect the massive amount of personal data collected by wearable devices. Companies will also need to develop better "privacy-by-design" and "security-by-design" strategies to "bake-in" best practices for data handling and use. Underwriters Labs is developing certification standards for wearable safety, security, and privacy.[54]

Other targeted laws or liability norms already exist that can address particular egregious misuses of wearable devices, like "Peeping Tom" laws and other privacy torts that address surreptitious surveillance. But policymakers should avoid preemptively regulating wearables based on worst-case hypotheticals about misuse.

These case studies illustrate how, more often than not, society has found ways to adapt to new technological changes by employing a variety of coping mechanisms or new social norms.[55] Technologies that are originally viewed as intrusive or annoying often become not just accepted but even essential in fairly short order. These examples should give us hope that we will also find ways of adapting to the challenges presented by other new innovations.

"Dynamists avoid panic in the face of new ideas," notes Postrel. "They realize that people get used to new developments, that they adjust," she says.[56] Thus, just as policymakers did not preemptively foreclose innovation with previous information technologies, they should not artificially restrict other forms of innovation today with overly prescriptive privacy, security, or safety regulations. Let innovation continue, and address tangible harms as they develop, if they do at all.

D. HOW NORMS "REGULATE"

Chapter VI will consider the role public policy should play in responding to technological disruptions. First, however, it is important to note that new technologies can be regulated by more than law.[57] Social pressure and private norms of acceptable use often act as a "regulator" of the uses (and misuses) of new technologies because, quite often, "norms dissuade many practices that are feasible but undesirable."[58]

Cass Sunstein defines norms as "social attitudes of approval and disapproval, specifying what ought to be done and what ought not to be done."[59] These social norms, and corresponding social sanctions, often act as powerful regulators of behavior. He notes that

> social norms are enforced through social sanctions; these sanctions create a range of unpleasant (but sometimes pleasant) emotional states in the minds of people who have violated them. If someone behaves in a way inconsistent with social norms, public disapproval may produce shame and a desire to hide.[60]

And, as Sunstein explains, the costs of violating social norms can be quite high because the unpleasant feelings brought about are intense, and the social consequences can be profound.[61] In some cases, norms rather than formal legal rules dictate how individuals will interact with one another.

Cristina Bicchieri, an expert on social norms and how they are formed, refers to these arrangements as "covenants without swords." She explains that "covenants are made and kept even in the absence of obvious sanctions. The very act of promising . . . might be enough to induce many of us to behave contrary to narrow self-interest. A social norm has been activated, and, under the right circumstances, we are prepared to follow it."[62] Bicchieri goes so far as to call social norms "the grammar of society":

> Like a collection of linguistic rules that are implicit in a language and define it, social norms are implicit in the operations of a society and make it what it is. Like a grammar, a system of norms specifies what is acceptable and what is not in a social group. And analogously to a grammar, a system of norms is not the product of human design and planning.[63]

Thus, whether they are born out of an obligation to keep promises or to avoid punishment or social sanction, norms act as a powerful check on bad behavior.[64] Norms played an important role in shaping acceptable social uses of the camera and other technologies discussed earlier in this chapter. But it happens in other modern contexts as well.

Consider how we are currently witnessing the development of social constraints on the use of mobile phones in various environments. For example, the use of mobile devices in some restaurants and most movie theaters is frowned upon and actively discouraged. Some of these norms or social constraints are imposed by establishments in the form of notices and restrictions on mobile device usage. Some establishments have even created incentives for compliance by offering discounts for patrons who voluntarily check in their devices.[65] Similar smartphone rules and norms have been established in other contexts; "quiet cars" on trains are one example. Restrictions on the use of camera phones in gym locker rooms is another.

In many cases, these norms or social constraints are purely bottom-up and group-driven. In many cinemas, for example, it is not uncommon to hear someone "shush" disruptive patrons who chat on their phones. And anyone casually snapping pictures in bathrooms or locker rooms is sure to draw the immediate reprobation of other patrons. Other social norm innovations are always developing. For example, "phone-stacking" refers to a new social convention in which friends having dinner agree to stack their phones in a pile in the middle of the table to minimize distraction during a meal. To encourage compliance with the informal rule, the first person who touches their phone must pick up the check for the entire table.[66]

Norms are also influenced by the social pressure exerted by advocacy organizations. Media watchdogs and online safety groups have been quite successful in shaping media norms over the past two decades. Groups like Common Sense Media have influenced content decisions through the pressure they have brought to bear on media providers in the marketplace. Common Sense Media not only encouraged and influenced the development of private content rating systems for video games, but the group also developed its own content rating system for games, TV, and movies to provide parents and others with useful information. Similarly, the Parents Television Council (PTC) awards a "seal of approval" to advertisers and programmers that support only programs that the PTC classifies as family-friendly.[67] The organization also encourages parents to send letters and emails to advertisers that support programming they find objectionable and encourage those advertisers to end their support of those shows.

In recent years, privacy advocates have also become more visible and gained influence that closely mirrors what occurred with online child safety organizations in the previous two decades. Although both sets of advocates were slow to gain influence at first, their power grew steadily as their respective issues gained more prominence. In addition to their activism and outreach efforts, nonprofit organizations— including the Electronic Privacy Information Center,[68] Privacy Rights

Clearinghouse,[69] American Civil Liberties Union,[70] and others—offer instructional websites and tips for how privacy-sensitive consumers can take steps to protect their personal information online. Going forward, we can expect privacy policies—both legal enactments and informal corporate standards—to be significantly influenced by the pressure that these advocates exert on the process.

Finally, the media offers a powerful check on mistakes and misbehavior. Technology developers today face near-constant scrutiny, not just from large media outlets, but also from what blogging pioneer Glenn Reynolds and *We the Media* author Dan Gillmor refer to as the rise of "we-dia"—user-generated content and citizen journalism—that is an increasingly important part of the modern media landscape.[71] Gillmor, a former *San Jose Mercury News* columnist, speaks of "a modern revolution . . . because technology has given us a communications toolkit that allows anyone to become a journalist at little cost and, in theory, with global reach. Nothing like this has ever been remotely possible before," he argues.[72] Notes Yochai Benkler, author of *The Wealth of Networks*, "We are seeing the emergence of new, decentralized approaches to fulfilling the watchdog function and to engaging in political debate and organization."[73]

Similarly, a recent *Ars Technica* essay offered some powerful examples of how, when "shamed on Twitter, corporations do an about-face."[74] Now that the public has more tools at its disposal to sound off, it is not uncommon for people to use social media as the equivalent of a public complaint box. This creates a powerful incentive for corporations, governments, and other organizations to improve their customer service.

In sum, this combination of social norms, media attention, and public pressure provides a powerful check on abuses of new technologies. "Manners are of more importance than laws," the English statesman and philosopher Edmund Burke once noted, because they are in "constant, steady, uniform, insensible operation, like that of the air we breathe in."[75] In other words, more than laws can regulate behavior—whether it is organizational behavior or individual behavior. Again, it's another way we learn to cope with technological change and "muddle through."

INNOVATION OPPORTUNITY: Immersive Technology

Immersive technology refers to services that utilize wearable devices such as a head-mounted display (HMD) or headset to expose users to digital content such as virtual worlds, virtual objects, or hologram-like projections. Immersive technology can be separated into two different, but related groups: virtual reality (VR) and augmented reality (AR).[76] Taken together, these two technologies are expected to generate about $150 billion in revenue by 2020 according to a report by Manatt Digital Media.[77]

VR tricks users' brains into thinking that they are in a virtual world by using two offset video streams or images placed beside one another and viewed through a lens to generate a stereoscopic effect.[78] AR, on the other hand, is more difficult to define owing to graduations in how "augmented" reality can be. Wearable AR headsets like Google's Glass, Microsoft's Hololens, or Magic Leap's unnamed project differ from VR HMDs like Facebook's Oculus, Valve and HTC's Vive, or Sony's newly dubbed PlayStation VR in that the devices lay images over actual reality as opposed to placing the user into a fully computer-generated world.[79]

Although gaming applications are driving VR, the technology is being used for more than just entertainment. VR and AR are increasingly changing how the medical profession approaches such situations as treating phobias and posttraumatic stress disorder in virtual spaces by controlled exposure to fear triggers.[80] Doctors are transforming traditional imaging methods like MRIs and CT scans by converting the resulting 2-D images into 3-D models to explore and manipulate the body before surgery.[81] These types of alternate training methods have reduced elderly care facilities' costs to teach procedures such as tracheal insertions from $3,000 per employee to $40 per employee.[82] VR and AR are also being used to reduce phantom-limb pain[83] and correct eye disorders,[84] and as a method of alleviating burn patients' pain during treatments.[85] Immersive technology is revolutionizing the training of medical professionals and students alike, but this learning process is not relegated to the medical field alone.

Immersive technologies are steadily making their way into education as tech companies use easy-to-access VR HMDs in the form of Google's own Cardboard or Mattel's View Master to take students on virtual field trips.[86] "Museums are flirting with change that may be more revolutionary than at any other point in their history" by using VR technologies, notes a recent *Wall Street Journal* report.[87] Educators are using VR to teach subjects like biology by taking students on a virtual tour of the bloodstream.[88] Meanwhile,

Discovery has launched a VR experience of wilderness survival and urban adventures with real recordings of undersea wrecks and shark dives.[89]

Commercially speaking, retailers can use VR to offer prospective customers virtual representations of products for sale[90] and realtors can offer clients virtual tours of homes.[91] Journalists are experimenting with VR to capture footage of war-torn areas using 360-degree video.[92] Automotive engineers[93] and architects are also using VR to virtually model and prototype their designs.[94]

The continued growth of immersive technologies such as these could raise some policy concerns. The peer-to-peer surveillance capabilities of Google Glass and other wearables like the "Narrative" clip-on camera have already spawned a variety of privacy fears.[95] How much data will these devices collect about us? How might they be used? Answers to these questions remain unclear at this point, but equally unclear is how many beneficial uses and applications might flow from such technologies.[96] Academics are already wondering how to enforce "notice and consent" privacy norms and rules in a world where everyone is wearing miniature body cams and heads-up displays in their sunglasses.

In terms of privacy fears and etiquette issues, the power of social norms in this context could become a crucial determinant of the success of AR technologies. As noted above, sometimes cultural norms, public pressure, and spontaneous social sanctions are a far more powerful "regulator" of innovations and how people use new tools when compared with laws and regulations.

Because VR technologies are not yet in widespread public use, the policy issues here have yet to come into clear focus. But it wouldn't be surprising if safety concerns end up driving some policy proposals as critics grow concerned about the psychological implications of people (especially kids) spending more and more time in immersive virtual worlds. In that sense, we might see a replay of the earlier debates over violent video games and video game addiction.

If distraction or even addiction *does* become the primary policy concern surrounding VR technologies, the better way to address that issue is with educational efforts, or, if the problem is more serious, counseling or behavioral therapy efforts. Generally speaking, however, policymakers should avoid burdening AR and VR technologies based on hypothetical worst-case scenarios. They should instead wait to see what sort of problems develop and determine whether less restrictive remedies are available.

CHAPTER V
WHAT ISSUES PROMPT PRECAUTIONARY THINKING AND POLICY TODAY?

T his chapter will identify some of the specific concerns related to new information technologies and the emerging next great industrial revolution. The most notable concerns relate to privacy, safety, security, and various types of economic disruptions.

A. PLANNING FOR EVERY WORST CASE MEANS THE BEST CASE NEVER COMES ABOUT

Before discussing those concerns, however, one paradox about technological innovation must be reiterated: *technology giveth and the technology taketh away.*[1] In order to move forward and prosper, we must sometimes learn to tolerate the disruptive effects associated with certain new technologies, or else progress becomes impossible.

For example, the great blessing of the Internet and modern digital platforms is that they are highly interconnected, ubiquitous, and generally quite open. Speech and commerce flow freely. On the other hand, you cannot have the most open, accessible, and interactive communications platform that humanity has ever known without also having some serious privacy, security, and safety issues creep up on occasion. Simply put, openness and interconnectedness offer us enormous benefits, but they also force us to confront gut-wrenching disruptions of both a social and economic nature. That is the price of admission to this wonderful new world of abundant content and communications opportunities. This tension will only be exacerbated by the rise of the next industrial revolution, the Internet of Things, and an even more interconnected, interactive economy.

Unfortunately, many of the scholars, regulatory advocates, and policymakers who fear the social and economic disruptions associated with these changes will often recommend preemptive steps to head off any number of hypothetical worst-case scenarios. While they likely have the best of intentions when they recommend such precautionary steps, the most serious flaw in their thinking has already been noted above: *trying to preemptively plan for every hypothetical worst-case scenario means that many best-case scenarios will never come about.* That is, the benefits that accompany the freedom to experiment will be sacrificed if fear paralyzes our innovative spirit. Progress and prosperity will be stifled as a result.[2]

Finally, as already noted, because it is typically based on fear and ignorance, such worst-case thinking "can lead to hasty and dangerous acts," notes Internet security expert Bruce Schneier. "You can't wait for a smoking gun, so you act as if the gun is about to go off. Rather than making us safer, worst-case thinking has the potential to cause dangerous escalation," he says.[3] And, as we'll see in this chapter, it can also lead to myriad other unintended consequences that can deter life-enriching innovation or set back social and economic progress in other ways.

With that admonition in mind, each major policy concern will be discussed in turn.

B. PRIVACY AND DISCRIMINATION CONCERNS

To appreciate how precautionary logic increasingly dominates the public policy dialog about new information technologies, we'll first consider concerns about privacy and "digital discrimination."[4]

Consider a summer 2013 speech by Federal Trade Commission Chairwoman Edith Ramirez on "The Privacy Challenges of Big Data: A View from the Lifeguard's Chair." In it, Ramirez focused her attention on privacy and security fears about the growth of "big data."[5] Ramirez made several provocative assertions in the speech, but the one "commandment" she issued warrants attention. Claiming that "one risk is that the lure of 'big data' leads to the indiscriminate collection of personal information," Ramirez went on to argue:

> The indiscriminate collection of data violates the First Commandment of data hygiene: Thou shall not collect and hold onto personal information unnecessary to an identified purpose. Keeping data on the offchance that it might prove useful is not consistent with privacy best practices. And remember, not all data is created equally. Just as there is low quality iron ore and coal, there is low quality, unreliable data. And old data is of little value.[6]

She continued on, arguing that "information that is not collected in the first place can't be misused" and then outlined a parade of "horribles" that will occur if such data collection is allowed at all.[7] She was particularly concerned that all this data might somehow be used by companies to discriminate against certain classes of customers. Some legal scholars today decry what Ryan Calo of the University of Washington School of Law calls "digital market manipulation," or the belief that "firms will increasingly be able to trigger irrationality or vulnerability in consumers—leading to actual and perceived harms that challenge the limits of consumer protection law, but which regulators can scarcely ignore."[8] Others fear "power asymmetries" between companies and consumers and even suggest that consumers' apparent lack of concern about sharing information means that people may not be acting in their own best self-interest when it comes to online safety and digital privacy choices.[9]

For example, Professor Siva Vaidhyanathan says consumers are being tricked by the "smokescreen" of "free" online services and "freedom of choice."[10] Although he admits that no one is forced to use online services and that consumers can opt out of most of these services or data collection practices, Vaidhyanathan argues that "such choices mean very little" because "the design of the system rigs it in favor of the interests of the company and against the interests of users."[11] He suggests that online operators are sedating consumers using the false hope of consumer choice.[12] "Celebrating freedom and user autonomy is one of the great rhetorical ploys of the global information economy," he says.[13] "We are conditioned to believe that having more choices—empty though they may be— is the very essence of human freedom. But meaningful freedom implies real control over the conditions of one's life."[14]

Paternalistic claims such as these clash mightily with the foundational principles of a free society—namely, that individuals are autonomous agents who should be left free to make choices for themselves, even when some of those choices strike others as unwise.[15] The larger problem with such claims is: Where does one draw the line in terms of the policy action they seem to counsel? Taken to the extreme, such reasoning would open the door to almost boundless controls on the activities of consumers.

Consumer protection standards have traditionally depended on a clear showing of actual, not prospective or hypothetical, harm. It is not enough to claim, "Well, it could happen!" In some cases, when the potential harm associated with a particular practice or technology is extreme in character and poses a direct threat to physical well-being, laws have preempted the general presumption that ongoing experimentation and innovation should be allowed by default. But these are extremely rare scenarios, at least in American law, and they mostly involved health and safety measures aimed at preemptively avoiding catastrophic harm to individual or environmental well-being. In the vast majority of other cases, our culture has not accepted that paternalistic idea that the law must "save us from ourselves" (i.e., our own irrationality or mistakes).[16]

But it's not just that this logic rejects personal responsibility, it's that it ignores the costs of preemptive policy action. After all, regulation is not a costless exercise. It imposes profound tradeoffs and opportunity costs that must always be considered.[17]

Unfortunately, many scholars don't bother conducting such a review of the potential costs of their proposals. As a result, preemptive regulation is almost always the preferred remedy to any alleged, hypothetical harm. "By limiting or conditioning the collection of information, regulators can limit market manipulation at the activity level," Calo says.[18] "We could imagine the government fashioning a rule perhaps inadvisable for other reasons that limits the collection of information about consumers in order to reduce asymmetries of information."[19] Ultimately, Calo does not endorse such a rule. Nonetheless, the corresponding cost of such regulatory proposals must be taken into account. If preemptive regulation slowed or ended certain information flows, it could stifle the provision of new and better services that consumers demand.[20]

The views set forth by some of these scholars as well as Chairwoman Ramirez represent a rather succinct articulation of precautionary principle thinking as applied to modern data collection practices. They are essentially claiming that—because there are various privacy risks associated with commercial data collection and aggregation—we must consider preemptive and potentially highly restrictive approaches to the initial collection and aggregation of data by private actors.

The problem with that logic should be fairly obvious and it was perfectly identified by Aaron Wildavsky when he noted, "If you can do nothing without knowing first how it will turn out, you cannot do anything at all."[21] Again, the best-case scenarios will never develop if we are gripped with fear by the worst-case scenarios and try to preemptively plan for them with policy interventions.

In his work, Wildavsky correctly noted that "'worst case' assumptions can convert otherwise quite ordinary conditions . . . into disasters, provided only that the right juxtaposition of unlikely factors occur."[22] In other words, creative minds can string together some random anecdotes or stories and concoct horrific-sounding scenarios about the future that leave us searching for preemptive solutions to problems that haven't even developed yet.

Again, consider Ramirez's speech. When she argues that "information that is not collected in the first place can't be misused," that is undoubtedly true. But it is equally true that information that is not collected at all is information that might have been used to provide us with the next "killer app" or the great gadget or digital service that we cannot currently contemplate but that some innovative entrepreneur out there might be looking to develop.

Likewise, claiming that "old data is of little value" and issuing the commandment that "thou shall not collect and hold onto personal information unnecessary to an identified purpose" reveals a rather shocking arrogance about the possibility of serendipitous data discovery. The reality is that the cornucopia of innovative information options and opportunities we have at our disposal today was driven in large part by data collection, including personal-data collection. And often those innovations were not part of some initial grand design; instead they came about through the discovery of new and interesting things that could be done with data after the fact.

Examples include many of the information services and digital technologies that we enjoy and take for granted today, such as language translation tools, mobile traffic services, digital mapping technologies, spam and fraud detection tools, and instant spell-checkers. As Viktor Mayer-Schönberger and Kenneth Cukier point out in their recent book, *Big Data: A Revolution That Will Transform How We Live, Work, and Think,* "data's value needs to be considered in terms of all the possible ways it can be employed in the future, not simply how it is used in the present." They also note, "In the big-data age, data is like a magical diamond mine that keeps on giving long after its principal value has been tapped."[23]

In any event, if the new policy in the United States is to follow Ramirez's pronouncement that "[k]eeping data on the offchance that it might prove useful is not consistent with privacy best practices," then much of the information economy as we know it today will need to be shut down. At a minimum, entrepreneurs will have to start hiring a lot more lobbyists who can sit in Washington and petition the FTC or other policymakers for permission to innovate whenever they have an interesting new idea for how to use data to offer a new service other than the one for which it was initially collected. Again, this is "Mother, May I" regulation and we had better get used to a lot more of it if we go down the path Ramirez is charting.

It is useful to contrast Ramirez's approach with that of her fellow FTC Commissioner Maureen K. Ohlhausen. In an October 2013 speech titled "The Internet of Things and the FTC: Does Innovation Require Intervention?" Ohlhausen noted, "The success of the Internet has in large part been driven by the freedom to experiment with different business models, the best of which have survived and thrived, even in the face of initial unfamiliarity and unease about the impact on consumers and competitors."[24]

More importantly, Ohlhausen went on to highlight another crucial point about why the precautionary mindset is dangerous when enshrined into laws or regulations. Put simply, many elites and regulatory advocates ignore *regulator irrationality or regulatory ignorance.* That is, they spend so much time focused on the supposed irrationality of consumers and their openness to persuasion or "manipulation" that they ignore the more concerning problem of the irrationality or ignorance of those who (incorrectly) believe they are always in the best position to solve every complex problem. Regulators simply do not possess the requisite knowledge to perfectly plan for every conceivable outcome. This is particularly true for information technology markets, which generally evolve much more rapidly than other sectors, and especially more rapidly than the law itself.

That insight leads Ohlhausen to issue a wise word of caution to her fellow regulators:

> It is . . . vital that government officials, like myself, approach new technologies with a dose of regulatory humility, by working hard to educate ourselves and others about the innovation, understand its effects on consumers and the marketplace, identify benefits and likely harms, and, if harms do arise, consider whether existing laws and regulations are sufficient to address them, before assuming that new rules are required.[25]

This again suggests that Ohlhausen's approach to technological innovation is consistent with the permissionless innovation approach whereas Ramirez's is based on precautionary principle thinking. Again, this tension dominates almost all policy debates over new technology today, even if it is not always on such vivid display as it is here with the views of these two FTC officials.

The fact is, almost every new media or communications technology raises some sort of privacy-related concern. Although privacy is a highly subjective value, most everyone can find a new technology or service that they find "creepy" because it violates their visceral sense of privacy.[26] But as "history has shown, many of the overinflated claims about loss of privacy have never materialized."[27] Moreover, as noted in chapter IV, more often than not, we humans prove particularly good at adapting to new technologies and finding ways to sensibly assimilate them into our lives over time.

C. SAFETY AND SPEECH CONCERNS

Many parents and policymakers worry about how new information technologies and other modern innovations might expose their children to objectionable content or communications. Primary concerns include online pornography, hate speech, and controversial ideas.[28]

The first great wave of Internet innovation in the early and mid-1990s gave rise to intense online safety concerns. As the Internet expanded quickly in the mid-1990s, a technopanic over online pornography developed just as quickly.[29] Unfortunately, the inflated rhetoric surrounding "the Great Cyberporn Panic of 1995"[30] turned out to be based on a single study with numerous methodological flaws.[31]

Similarly, a decade later, as social networking sites began growing in popularity, in 2005–06 several state attorneys general and lawmakers began claiming that sites like MySpace and Facebook represented a "predators' playground," implying that youth could be groomed for abuse or abduction by visiting those sites.[32] Regulatory efforts were pursued to remedy this supposed threat, including a proposed federal ban on access to social networking sites in schools and libraries as well as mandatory online age verification, which was endorsed by many state attorneys general.[33] These measures would have affected a wide swath of online sites and services with interactive functionality.[34]

Unsurprisingly, the bill proposing a federal ban on social networks in schools and libraries was titled Deleting Online Predators Act of 2006.[35] That year, the measure received 410 votes in the US House of Representatives before finally dying in the Senate.[36] The bill was introduced in the following session of Congress, but did not see another floor vote and was never implemented.[37] During this same period, many states floated bills that also sought to restrict underage access to social networking sites. However, none of the underage access restrictions introduced with these bills were ultimately enacted as law.[38]

Despite the heightened sense of fear aroused by policymakers over this issue, there was almost no basis for the predator panic. It was based almost entirely on threat inflation. "As with other moral panics, the one concerning MySpace had more to do with perception than reality," concluded social media researcher Danah Boyd.[39] Furthermore, she states, "As researchers began investigating the risks that teens faced in social network sites, it became clear that the myths and realities of risk were completely disconnected."[40]

Generally speaking, the fear about strangers abducting children online was always greatly overstated, since it is obviously impossible for abductors to directly "snatch" children by means of electronic communication. Abduction after Internet contact requires long-term, and usually long-distance, grooming and meticulous planning about how to commit the crime.[41] This is not to say there were no cases of abduction that involved Internet grooming, but such cases did not represent the epidemic that some suggested.[42]

Lenore Skenazy, author of *Free-Range Kids: Giving Our Children the Freedom We Had without Going Nuts with Worry*, puts things in perspective: "[T]he chances of any one American child being kidnapped and killed by a stranger are almost infinitesimally small: .00007 percent."[43] A May 2010 report by the Department of Justice confirmed that "family abduction [remains] the most prevalent form of child abduction in the United States."[44] These facts are not intended to trivialize the seriousness of abduction by family members or family acquaintances, but they make it clear that the panic over strangers using social networks to groom and abduct children was based on a faulty premise that kidnappings resulting from online grooming by sexual predators are commonplace and demand preemptive Internet controls. Regardless, as with all other technopanics, the predator panic eventually ran its course, although some of the aforementioned fears remain in the public consciousness.

Importantly, many individuals and organizations have worked together to empower and educate the public on how to deal with underage access to objectionable online material.[45] And many industry trade associations and nonprofit advocacy groups have established industry best practices and codes of conduct to ensure users of all ages have a safer and more secure online experience. For example, the Family Online Safety Institute, which coordinates online safety campaigns with various online operator and child safety advocacy groups, sponsors the Broadband Responsibility Awareness Campaign.[46] The effort includes "A Blueprint for Safe and Responsible Online Use" that encourages member organizations to help create a culture of online responsibility by adopting various education and empowerment-based efforts.[47]

Concerns about online "hate speech" often lead to calls for preemptive speech controls as well.[48] Many academics,[49] pundits,[50] and advocacy groups have pushed governments across the globe to clamp down on various types of offensive online speech. Sometimes, concerns about controversial or potentially false online information raise similar calls for preemptive action, sometimes in a completely contradictory fashion.

For example, Evgeny Morozov has argued that online intermediaries should be doing both more and less to police online speech and content. In a January 2012 *Slate* essay, Morozov argued that steps be taken to root out lies, deceptions, and conspiracy theories on the Internet.[51] Morozov was particularly worried about "denialists of global warming or benefits of vaccination," but he also wondered how we might deal with 9/11 conspiracy theorists, the anti-Darwinian intelligent design movement, and those that refuse to accept the link between HIV and AIDS.[52]

He recommended that Google "come up with a database of disputed claims" or "exercise a heavier curatorial control in presenting search results," to weed out such things.[53] He suggested that the other option "is to nudge search engines to take more responsibility for their index and exercise a heavier curatorial control in presenting search results for issues" that someone (he never says who) determines to be conspiratorial or antiscientific in nature.[54]

Yet, less than a year later in a *New York Times* op-ed, Morozov claimed that Silicon Valley is imposing a "deeply conservative" "new prudishness" on modern society.[55] The cause, he says, is "dour, one-dimensional algorithms, the mathematical constructs that automatically determine the limits of what is culturally acceptable."[56] He proposed that some form of external algorithmic auditing be undertaken to counter this supposed problem.

Taken together, Morozov's two essays may initially appear intellectually schizophrenic. Yet, what unifies them is his technocratic tendency to think there is some sort of Goldilocks-like formula to getting things *just right* as they pertain to online free speech. Morozov is vague on the details of his proposed regime, however. "Is it time for some kind of a quality control system [for the Internet]?" he asked in *Slate*. Perhaps that would be the algorithmic auditors he suggests in his *New York Times* essay. But who, exactly, are those auditors? What is the scope of their powers? Again, like so many other technocratic, precautionary principle–minded pundits, Morozov refuses to let us in on the details. We are supposed to instead be content to trust him or some other group of technocratic philosopher kings to make wise decisions on our behalf and guide online speech and content down some supposedly better path.

D. SECURITY CONCERNS

Viruses, malware, spam, data breeches, and critical system intrusions are just some of the security-related concerns that often motivate precautionary thinking and policy proposals.[57] But as with privacy- and safety-related worries, the panicky rhetoric surrounding these issues is usually unfocused and counterproductive.

In today's cybersecurity debates, for example, it is not uncommon to hear frequent allusions to the potential for a "digital Pearl Harbor,"[58] a "cyber cold war,"[59] or even a "cyber 9/11."[60] These analogies are made even though these historical incidents resulted in death and destruction of a sort not comparable to attacks on digital networks. Others refer to "cyber bombs" or technological "time bombs," even though no one can be "bombed" with binary code.[61] Michael McConnell, a former director of national intelligence, went so far as to say that this "threat is so intrusive, it's so serious, it could literally suck the life's blood out of this country."[62]

Such outrageous statements reflect the frequent use of "threat inflation" rhetoric in debates about online security.[63] Threat inflation has been defined as "the attempt by elites to create concern for a threat that goes beyond the scope and urgency that a disinterested analysis would justify."[64] Unfortunately, such bombastic rhetoric often conflates minor cybersecurity risks with major ones. For example, dramatic doomsday stories about hackers pushing planes out of the sky misdirects policymakers' attention from the more immediate, but less gripping, risks of data extraction and foreign surveillance. Well-meaning skeptics might then conclude that our real cybersecurity risks are also not a problem. In the meantime, outdated legislation and inappropriate legal norms continue to impede beneficial defensive measures that could truly improve security.

Meanwhile, similar concerns have already been raised about security vulnerabilities associated with the Internet of Things[65] and driverless cars.[66] Legislation has already been floated to address the latter concern through federal certification standards.[67] More broad-based cybersecurity legislative proposals have also been proposed, most notably the Cybersecurity Information Sharing Act, which would extend legal immunity to corporations that share customer data with intelligence agencies.[68]

Ironically, these efforts to expand federal cybersecurity authority come before the federal government has even gotten its own house in order. According to a recent report, federal information security failures had increased by an astounding 1,169 percent, from 5,503 in fiscal year 2006 to 69,851 in fiscal year 2014.[69] Of course, many of these same agencies would be tasked with securing the massive new datasets containing personally identifiable details about US citizens' online activities that legislation like the Cybersecurity Information Sharing Act would authorize. In the worst-case scenario, such federal data storage could counterintuitively encourage more attacks on government systems.

It's important to put all these security issues in some context and to realize that proposed legal remedies are often inappropriate to address online security concerns and sometimes end up backfiring. In his research on the digital security marketplace, my Mercatus Center colleague Eli Dourado has illustrated how we are already able to achieve "Internet Security without Law."[70] Dourado documented the many informal institutions that enforce network security norms on the Internet to show how cooperation among a remarkably varied set of actors improves online security without extensive regulation or punishing legal liability. "These informal institutions carry out the functions of a formal legal system—they establish and enforce rules for the prevention, punishment, and redress of cybersecurity-related harms," Dourado says.[71]

For example, a diverse array of computer security incident response teams (CSIRTs) operate around the globe, sharing their research on and coordinating responses to viruses and other online attacks. Individual Internet service providers (ISPs), domain name registrars, and hosting companies work with these CSIRTs and other individuals and organizations to address security vulnerabilities.

Encouraging the development of robust and lawful software vulnerability markets would provide even more effective cybersecurity reporting. Some private companies and nonprofit security research firms have offered financial incentives for hackers to find and report software vulnerabilities to the proper parties for years now.[72] Such "bug bounty" and "vulnerability auction" programs better align hackers' monetary incentives with the public interest. By allowing a space for security researchers to responsibly report and profit from discovered bugs, these markets dissuade hackers from selling vulnerabilities to criminal or state-backed organizations.[73]

A growing market for private security consultants and software providers also competes to offer increasingly sophisticated suites of security products for businesses, households, and governments. "Corporations, including software vendors, antimalware makers, ISPs, and major websites such as Facebook and Twitter, are aggressively pursuing cyber criminals," notes Roger Grimes of *Infoworld*.[74] "These companies have entire legal teams dedicated to national and international cyber crime. They are also taking down malicious websites and bot-spitting command-and-control servers, along with helping to identify, prosecute, and sue bad guys," he says.[75] Meanwhile, more organizations are employing "active defense" strategies, which are "countermeasures that entail more than merely hardening one's own network against threats and instead seek to unmask one's attacker or disable the attacker's system."[76]

A great deal of security knowledge is also "crowd-sourced" today via online discussion forums and security blogs that feature contributions from experts and average users alike. University-based computer science and cyber law centers and experts have also helped by creating projects like Stop Badware, which originated at Harvard University but then grew into a broader nonprofit organization with diverse financial support.[77] Meanwhile, informal grassroots security groups like The Cavalry have formed to build awareness about digital security threats among developers and the general public and then devise solutions to protect public safety.[78]

The recent debacle over the Commerce Department's proposed new export rules for so-called cyberweapons provides a good example of how poorly considered policies can inadvertently undermine such beneficial emergent ecosystems. The agency's new draft of US "Wassenaar Arrangement" arms control policies would have unintentionally criminalized the normal communication of basic software bug-testing techniques that hundreds of companies employ each day.[79] The regulators who were drafting the new rules had good intentions. They wanted to crack down on cyber criminals' abilities to sell malware to hostile state-backed initiatives. However, their lack of technical sophistication led them to unknowingly write a proposal that would have compelled software engineers to seek Commerce Department permission before communicating information about minor software quirks. Fortunately, regulators wisely heeded the many concerned industry comments and rescinded the initial proposal.[80]

Dourado notes that informal, bottom-up efforts to coordinate security responses offer several advantages over top-down government solutions such as administrative regulatory regimes or punishing liability regimes. First, the informal cooperative approach "gives network operators flexibility to determine what constitutes due care in a dynamic environment." "Formal legal standards," by contrast, "may not be able to adapt as quickly as needed to rapidly changing circumstances," he says.[81] Simply put, markets are more nimble than mandates when it comes to promptly patching security vulnerabilities.

Second, Dourado notes that "formal legal proceedings are adversarial and could reduce ISPs' incentives to share information and cooperate."[82] Heavy-handed regulation or threatening legal liability schemes could have the unintended consequence of discouraging the sort of cooperation that today alleviates security problems swiftly.

Indeed, there is evidence that existing cybersecurity law prevents defensive strategies that could help organizations to more quickly respond to system infiltrations. For example, some argue that private individuals and organizations should be allowed to defend themselves using special measures to expel or track system infiltrators, often called "hacking back" or "active defense." Anthony Glosson's analysis for the Mercatus Center discusses how the Computer Fraud and Abuse Act currently prevents computer security specialists from utilizing defensive hacking techniques that could improve system defenses or decrease the number of attempted attacks.[83]

Third, legal solutions are less effective because "the direct costs of going to court can be substantial, as can be the time associated with a trial," Dourado argues.[84] By contrast, private actors working cooperatively "do not need to go to court to enforce security norms," meaning that "security concerns are addressed quickly or punishment . . . is imposed rapidly."[85] For example, if security warnings don't work, ISPs can "punish" negligent or willfully insecure networks by "de-peering," or terminating network interconnection agreements. The very threat of de-peering helps keep network operators on their toes.

Finally, and perhaps most importantly, Dourado notes that international cooperation between state-based legal systems is limited, complicated, and costly. By contrast, under today's informal, voluntary approach to online security, international coordination and cooperation are quite strong. The CSIRTs and other security institutions and researchers mentioned above all interact and coordinate today as if national borders did not exist. Territorial legal system and liability regimes don't have the same advantage; enforcement ends at the border.

Dourado's model has ramifications for other fields of tech policy. Indeed, as noted above, these collaborative efforts and approaches are already at work in the realms of online safety and digital privacy. Countless organizations and individuals collaborate on educational initiatives to improve online safety and privacy. And many industry and nonprofit groups have established industry best practices and codes of conduct to ensure a safer and more secure online experience for all users. The efforts of the Family Online Safety Institute were discussed above. Another example comes from the Future of Privacy Forum, a privacy think tank that seeks to advance responsible data practices. The think tank helps create codes of conduct to ensure privacy best practices by online operators and also helps highlight programs run by other organizations.[86] Likewise, the National Cyber Security Alliance helps promote Internet safety and security efforts among a variety of companies and coordinates National Cyber Security Awareness Month (every October) and Data Privacy Day (held annually on January 28).[87]

What these efforts prove is that not every complex social problem requires a convoluted legal regime or heavy-handed regulatory response. We can achieve *reasonably effective* safety and security without layering on more and more law and regulation.[88] Indeed, the Internet and digital systems could arguably be made *more* secure by reforming outdated legislation that prevents potential security-increasing collaborations. "Dynamic systems are not merely turbulent," Postrel notes. "They respond to the desire for security; they just don't do it by stopping experimentation."[89] She adds, "Left free to innovate and to learn, people find ways to create security for themselves. Those creations, too, are part of dynamic systems. They provide personal and social resilience."[90]

Education is a crucial part of building resiliency in the security context as well. People and organizations can prepare for potential security problems rationally if given even more information and better tools to secure their digital systems and to understand how to cope when problems arise. Again, many corporations and organizations already take steps to guard against malware and other types of cyberattacks by offering customers free (or cheap) security software. For example, major broadband operators offer free antivirus software to customers and various parental control tools to parents. In the context of "connected car" technology, automakers have banded together to come up with privacy and security best practices to address worries about remote hacking of cars as well as concerns about how much data they collect about our driving habits.[91]

Thus, although it is certainly true that "more could be done" to secure networks and critical systems, panic is unwarranted because much is already being done to harden systems and educate the public about risks.[92] Various digital attacks will continue, but consumers, companies, and others organizations are learning to cope and become more resilient in the face of those threats through creative "bottom-up" solutions instead of innovation-limiting "top-down" regulatory approaches.

INNOVATION OPPORTUNITY: Autonomous Vehicles and "Smart Cars"

Our cars are getting smarter and eventually they may all drive themselves so that we don't have to. Autonomous or completely "driverless" vehicles could also have many benefits if they are allowed on the roads.[93] "This new technology has the potential to reduce crashes, ease congestion, improve fuel economy, reduce parking needs, bring mobility to those unable to drive, and over time dramatically change the nature of US travel," notes the Eno Center for Transportation.[94]

"These impacts will have real and quantifiable benefits," the group notes, because more than 30,000 people die each year in the United States in automobile collisions, and "driver error is believed to be the main reason behind over 90 percent of all crashes."[95] These driver errors include drunk driving, distracted operators, failure to remain in one's lane, and failure to yield the right of way.[96] The total annual costs of such accidents amount to over $300 billion, or 2 percent of US GDP.[97] "Automation on the roads could be the great public-health achievement of the 21st century," notes Adrienne LaFrance of the *Atlantic*, because "nearly 300,000 fatalities [could be] prevented over the course of a decade, and 1.5 million lives saved in a half-century."[98]

More generally, autonomous vehicles could greatly enhance convenience and productivity for average Americans by potentially reducing traffic congestion and freeing up time spent behind the wheel. The US Census Bureau estimates that Americans annually spend over 23.5 billion hours driving to work alone, which equates to over 210 hours per person. That's time that could be used for productive or recreational purposes. A November 2013 report from Morgan Stanley estimated that autonomous cars could contribute $1.3 trillion in annual savings to the US economy, with global savings estimated at more than $5.6 trillion.[99] A decline in costs for fuel and accidents, as well as $507 billion in annual productivity gains, would drive these savings, notes Morgan Stanley. Ironically, the benefits of intelligent vehicle technologies are so profound that some now want to ban human drivers altogether![100]

Despite these benefits, plenty of critics are already worried about the societal implications of autonomous vehicles.[101] Security and liability concerns tend to dominate. Conflicting state and local laws and liability standards could also limit the growth of these technologies.[102] And some philosophers have raised ethical issues surrounding the decisions that algorithms powering autonomous systems are programmed to make in life-and-death situations.[103] Finally, concerns over remote car hacking have already promoted the introduction of congressional legislation that would impose federal standards, and the threat of class action lawsuits looms large.[104]

Such regulatory efforts could slow the adoption of intelligent vehicles and delay the many benefits they will bring.[105] Manufacturers have powerful reputational incentives to continuously improve the security of their systems and to adopt best practices within the industry, much as the information technology sector has taken steps to secure its networks.

But law could have a hard time keeping up with the rapid pace of innovation in this space. "Technology is always running ahead of the law, but in this case, it is running way ahead of the law," says Carl Tobias, a law professor at the University of Richmond.[106] That's probably not a bad thing in light of the profound benefits associated with intelligent vehicle technology. But today's legitimate safety and security concerns about smart cars will be worked out over time through ongoing trial-and-error experimentation, and legal standards will evolve to address accidents or security lapses with these systems. This is what the tort system is for; it deals with product liability and accident compensation in an evolutionary way through a variety of mechanisms, including strict liability, negligence, design-defects law, failure to warn, breach of warranty, and so on.[107]

E. ECONOMIC DISRUPTION AND AUTOMATION CONCERNS

A world of permissionless innovation is one that will ultimately disrupt many sectors, professions, and ways of doing business. Business models and jobs that were once considered "safe" may suddenly become vulnerable, even to the point where they can disappear in fairly short order.[108]

As already noted, Schumpeter's "gales of creative destruction" reverberate all around us in the modern tech economy, and the effects ripple throughout the broader economy. New products and services flow from many unexpected quarters as some innovators launch groundbreaking products and services while others devise new ways to construct cheaper and more efficient versions of existing technologies, and still others see opportunities to commercialize and attract consumers to all of them. Change has been constant, uneven, and highly disruptive, but it has also been the secret to the progress and innovation we have seen flowing from the information sector over the past two decades.

The rapid rise of the sharing economy provides one of the most recent and extreme examples of this sort of cycle in action, as the adjoining case study makes clear.[109] Yet, some critics worry that this "gig economy" will undermine the social contract between employers and employees, or various worker protections.[110] Meanwhile, concerns have been growing about the "rise of the robots"[111] and the impact of automation on the workforce.[112]

In one sense, such concerns about job disruption or displacement are nothing new. "There have been periodic warnings in the last two centuries that automation and new technology were going to wipe out large numbers of middle class jobs," notes MIT economist David H. Autor.[113] Luckily, those dire predictions have not come to pass. This is because shortsighted skeptics failed to appreciate how as new technologies obliterated old businesses and jobs, they simultaneously opened up many more opportunities that were impossible to predict in advance.[114] For every factory worker who lost a job due to technological innovation, new jobs opened up in entirely new sectors that usually offered workers better wages, a safer work environment, and more leisure time.[115]

In late 2014, economists at Deloitte LLP published a sweeping survey of the impact of technology and jobs over the past 200 years and found that "[t]echnology has transformed productivity and living standards, and, in the process, created new employment in new sectors."[116] This is because human needs and wants constantly change and, therefore, "[t]he stock of work in the economy is not fixed; the last 200 years demonstrates that when a machine replaces a human, the result, paradoxically, is faster growth and, in time, rising employment."[117] While it is easy for critics to highlight disruptions in some notable sectors where machines replaced human labor, fewer media reports or panicky books discuss the many new sectors where people have found new opportunities.[118]

And despite "a resurgence of automation anxiety"[119] in recent years, that historic trend still generally holds true.[120] Critics will repeat the old argument that *this time it's different!*, but the historical evidence suggests that there are good reasons to have faith that humans will once again muddle through and prevail in the face of turbulent, disruptive change. As venture capitalist Marc Andreessen has noted when addressing the fear that automation is running amok and that robots will eat all our jobs,

> We have no idea what the fields, industries, businesses, and jobs of the future will be. We just know we will create an enormous number of them. Because if robots and AI [artificial intelligence] replace people for many of the things we do today, the new fields we create will be built on the huge number of people those robots and AI systems made available. To argue that huge numbers of people will be available but we will find nothing for them (us) to do is to dramatically short human creativity. And I am way long [on] human creativity.[121]

Some tech critics may reject Andreessen's bullish optimism about human resiliency, but real-world evidence already supports his conclusion that we'll learn to adapt to a world full of robots and robotic systems. A 2015 economic analysis from Colin Lewis, a behavioral economist who runs *RobotEnomics*, a blog about how robotics, behavior, and culture are shaping the future, showed that "despite the headlines, companies that have installed industrial robots are actually increasingly employing more people whilst at the same time adding more robots." His research revealed that 1.25 million new jobs had been added by companies that make extensive use of industrial robots over the previous six years.[122] He also found that this trend held among more recently developed firms like Amazon and Tesla Motors, as well as older and more established companies like Chrysler, Daimler, Philips Electronics and others.[123]

It's also worth noting how difficult it is to predict future labor market trends. In early 2015, Glassdoor, an online jobs and recruiting site, published a report on the 25 highest paying jobs in demand today. Many of the job titles identified in the report probably weren't considered a top priority 40 years ago, and some of these job descriptions wouldn't even have made sense to an observer from the past. For example, some of those hotly demanded jobs on Glassdoor's list include[124] software architect (#3), software development manager (#4), solutions architect (#6), analytics manager (#8), IT manager (#9), data scientist (#15), security engineer (#16), quality assurance manager (#17), computer hardware engineer (#18), database administrator (#20), UX designer (#21), and software engineer (#23).

Looking back at reports from the 1970s and '80s published by the US Bureau of Labor Statistics, the federal agency that monitors labor market trends, one finds no mention of these computing and information technology–related professions because they had not yet been created or even envisioned.[125] So, what will the most important and well-paying jobs be 30 to 40 years from now? If history is any guide, we probably can't even imagine many of them right now.

Of course, as with previous periods of turbulent technological change, many of today's jobs and business models will be rendered obsolete, and workers and businesses will need to adjust to new marketplace realities. That transition takes time, but as James Bessen points out in his book *Learning by Doing*, for technological revolutions to take hold and have a meaningful impact on economic growth and worker conditions, large numbers of ordinary workers must acquire new knowledge and skills. But "that is a slow and difficult process, and history suggests that it often requires social changes supported by accommodating institutions and culture."[126] Luckily, however, history also suggests that, time and time again, society has adjusted to technological change and the standard of living for workers and average citizens alike improve at the same time.[127]

F. SUMMARY: OPENNESS TO CHANGE IS ESSENTIAL FOR PROGRESS

The social and economic concerns discussed in this chapter will likely continue to prompt calls for preemptive and precautionary controls on new forms of technological innovation. But we must not let those fears trump ongoing experimentation and innovation. "There is no way to get increased prosperity without being willing to try new technologies, even if they may sometimes bring short-term questions," notes Michael Mandel, chief economic strategist at the Progressive Policy Institute.[128] Economic and social progress requires an openness to constant change and a willingness to embrace new ideas, norms, business models, and public policies.[129]

Of course, problems *will* develop. But *how* these concerns are dealt with matters deeply. We should exhaust all other potential nonregulatory remedies first before resorting to prophylactic controls on new forms of innovation. Generally speaking, ex post (or after the fact) solutions should generally trump ex ante (before the fact) controls. Companies, advocacy groups, and the government should all work together to educate consumers about proper use and corporate and personal responsibility to head off those problems to the maximum extent possible. When abuse occurs, some rules may become necessary or, more likely, litigation will be used to punish misbehavior, the same way it has in one industry after another and for one technology after another for many years now. There's no reason information technology should be any different in that regard.[130] Other solutions such as these will be discussed in the next chapter.

INNOVATION OPPORTUNITY: The "Sharing Economy"

One of the best examples of permissionless innovation in action today can be seen in the "sharing economy."[131] Just a few years ago, most of us had not heard the term, but today the sharing economy is growing faster than ever and offering consumers a growing array of new service options.[132] Sadly, some policymakers want to stop this sort of pro-consumer permissionless innovation.[133]

The sharing economy refers to any marketplace that uses the Internet to bring together distributed networks of individuals to share or exchange otherwise underutilized assets.[134] It encompasses all manner of goods and services shared or exchanged for both monetary and nonmonetary benefit. In practice, the sharing economy is enabling people to take things they may not be using all the time (cars, bedrooms, etc.) and put them to productive use by finding others in need of those items.

PricewaterhouseCoopers "estimates that global revenue from sharing economy companies, which is roughly $15 billion today, will increase to around $335 billion by 2025."[135] Almost every sector of the US economy is now affected by the sharing economy, especially transportation, hospitality, dining, goods, finance, and personal services.

Policymakers have acknowledged the benefits of the sharing economy. The Federal Trade Commission recently noted that "the development of the sharing economy can stimulate economic growth by encouraging entrepreneurship and promoting more productive and efficient use of assets."[136] More specifically, the sharing economy is creating value for both consumers and producers in five ways.[137] First, by giving people an opportunity to use others' cars, kitchens, apartments, and other property, it allows underutilized assets or "dead capital" to be put to more productive use.[138] Second, by bringing together multiple buyers and sellers, it makes both the supply and demand sides of its markets more competitive and allows greater specialization.[139] Third, by lowering the cost of finding willing traders, haggling over terms, and monitoring performance, it cuts transaction costs and expands the scope of trade. Fourth, by aggregating the reviews of past consumers and producers and putting them at the fingertips of new market participants, it can significantly diminish the problem of asymmetric information between producers and consumers.[140] Last, by offering an "end-run" around regulators who are captured by existing producers, it allows suppliers to create value for customers long underserved by those incumbents that have become inefficient and unresponsive because of their regulatory protections.[141]

Some policymakers insist that existing regulations should be strictly applied to new sharing economy innovators and that they should seek permission before disrupting existing sectors.[142] But while those traditional regulations may have been put on the books with the best of intentions in mind, ultimately, they failed to protect consumers and simply advanced producer welfare instead.[143] Competition and ongoing innovation are always the better consumer protections, and the rise of the sharing economy has made that possible. This may explain why, when recently surveyed by PricewaterhouseCoopers, 64 percent of US consumers said that in the sharing economy, peer regulation is more important than government regulation.[144]

CHAPTER VI
A BLUEPRINT FOR PRESERVING PERMISSIONLESS INNOVATION

We are now in a position to think more concretely about the policy implications associated with the distinct approaches to thinking about innovation identified above. Building on the discussion in previous chapters, we can identify four types of responses to new forms of technology and technological risk and plot them along a "risk response continuum." The first two general responses are motivated by the precautionary principle mindset. The latter two are driven by the permissionless innovation vision.[1]

1. **Prohibition:** Prohibition attempts to eliminate potential risk through suppression of technology, product or service bans, information controls, or outright censorship.

2. **Anticipatory regulation:** Anticipatory regulation controls potential risk through preemptive, precautionary safeguards, including administrative regulation, government ownership or licensing controls, or restrictive defaults. Anticipatory regulation can lead to prohibition, although that tends to be rare, at least in the United States.

3. **Resiliency:** Resiliency-based efforts aim to address potential technological risk through education, awareness building, transparency and labeling, empowerment

efforts, and perhaps even industry self-regulation and best practices.

4. **Adaptation:** Adaptation involves learning to live with risk through trial-and-error experimentation, experience, coping mechanisms, and social norms. Adaptation strategies often begin with, or evolve out of, resiliency-based efforts.

While these risk-response strategies could also describe the possible range of responses that individuals or families might employ to cope with technological change, generally speaking, we are using this framework to consider the theoretical responses by society at large or by governments.

The adjoining image depicts this range of possible policy responses to new innovations and risks. It illustrates how precautionary or "permissioned" responses (such as prohibition or anticipatory regulation) tend to be more "top-down" in character, focusing on prohibitionary policy solutions or anticipatory regulation. Such solutions tend to be centrally planned and command-and-control in nature.

By contrast, permissionless innovation approaches (resiliency and adaptation) are more "bottom-up" in character, evolving more organically in response to new challenges. To summarize, the case for the permissionless innovation approach is premised on the conclusions that

1. Society is better off when innovation is not preemptively restricted;

2. Trial-and-error experimentation, the evolution of norms, and the development of educational solutions and coping mechanisms should be the initial responses to new technologies and the risks they pose;

3. Accusations of harm and calls for policy responses should not be premised on hypothetical, worst-case scenarios; and

4. Policy remedies for actual harms should be narrowly tailored so that beneficial uses of technology are not derailed.

The Risk Response Continuum
A Range of Responses to Technological Risk

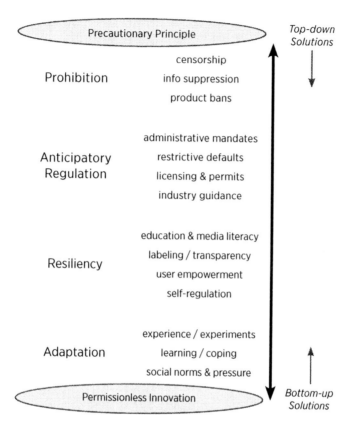

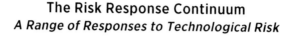

Source: Adam Thierer, Mercatus Center at George Mason University.

We can translate these principles into some general lessons for public policy in order to nurture technological innovation and progress. "If there is a lesson to be learned from the history of technology it is that Schumpeterian growth," as Mokyr correctly observes, "cannot and should not be taken for granted."[2] This is why getting policy right is so important and why government officials must be willing to adapt if they hope to foster a more innovation-enhancing policy environment.[3]

The following principles can help guide that process.

A. APPRECIATE THE VIRTUES OF PATIENCE AND FORBEARANCE (OR, "FIRST, DO NO HARM")

At the most abstract level, the most sensible response to a world full of turbulent, dynamic change comes down to patience and tolerance. As Postrel counseled:

> While dynamism requires many private virtues, including the curiosity, risk taking, and playfulness that drive trial-and-error progress, its primary public virtues are those of *forbearance*: of inaction, of not demanding a public ruling on every new development. These traits include tolerance, toughness, patience, and good humor.[4]

This philosophy of forbearance can be applied right down to the individual level, Postrel notes. It comes down to having "the self-restraint not to impose your own idea of the one best way on others [and] not to use political power to short-circuit trial-and-error learning."[5] It is a "tolerance that permits peaceful differences. . . . It means accepting that we cannot always have things our own way and that we must not limit our neighbors' experiments, aspirations, or ideas just because they might make us feel bad."[6]

More importantly, the philosophy of forbearance should guide public policy because, as legal scholars Geoffrey Manne and Joshua Wright argue, "the ratio of what is known to what is unknown with respect to the relationship between innovation, competition, and regulatory policy is staggeringly low."[7] Regulators lack enough knowledge of all the developments occurring in fast-moving technology markets to be able to forecast everything that lies ahead.[8]

In practice, this philosophy of forbearance should take the form of the timeless principle of "first, do no harm." As economic historian Nathan Rosenberg once noted, "The essential feature of technological innovation is that it is an activity that is fraught with many uncertainties," and, therefore, policymakers should generally exercise restraint and resist the urge to try to plan the future and all the various scenarios—good or bad—that might come about.[9]

Again, we earlier saw the philosophy of forbearance at work in the remarks of FTC Commissioner Ohlhausen when she argued for "a dose of regulatory humility," and the need to try harder "to educate ourselves and others about the innovation, understand its effects on consumers and the marketplace, identify benefits and likely harms, and, if harms do arise, consider whether existing laws and regulations are sufficient to address them, before assuming that new rules are required."[10]

B. LIBERALIZE MARKETS BY APPLYING MOORE'S LAW TO POLICY

One way to translate the philosophy of forbearance into policy is by imposing a variant of "Moore's Law" to technology laws and regulations.[11] Moore's Law is the principle named after Intel cofounder Gordon E. Moore, who first observed that, generally speaking, the processing power of computers doubles roughly every 18 months while prices remain fairly constant.[12]

Moore's Law has profound ramifications for high-tech policy-making.[13] Technology policy expert Larry Downes has shown how lawmaking in the information age is inexorably governed by the "law of disruption" or the fact that "technology changes exponentially, but social, economic, and legal systems change incrementally."[14] This law is "a simple but unavoidable principle of modern life," he said, and it will have profound implications for the way businesses, government, and culture evolve going forward.[15] "As the gap between the old world and the new gets wider," he argues, "conflicts between social, economic, political, and legal systems" will intensify and "nothing can stop the chaos that will follow."[16]

To illustrate, consider this cautionary tale told by Jonathan Askin, a technology lawyer and former FCC attorney. In the early 2000s, Askin served as legal counsel to Free World Dialup (FWD), "a startup that had the potential to dramatically disrupt the telecom sector" with its peer-to-peer Internet protocol-based network that could provide free global voice communications.[17] Askin notes that "FWD paved the way for another startup—Skype. But FWD was Skype before Skype was Skype. The difference was that FWD had U.S. attorneys who put the reigns [sic] on FWD to seek FCC approvals to launch free of regulatory constraints."[18] Here's what happened to FWD:

> In lightning regulatory speed (18 months), the FCC acknowledged that FWD was not a telecom provider subject to onerous telecom regulations. Sounds like a victory, right? Think again. During the time it took the FCC to greenlight FWD, the foreign founders of Skype proceeded apace with no regard for U.S. regulatory approvals. The result is that Skype had a two-year head start and a growing embedded user base, making it difficult for FWD, constrained by its U.S.-trained attorneys, to compete.[19]

FWD would eventually shut down while Skype still thrives.

This shows that no matter how well-intentioned any particular laws or regulation may be, they will be largely ineffective and possibly quite counterproductive when stacked against the realities of the fundamental "law of disruption" because they simply will not be able to keep up with the pace of technological change.[20] "Emerging technologies change at the speed of Moore's Law," Downes notes, "leaving statutes that try to define them by their technical features quickly out of date."[21] Sofia Ranchordás similarly observes, "Law will necessarily lag behind innovation since it cannot be adapted at innovation's speed."[22]

Good examples today can be found in the fields of commercial drones,[23] autonomous (self-driving) car technology,[24] the sharing economy,[25] and advanced medical device innovation.[26] With these markets evolving at the speed of Moore's Law, we should demand that public policy do so as well. We can accomplish that by applying a variant of Moore's Law to all current and future technology policy laws and regulations through two simple principles:

- **Principle #1:** Every new technology proposal should include a provision sunsetting the law or regulation 18 months to two years after enactment. Policymakers can always reenact the rule if they believe it is still sensible.[27]
- **Principle #2:** Reopen all existing technology laws and regulations and reassess their worth. If no compelling reason for their continued existence can be identified and substantiated, those laws or rules should be repealed within 18 months to two years. If a rationale for continuing existing laws and regulations can be identified, the rule can be reimplemented and Principle #1 applied to it.

If critics protest that some laws and regulations are "essential" and they can make the case for new or continued action, Congress can always legislate to continue those efforts. But when it does, Congress should always include a sunset provision to ensure that those rules and regulations are given a frequent fresh look.

Better yet, we should just be doing a lot less legislating and regulating in these areas. The only way to ensure that more technologies and entrepreneurs don't end up like FWD is to make sure they don't have to deal with mountains of regulatory red tape from the beginning.

C. LEVEL THE PLAYING FIELD BY "DEREGULATING DOWN," NOT REGULATING UP

Sometimes it is impossible to completely liberalize certain sectors or deregulate various technologies. Traditional rules and regulations might predate new innovations by many decades and already cover firms in related industries. This raises reciprocity and fairness concerns since marketplace rivals may be regulated differently.

This is a fundamental policy problem raised by the sharing economy, for example.[28] Ride-sharing services (Uber and Lyft, for example) have begun competing against incumbent taxi operators in many cities across the United States and the world. This leads incumbents that oppose new entry by innovators to argue that they still face various regulatory burdens—including licensing requirements, price controls, service area requirements, marketing limitations, and technology standards—that new entrants are evading. In theory, these burdens could place incumbents at a disadvantage relative to new sharing economy start-ups that might not face the same regulations (even though those same regulations could simultaneously be used to keep smaller start-ups out of the market). This sort of "level playing field" problem often develops in any sector undergoing rapid technological change.

One option is to just "wait it out" and see where the chips fall, even if competitors are playing by slightly different rules. Nevertheless, such regulatory asymmetries represent a legitimate policy problem that usually must be dealt with to ensure fairness for all rivals.

The best solution, however, is not to punish new innovations by simply rolling old regulatory regimes onto new technologies and sectors. The better alternative is to level the playing field by "deregulating down" to put everyone on equal footing, not by "regulating up" to achieve parity.[29] Policymakers should relax old rules on incumbents as new entrants and new technologies challenge the status quo.

D. EMBRACE "EDUCATE AND EMPOWER"–BASED SOLUTIONS

"Legislate and regulate" responses are not productive approaches to safety, security, or privacy concerns because preemptive and prophylactic regulation of technology can be costly, complicated, and overly constraining. The better approach might be labeled "educate and empower," which refers to strategies that can help build individual resiliency and ensure proper assimilation of new technologies into society. This approach is built on media literacy and "digital citizenship" and focuses on encouraging better social norms and coping strategies.[30]

For example, regarding online safety and proper online behavior, we need to assimilate children gradually into online environments and use resiliency strategies to make sure they understand how to cope with the challenges they will face in the digital age. Teaching our kids smarter online hygiene and "Netiquette" is vital. "Think before you click" should be lesson number one.

They should also be encouraged to delete unnecessary online information occasionally.[31]

In recent years, many child safety scholars and child development experts have worked to expand traditional online education and media literacy strategies, to place the notion of digital citizenship at the core of their lessons.[32] Online safety expert Anne Collier defines digital citizenship as "critical thinking and ethical choices about the content and impact on oneself, others, and one's community of what one sees, says, and produces with media, devices, and technologies."[33]

A 2014 Obama administration report on "big data" issues included a short section on the need to "recognize digital literacy as an important 21st century skill" and defined it as "understanding how personal data is collected, shared, and used."[34] The report stated, "In order to ensure students, citizens, and consumers of all ages have the ability to adequately protect themselves from data use and abuse, it is important that they develop fluency in understanding the ways in which data can be collected and shared, how algorithms are employed and for what purposes, and what tools and techniques they can use to protect themselves."[35] The administration recommended that digital literacy "should be recognized as an essential skill in K-12 education and be integrated into the standard curriculum."[36]

This approach should be at the center of child safety debates going forward to encourage ethical online behavior and promote online civility and respect. Only by teaching our children to be good cyber-citizens can we ensure they are prepared for life in an age of information abundance. Moreover, many of these same principles and strategies can help us address privacy and security concerns for both kids and adults. "Again, the solution is critical thinking and digital citizenship," argues online safety expert Larry Magid.[37] He continues, "We need educational campaigns that teach kids how to use whatever controls are built-in to the browsers, how to distinguish between advertising and editorial content and how to evaluate whatever information they come across to be able to make informed choices."[38]

In 2013, scholars affiliated with the Center on Law and Information Policy at the Fordham University School of Law released a good model for how to operationalize this vision. They launched a privacy education program "aimed at engaging middle school students in discussions about privacy and its relevance in their lives."[39] The resulting Volunteer Privacy Educators Program offers students lessons about how to deal with social media and how to actively manage their digital reputation, as well as how to establish strong passwords and avoid behavioral advertising, if they were so inclined.[40]

Companies also have an important role to play in creating "well-lit neighborhoods" online where users will be safe and can feel that their information is relatively secure. Many companies and trade associations are also taking steps to raise awareness among their users about how they can better protect their privacy and security.[41] Online operators should also be careful about what (or how much) information they collect—especially if they primarily serve young audiences. Most widely trafficked social networking sites and search engines already offer a variety of privacy controls and allow users to delete their accounts.

Many other excellent online safety- and privacy-enhancing tools already exist for people seeking to safeguard their child's online experiences or their own online privacy. A host of tools are available to block or limit various types of data collection, and every major web browser has cookie-control tools to help users manage data collection. Many nonprofits—including many privacy advocates—offer instructional websites and videos explaining how privacy-sensitive consumers can take steps to protect their personal information online.

Taken together, this amounts to a "layered approach" to addressing concerns about safety, security, and privacy. Only by using many tools, methods, strategies, social norms, and forms of market pressure can we ensure that youngsters and even adults are safe online while they learn to cope with new technology and adapt to the changing world around them.

Governments can also contribute to users' online safety by facilitating learning and resiliency through educational and empowerment-based solutions, instead of heavy-handed, silver-bullet regulatory solutions. Governments are uniquely positioned to get the word out about new technologies—both the benefits and dangers—and can develop messaging—especially to youngsters still in school—about appropriately using new technologies. The FTC notes, "Consumer and business education serves as the first line of defense against fraud, deception, and unfair practices."[42]

Toward that end, the FTC hosts a collaborative online education effort with more than a dozen other federal agencies called "OnGuard Online," which presents a savvy approach to raising awareness about various online threats.[43] The FTC has also created a YouTube page that features informational videos on these issues.[44] The FCC also offers smartphone security advice on its website.[45] Many privacy activists and privacy professionals already offer extensive educational programs and advice.[46]

Beyond classroom media literacy and digital citizenship efforts, government can undertake broad-based public awareness campaigns. Officials at the federal, state, and local levels should work together to devise media literacy campaigns focused on online safety, understanding the existing rating systems, how to use parental controls, and so on. These campaigns should include broadcast (radio and TV) ads, Internet websites and advertising, and promotional posters and brochures that could be distributed at schools and government institutions. Government has undertaken (or lent its support to) such public awareness campaigns to address other concerns in the past and had a great deal of success, including forest fire prevention (i.e., "Smokey the Bear");[47] antilittering ("Give a Hoot, Don't Pollute");[48] crime prevention ("McGruff the Crime Dog");[49] and seat-belt safety.[50]

All of these efforts represent a more constructive, bottom-up way of addressing safety, security, and privacy concerns as compared with heavy-handed regulatory approaches. Moreover, education teaches lessons that can serve people well for a lifetime, whereas regulatory approaches are increasingly too slow to address these concerns.

E. ENCOURAGE PRIVACY, SAFETY, AND SECURITY "BY DESIGN" EFFORTS

One of the hottest concepts in the field of information policy today is "privacy by design."[51] Privacy by design refers to efforts by organizations to "embed privacy into the architecture of technologies and practices."[52] Amazing strides have already been made in this regard, and progress—though slow—will continue. "The signs are already beginning to appear," says Ann Cavoukian, who is widely credited with coining the phrase. "Market leaders are embracing *Privacy by Design*, and are, in turn, reaping the benefits."[53] Examples of privacy by design would include efforts by designers and vendors to ensure that consumers know what data are being collected about them and why, making reasonable efforts to protect user confidentiality and secure consumer data, and asking for explicit permission from consumers before sharing information with third parties.[54]

The growth of privacy-by-design efforts reflects a renewed focus on evolving industry self-regulation and codes of conduct. Policymakers and the general public are increasingly demanding that privacy professionals be included in information-gathering institutions and take steps to better safeguard private information flows.[55] The rapid expansion of the ranks of the International Association for Privacy Professionals reflects that fact.[56] The association was formed in 2000 and has rapidly grown from just a few hundred members to almost 14,000 members in 83 countries by 2013.[57] As a result, a growing class of privacy professionals exists throughout the corporate world, as professors Kenneth Bamberger and Deirdre Mulligan summarize:

> The individuals managing corporate privacy have an applicant pool of trained professionals to draw from. There is ongoing training, certification, and networking. A community of corporate privacy managers has emerged. Ready evidence suggests that substantial effort is made to manage privacy.[58]

But these efforts aren't limited to privacy. Similar efforts have been underway for many years, on the online safety front. Various online safety advocates and child safety experts have pushed companies to adopt various online safety best practices to ensure that digital sites and services offer users safer online experiences.[59]

Similar "security-by-design" efforts have been going on for years as well.[60] Corporations and other organizations have a vested interest in keeping their systems and devices secure from viruses, malwares, breaches, spam, and so on.

We should continue to consider how we might achieve privacy by design before new services are rolled out, but the reality is that "privacy on the fly" and "privacy by ongoing norm-shaping" may become even more essential. This is where the role of privacy, safety, and security professionals will be absolutely essential.[61] As Bamberger and Mulligan have noted, increasingly, it is what happens "on the ground"—the day-to-day management of privacy and security decisions through the interaction of privacy and security professionals, engineers, outside experts, and regular users—that is really important. They stress how "governing privacy through flexible principles" is the new norm.[62] They note that "privacy work takes many forms in the firm" today, with privacy professionals responding on the fly to breaking developments, many of which could not have been foreseen.[63] To continuously improve on this model, they argue that the "daily work [of privacy professionals] requires trusted insider status" and "full and early access and ongoing dialogue with business units."[64] Success, they note, "is best accomplished by a diverse set of distributed employees with privacy training who are nonetheless viewed as part of the business team."[65]

That is exactly right. Moreover, going forward, privacy and safety professionals within firms and other organizations will need to be on the front lines of this rapidly evolving technological landscape to solve the hard problems presented by new technologies, such as the Internet of Things, wearable technologies, 3-D printing, facial recognition, driverless cars, and private drones. These professionals will need to be responsive to user concerns and continuously refine corporate practices to balance the ongoing services that the public demands against the potential negative impacts associated with these technologies. They will need to get creative about data use and deletion policies and simultaneously work to educate the public about appropriate use of these new tools.

INNOVATION OPPORTUNITY: 3-D Printing and Additive Manufacturing

3-D printing, or what is more accurately labeled "additive manufacturing," refers to technology that "moves us away from the Henry Ford era mass production line, and will bring us to a new reality of customizable, one-off production."[66] Working from digital blueprints, 3-D printers let users fabricate or replicate almost any product imaginable using various materials.[67]

3-D printers are gaining more widespread adoption and promise to significantly alter the way many goods are manufactured.[68] In mid-2013, technology researchers at Gartner estimated a 49 percent jump in sub-$10,000 3-D printer sales over the previous year and projected sales to double in each of the following two years,[69] and they estimate that shipments of 3-D printers will exceed 490,000 units in 2016.[70] Wohlers Associates Inc. reports that the additive manufacturing market grew by a compound annual growth rate of 35.2 percent to $4.1 billion in 2014.[71] "Once we link together innovations like 3D printing, the Internet of Things, and Big Data, the sky's the limit on what we can dream up. We won't just be able to build any object we need—it will instantly become part of our networked world," says Brian Proffitt of ReadWrite.[72]

As the costs to produce 3-D printing items continue to fall, marketplaces are emerging to facilitate transactions. For example, Shapeways is an online marketplace that has an ever-growing selection of over 120,000 3-D-printed products using over 55 materials from over 150,000 unique designs that are shipped every month to a community base of over 625,000 members from over 140 countries.[73]

The ramifications of 3-D printing could be enormous. "The Internet changed the balance of power between individuals and institutions," notes digital visionary Esther Dyson, "[and] I think we will see a similar story with 3D printing, as it grows from a novelty into something useful and disruptive—and sufficiently cheap and widespread to be used for (relatively) frivolous endeavors as well. We will print not just children's playthings, but also human prostheses—bones and even lungs and livers—and ultimately much machinery, including new 3D printers."[74] Notes Proffitt, "[v]ery soon the day will come when a patient in need of a custom medical device, such as a prosthesis or stent, can have such an object manufactured within minutes right at the healthcare facility, instead of waiting for days to get the device delivered from a factory."[75]

In fact, 3-D-printed medical devices are already being used to improve and even save lives.[76] Researchers at the University of Michigan have 3-D-printed splints to help children with rare breathing disorders.[77] Splints are not the only such instance of 3-D-printed medical devices being inserted into the human body. Doctors in Spain have successfully implanted a 3-D-printed titanium sternum and ribs into a cancer patient.[78]

Meanwhile, average citizens are using 3-D printing to help others. Michael Balzer, a software engineer, used 3-D imaging software combined with a 3-D printer to create life-size replicas of his wife's skull in an attempt to seek less invasive approaches to her impending cranial surgery.[79] This allowed 95 percent of her tumor to be removed and helped save her sight. And prosthetic hands and arms are being 3-D-printed by volunteers to help victims of war[80] and children born with limb deficiencies.[81] Prosthetics are medical devices in a traditional regulatory sense, but few people are asking the FDA for permission to create new 3-D-printed limbs.[82] Instead, they are just going ahead and engaging in this sort of life-enriching innovation.

Of course, decentralized production of medical devices will raise policy concerns, not just at the FDA but with many other regulatory bodies. The FDA has not yet regulated 3-D printing, even though the agency already regulates comparable commercial devices. It is unclear, however, how the FDA or other regulators can stop such innovation given its highly decentralized and even noncommercial nature.[83]

But the growth of additive manufacturing has also raised other policy concerns.[84] For example, what is the future of intellectual property when products can be so easily replicated by not just companies but average citizens?[85] Meanwhile, proposals to regulate 3-D-printed guns have already been introduced in the state of New York.[86] More efforts to preemptively regulate 3-D printers are likely to surface as additive manufacturing technologies grow more popular.

As with other technologies discussed throughout this book, the best policy approach for 3-D printing is one rooted in patience and regulatory humility. While 3-D printing could create some new and unique policy challenges, regulation should not be premised on hypothetical worst-case outcomes. Instead, policymakers should be patient and see if the common law and other existing legal remedies can solve problems that develop.

F. RELY ON "SIMPLE RULES FOR A COMPLEX WORLD" WHEN REGULATION IS NEEDED

But don't we need some regulation? Yes, of course we do. As chapter III already noted, regulation is sometimes needed to prevent or remedy the harms that businesses or other organizations might impose on customers or third parties. But, again, how we go about preventing or remedying those harms matters profoundly. And that regulation needn't always be preemptive in character.

We should first look to the sort of less restrictive remedies to complex social problems described above before we resort to heavy-handed, legalistic solutions. Let us briefly recall the problem with traditional regulatory systems. These tend to be overly rigid, bureaucratic, inflexible, and slow to adapt to new realities. They focus on preemptive remedies that aim to predict the future, and future hypothetical problems that may not ever come about. Worse yet, administrative regulation generally preempts or prohibits the beneficial experiments that yield new and better ways of doing things.[87] Regardless of whether the technical specifications for permitted products and services are published in advance or firms must seek special permission before they offer a new product or service, both varieties of preemptive regulation have the same effect: they raise the cost of starting or running a business or nonbusiness venture; therefore they discourage activities that benefit society.

Philip K. Howard, chair of Common Good and the author of *The Rule of Nobody*, notes:

> Too much law, however, can have similar effects as too little law. People slow down, they become defensive, they don't initiate projects because they are surrounded by legal risks and bureaucratic hurdles. They tiptoe through the day looking over their shoulders rather than driving forward on the power of their instincts. Instead of trial and error, they focus on avoiding error.
>
> Modern America is the land of too much law. Like sediment in a harbor, law has steadily accumulated, mainly

since the 1960s, until most productive activity requires slogging through a legal swamp. It's degenerative. Law is denser now than it was 10 years ago, and will be denser still in the next decade. This growing legal burden impedes economic growth.[88]

This is why flexible, bottom-up approaches to solving complex problems, such as those outlined in the preceding sections, are almost always superior to top-down laws and regulations. For example, we have already identified how social norms and pressure from the public, media, or activist groups can "regulate" behavior and curb potential abuses. And we have seen how education, awareness-building, transparency, and empowerment-based efforts can often help alleviate the problems associated with new forms of technological change.

But there are other useful approaches that can be tapped to address or alleviate concerns or harms associated with new innovations. To the extent that other *public* policies are needed to guide technological developments, simple legal principles are greatly preferable to technology-specific, micromanaged regulatory regimes. Ex ante (preemptive and precautionary) regulation is often highly inefficient, even dangerous. Prospective regulation based on hypothesizing about future harms that may never materialize is likely to come at the expense of innovation and growth opportunities. To the extent that any corrective action is needed to address harms, ex post measures, especially via the common law, are typically superior.

In his 1983 book, *Technologies of Freedom: On Free Speech in an Electronic Age*, political scientist Ithiel de Sola Pool offered a passionate defense of technological freedom and freedom of speech in the electronic age. He set forth several "Guidelines for Freedom" to ensure that new information technologies could realize their full potential. Regarding regulation of information markets, Pool stressed that "enforcement must be after the fact, not by prior restraint" and that "regulation is a last recourse. In a free society, the burden of proof is for the least possible regulation of communication."[89]

That same principle can and should be applied to all technologies more generally.

What we should strive for—to borrow the title of Richard Epstein's 1995 book—are "simple rules for a complex world."[90] Many laws already exist that can be applied to new challenges before we look to impose new laws or more heavy-handed regulation. Those simple rules include

- **Torts, common law, and class action activity:**
  Traditionally, the common law has dealt with product liability and accident compensation in an evolutionary way through a variety of mechanisms, including strict liability, negligence, design defects law, failure to warn, and breach of warranty.[91] The common law of tort is centuries old and well tested. Under tort law, instead of asking for permission to introduce a potentially dangerous product, a firm must pay for the damages its dangerous product creates if it is found liable in court. Thus, because the tort system operates retrospectively, it is restitution-based, not permission-based. This also creates incentives for firms to make their products safer over time so they can avoid lawsuits.

  "[W]hen confronted with new, often complex, questions involving products liability, courts have generally gotten things right," notes Brookings Institution scholar John Villasenor. "Products liability law has been highly adaptive to the many new technologies that have emerged in recent decades." By extension, it will adapt to other technologies and developments as cases and controversies come before the courts.[92] There is no reason, therefore, to believe that the common law will not adapt to new technological realities, especially since firms have powerful incentives to improve the security of their systems and avoid punishing liability, unwanted press attention, and lost customers.

  When considering privacy-related concerns about new technologies, in particular, it is also important to remember how the United States "has a vibrant privacy litigation industry, led by privacy class actions."[93] Class action lawsuit activity is remarkably intense following not just major privacy violations but also data breaches,[94] and there is evidence that "[h]ow federal courts define the damages people suffer from data breaches is broadening dramatically, leaving unprepared companies at greater risk of big payouts in class-action lawsuits."[95] This disciplines firms that violate privacy and data security norms while sending a signal to other online operators about their data policies and procedures.[96]

Finally, specific privacy-related torts—including the tort of intrusion upon seclusion—could also evolve in response to technological change and provide more avenues of recourse to plaintiffs seeking to protect their privacy and data security.

- **Property law and other targeted remedies:** Federal and state laws already exist that could address perceived harms associated with many of the new technologies identified herein. For example, property law already governs trespass, and new court rulings may well expand the body of such law to encompass trespass by focusing on actual cases and controversies, not merely hypotheticals. Likewise, many states have "Peeping Tom" laws on the books that prohibit spying into homes and other spaces.[97] Antiharassment laws in every state address such activity. These laws could be adapted to cover developing privacy, safety, and security concerns before new regulations are enacted.

- **Contract law:** The enforcement of contractual promises is one of the most powerful ways to curb potential abuses of new technologies. When companies make promises to the public about new services or devices, the companies can and should be held to them. Again, class action lawsuits could come into play when firms do not live up to the promises they make to consumers.

- **FTC enforcement of "unfair and deceptive practices":**
  There are ways outside the courts to ensure that contractual promises get kept. The FTC possesses broad consumer protection powers under Section 5 of the Federal
  Trade Commission Act.[98] Section 5 prohibits "unfair or
  deceptive acts or practices in or affecting commerce."[99]
  The FTC formalized its process for dealing with unfairness claims in its 1984 *Policy Statement on Unfairness,*
  and noted, "To justify a finding of unfairness the injury
  must satisfy three tests. It must be substantial; it must not
  be outweighed by any countervailing benefits to consumers or competition that the practice produces; and it must
  be an injury that consumers themselves could not reasonably have avoided."[100] (Importantly, however, the *Policy
  Statement* stipulated that "the injury must be substantial.
  The Commission is not concerned with trivial or merely
  speculative harms. . . . Emotional impact and other more
  subjective types of harm . . . will not ordinarily make a
  practice unfair."[101]) In recent years, the FTC has brought
  and settled many cases involving its Section 5 authority
  to address identity theft and data security matters and,
  generally speaking, has been able to identify clear harms
  in each case.[102]

Moreover, targeted legislation already addresses the special
concerns raised by the collection or use of certain types of
health information,[103] financial information,[104] or information about children.[105] Of course, it is true that the potential privacy or data security harms in those contexts are
somewhat more concrete in nature. Privacy violations of
health and financial information, for example, can pose a
more direct and quantifiable threat to personal well-being
or property. Finally, state governments and state attorneys
general also continue to advance their own privacy and
data security policies, and those enforcement efforts are
often more stringent than federal law.[106]

- **Transparency:** If regulation is still deemed necessary, transparency and disclosure policies should generally trump the use of more restrictive rules. The push for better transparency has already led to progress in other contexts. Voluntary media content ratings and labels for movies, music, video games, and smartphone apps have given parents more information to make determinations about the appropriateness of content they or their children may want to consume.[107] And the push for better privacy information has led to more website privacy policies and disclosure statements. Consumers are better served when they are informed about online privacy and data collection policies of the sites they visit and the devices they use.[108]

G. PROTECT ONLINE INTERMEDIARIES FROM PUNISHING LIABILITY

A special word is required about the dangers of intermediary liability as a regulatory remedy to various perceived ills. When concerns are raised about the various technology issues addressed above, many regulatory advocates or policymakers are often quick to demand that special regulatory responsibilities be imposed on digital intermediaries. The goal of such proposals is to force online platforms, network providers, or application developers to take a more active role policing their systems for content or behavior that activists or policymakers want curtailed.

For example, some advocates want these intermediaries to "clean up" online hate speech, cyberbullying, or adult-oriented content or be punished for failing to do so.[109] Others want intermediaries to take additional steps to protect the privacy or security of individuals online.[110] Again, this is precautionary principle thinking.

Proposals such as these to "deputize the middleman" are always well-intentioned but they can be highly counterproductive and should, therefore, be extremely limited. In fact, as noted earlier, US law already does so via "Section 230" of the Telecommunications Act of 1996, a law that immunizes intermediaries from most of these policing responsibilities. Again, this was hugely beneficial in helping to promote online speech and commerce.[111] Had Section 230 not been put on the books, it is unclear whether many of today's most popular online sites and services could have survived because they might have been hit with huge lawsuits for the content and commerce that some didn't approve of on their platforms. For example, popular sites like eBay, Facebook, Wikipedia, Yelp, and YouTube all depend on Section 230's protections to shield them from punishing liability. But the law protects countless small sites and services just as much.

If problematic content or troublemaking users exist on some platforms, it is almost always better to address them directly and hold them accountable for their actions. Deputizing middlemen to do so or holding them accountable for the actions of others will disincentivize them from creating vibrant, open platforms for online speech and commerce. Permissionless innovation demands a rejection of such middleman deputization schemes.

H. QUANTIFY OPPORTUNITY COSTS BY REQUIRING STRICT BENEFIT-COST ANALYSIS

Finally, even when rules are deemed necessary, it does not mean they should be imposed without reference to the potential costs to consumers, commerce, or progress and liberty more generally.[112] We need to make sure that new rules make sense and that the "bang for the buck" is real, regardless of the concern being addressed by new laws or regulations.[113]

As discussed in chapter III, many cognitive biases predispose us toward pessimism and the precautionary principle mentality. We obviously don't want anything to go wrong and, therefore, many people often call for "steps to be taken" to head off troubles they believe lie ahead. But, as noted, all policy choices entail tradeoffs and have serious opportunity costs.

Cass Sunstein has written of "tradeoff neglect," or the general fact that "people fail to see the frequent need to weigh competing variables against one another."[114] Sunstein correctly observes that "people neglect the systemic effect of one-shot interventions" and instead "tend to assume that a change in a social situation would alter the part at issue but would not affect other parts."[115] In other words, all actions have consequences—especially policy interventions—but we often fail to consider the full extent of the opportunity costs at work.[116]

Bastiat's "seen and unseen" insights, which were discussed earlier, are worth recalling in this regard. People often discount unseen gains or opportunities and focus only on the immediately visible benefits or costs. When we choose one course of action, it necessarily means we have forgone others. As noted, politicians are often engaged in an elusive search for some magical Goldilocks-like formula to get things *just right* and preempt potential risks. But when we allow our leaders to ignore the opportunity costs of their actions, progress is stunted or at least artificially skewed.

The reality of opportunity costs and tradeoff neglect are particularly important to keep in mind when thinking about digital technology and information production and dissemination. These are probably the last technologies and sectors we would want regulators monkeying with, because planners lack the requisite knowledge of how to best guide the evolution of complex, dynamic, fast-moving information technologies. Moreover, the opportunity costs associated with error could be profound and derail the innovative, informative benefits that have thus far flowed from a largely unregulated digital sphere.

This is why it is essential that all proposals to regulate new technologies be subjected to strict benefit-cost analysis (BCA). BCA represents an effort to formally identify the tradeoffs or opportunity costs associated with regulatory proposals and, to the maximum extent feasible, quantify those benefits and costs.[117]

At the federal level in the United States, regulatory policymaking and the BCA process are directed by various presidential executive orders and guidance issued by the White House Office of Information and Regulatory Affairs (OIRA).[118] As part of any BCA review, OIRA demands "[a] statement of the need for the regulatory action" that includes "a clear explanation of the need for the regulatory action, including a description of the problem that the agency seeks to address."[119] As part of this step, OIRA specifies, "Agencies should explain whether the action is intended to address a market failure or to promote some other goal."[120] Second, "[a] clear identification of a range of regulatory approaches" is required "including the option of not regulating."[121] Agencies must also consider other alternatives to federal regulation, such as "[s]tate or local regulation, voluntary action on the part of the private sector, antitrust enforcement, consumer-initiated litigation in the product liability system, and administrative compensation systems."[122] Agencies are supposed to assess the benefits and costs of all these alternatives.[123] If federal regulation is still deemed necessary, flexible approaches are strongly encouraged by OIRA.[124] Finally, "[a]n estimate of the benefits and costs—both quantitative and qualitative" is required.[125] The quantification of benefits and costs is strongly encouraged but, when that is impossible, agencies are required to describe them qualitatively and make a clear case for action.[126]

Unfortunately, federal agency officials often ignore these requirements, or at least do not take them seriously enough. Worse yet for technology policy matters is the fact that many agencies, including the FTC and the FCC, are neither required to conduct BCA nor have their rulemaking activities approved by OIRA. This is like giving regulators a free pass to meddle with new innovation without any serious oversight.

All new proposed regulatory enactments should be subjected to strict BCA and, if they are formally enacted, they should also be retroactively reviewed to gauge their cost-effectiveness. Better yet, the sunsetting guidelines recommended above should be applied to make sure outdated regulations are periodically removed from the books so that innovation is not discouraged. Of course, as already noted above, every effort should be made to exhaust all other options before even entertaining a discussion about the need for new regulations and restrictions on technological innovation. Again, the default should be *innovation allowed.*

As noted in chapter III, the case for precautionary regulation sometimes can be made by advocates of preemptive control, but they must be able to make a compelling case that the benefits of intervention clearly outweigh the costs of ongoing experimentation. Until they can do so, permissionless innovation deserves the benefit of the doubt.

I. SUMMARY: POLICY MUST BE FLEXIBLE AND ADAPTIVE

This chapter has argued that, if we hope to preserve the benefits associated with permissionless innovation, we need *flexible* and *adaptive* policies going forward. We need diverse solutions for a diverse citizenry. We must avoid policy proposals that are top-down, one-size-fits-all, overly rigid, and bureaucratic. Instead, we need approaches that are bottom-up, flexible, and evolutionary in nature.

The challenges ahead will be formidable, but the payoff to society for getting this balance right will be enormous.

CONCLUSION
IT'S ABOUT FREEDOM, PROGRESS, AND PROSPERITY

It should be clear now that the case for permissionless innovation is synonymous with the case for human freedom more generally.

Indeed, in making the case against the stasis mentality and precautionary principle–based policies, we can link dynamism and permissionless innovation to the expansion of cultural and economic freedom throughout history. There is a symbiotic relationship between freedom and progress. In his book *History of the Idea of Progress*, Robert Nisbet writes of those who adhere to "the belief that freedom is necessary to progress, and that the goal of progress, from most distant past to the remote future, is ever-ascending realization of freedom."[1] That is the vision I have attempted to outline and defend here. Freedom, including technological freedom, is essential to achieving progress and human flourishing.

Few scholars better connected the dots between freedom and progress than F. A. Hayek and Karl Popper, two preeminent 20th century philosophers of history and politics. "Liberty is essential in order to leave room for the unforeseeable and the unpredictable," Hayek teaches us. "[W]e want it because we have learned to expect from it the opportunity of realizing many of our aims. It is because every individual knows so little and, in particular, because we rarely know which of us knows best that we trust the independent and competitive efforts of many to induce the emergence of what we shall want when we see it."[2]

In a similar vein, Popper explains that "the human factor is the ultimately uncertain and wayward element in social life and in all social institutions. Indeed this is the element which ultimately cannot be completely controlled by institutions . . . for every attempt at controlling it completely must lead to tyranny; which means, to the omnipotence of the human factor—the whims of a few men, or even one."[3]

These realities—the limits of our knowledge and our ability to plan for an uncertain future—have ramifications for public policy, obviously. "Despite his best intentions, the government planner will tend to live in the past, for only the past is sure and calculable," explains technology historian George Gilder.[4] "The most serious damage inflicted by excessive controls is the discouragement of innovation and entrepreneurship and the perpetuation of slightly laundered and government-approved obsolescence," he noted.[5]

It is vital that we embrace dynamism and leave a broad sphere for continued experimentation by individuals and organizations alike because freedom, broadly construed, is valuable in its own right— even if not all of the outcomes are optimal or equal. As Clay Shirky rightly notes in his 2008 book, *Here Comes Everybody*:

> This does not mean there will be no difficulties associated with our new capabilities—the defenders of freedom have long noted that free societies have problems peculiar to them. Instead, it assumes that the value of freedom outweighs the problems, not based on calculation of net value but because freedom is the right thing to want for society.[6]

The "value of freedom" is "the right thing to want for society" because it allows humans to grow, learn, prosper, and enjoy life. "Progress is movement for movement's sake," Hayek argues, "for it is in the process of learning, and in the effects of having learned something new, that man enjoys the gift of his intelligence."[7] Notes Matt Ridley, "The wonderful thing about knowledge is that it is genuinely limitless."[8] He concludes, "There is not even a theoretical possibility of exhausting the supply of ideas, discoveries and inventions. This is the biggest cause for all my optimism."[9]

Pessimistic critics will persist in their claims that our culture and economy can be guided down the proverbial "better path," but the path we're on right now isn't looking so bad and does not require the intrusive, freedom-crushing prescriptions that some critics call for.[10]

Of course, a world of permissionless innovation will not be perfect. Mistakes will be made and there will even be short-term spells of what many would regard as particularly difficult social and cultural disruptions. *The crucial question is how much faith we should place in precautionary thinking and preemptive planning, as opposed to evolving social norms and ongoing trial-and-error experimentation, to solve those problems.*[11] Those with an appreciation of liberty and the importance of trial-and-error experimentation will have more patience with technological change and be more willing to see how things play out.

This approach is rooted in the belief that social and economic disruptions are ultimately better addressed by voluntary, spontaneous, bottom-up responses than by coercive, top-down, centrally planned, technocratic approaches.[12] The decisive advantage of the bottom-up approach is its nimbleness. It is during what some might regard as the darkest hour when some of the most exciting innovations and creative solutions emerge.[13] People don't sit still; they respond to incentives and suboptimal cultural and economic challenges because, as Benjamin Franklin once noted, "man is a tool-making animal." And if we understand "technology" to be, in Frederick Ferré's phrasing, "practical implementations of intelligence,"[14] then we can appreciate how humans are constantly striving to create better tools to apply their intelligence to various problems and improve the human condition in the process.

But they can only do so if they are truly free from artificial constraint from government forces that, inevitably, are always one or two steps behind fast-moving technological developments. We shouldn't allow pessimistic techno-critics to sell us a version of "freedom" in which markets and cultural norms are constantly being reshaped and contorted through incessant regulatory interventions.[15] That isn't true freedom; that's control. Permissionless innovation offers us a more promising, freedom-preserving, and progress-enhancing way forward.

Finally, if permissionless innovation advocates hope to triumph over precautionary principle thinking, it is essential that we avoid falling prey to what philosopher Michael Sacasas refers to as "the Borg Complex," which, he says, is often "exhibited by writers and pundits who explicitly assert or implicitly assume that resistance to technology is futile."[16] Indeed, some Pollyannaish pundits adopt a cavalier attitude about the impact of technological change on individuals and society. That approach must be rejected.

Those of us who espouse the benefits of permissionless innovation must be mature enough to appreciate and address the occasional downsides of technological change. Adopting a blasé "just-get-over-it" attitude toward the challenges sometimes posed by technological change is never wise. In fact, it can be downright insulting. Advocates of permissionless innovation must instead listen to concerns about emerging technologies and offer constructive solutions to complex social and economic problems.

But we should also ask critics to think through the consequences of preemptively prohibiting technological innovation and to realize that not everyone shares their same values, especially values pertaining to privacy, safety, and security issues. We should encourage them to avoid imposing their subjective judgments on everyone else by force of law and instead ask them to work with us to find practical, bottom-up solutions that will help individuals, institutions, and society learn how to better cope with technological change over time. Using this approach, we will have a better chance of convincing them that we can embrace our dynamic future together and radically improve the human condition in the process.

APPENDIX
ADDITIONAL READINGS FROM ADAM THIERER

Journal articles and book chapters:

- "US Medical Devices: Choices and Consequences," (with Richard Williams and Robert Graboyes), October 21, 2015.

- "How the Internet, the Sharing Economy, and Reputational Feedback Mechanisms Solve the 'Lemons Problem,'" (with Christopher Koopman, Anne Hobson, and Chris Kuiper), May 26, 2015.

- "The Sharing Economy and Consumer Protection Regulation: The Case for Policy Change," (with Christopher Koopman and Matthew Mitchell), *The Journal of Business, Entrepreneurship & the Law* 8, no. 2 (2015).

- "The Internet of Things and Wearable Technology: Addressing Privacy and Security Concerns without Derailing Innovation," *Richmond Journal of Law and Technology* 21, no. 6 (2015).

- "Removing Roadblocks to Intelligent Vehicles and Driverless Cars," (with Ryan Hagemann), *Wake Forest Journal of Law & Policy* 5, no. 2 (2015): 339–91.

- "Technopanics, Threat Inflation, and the Danger of an Information Technology Precautionary Principle," *Minnesota Journal of Law, Science & Technology* 14 (2013): 309–86.

- "Privacy Law's Precautionary Principle Problem," *Maine Law Review* 66, no. 2 (2014).

- "The Pursuit of Privacy in a World Where Information Control Is Failing," *Harvard Journal of Law & Public Policy* 36 (2013): 409–55.

- "A Framework for Benefit-Cost Analysis in Digital Privacy Debates," *George Mason University Law Review* 20, no. 4 (Summer 2013): 1055–105.

- "The Case for Internet Optimism, Part 1: Saving the Net from Its Detractors," in *The Next Digital Decade: Essays on the Future of the Internet*, ed. Berin Szoka and Adam Marcus (Washington, DC: Tech Freedom, 2010), 57–87.

Testimony/Filings:

- Comments of the Mercatus Center to the Federal Trade Commission, "The Sharing Economy: Issues Facing Platforms, Participants, and Regulators," (with Christopher Koopman and Matthew Mitchell), May 26, 2015.

- Comments of the Mercatus Center to the FAA on Operation and Certification of Small Unmanned Aircraft Systems, (with Eli Dourado and Ryan Hagemann), April 24, 2015.

- Senate Testimony on Privacy, Data Collection & Do Not Track, April 24, 2013.

- Comments of the Mercatus Center to the FTC in Privacy & Security Implications of the Internet of Things, May 31, 2013.

- Comments of the Mercatus Center to FAA on commercial domestic drones, (with Jerry Brito and Eli Dourado), April 23, 2013.

NOTES

PREFACE
WHICH POLICY VISION WILL GOVERN THE FUTURE?

1. I wish to thank the following individuals for assisting in the preparation of this book: Ted Bolema, Jonathan Camp, Andrea Castillo, Eli Dourado, Ryan Hagemann, Sam Hammond, Christopher Koopman, Chris Kuiper, Matthew Mitchell, Brent Skorup, Caleb Watney, and the outstanding editing and production team at the Mercatus Center.

2. Mary Douglas and Aaron Wildavsky, *Risk and Culture* (Berkeley, CA: University of California Press, 1983), 67. ("The political argument over technology is conducted between the heavily risk averse and the risk takers.")

3. "Few issues in contemporary technology policy are as momentous (or contentious) as the precautionary principle," observes Andy Stirling. See Andy Stirling, "The Precautionary Principle," in *A Companion to the Philosophy of Technology*, ed. Jan Kyrre Berg Olsen, Stig Andur Pedersen, and Vincent F. Hendricks (Chichester, UK: Blackwell Publishing, 2009), 248.

4. Larry Downes, "Take Note Republicans and Democrats, This Is What a Pro-innovation Platform Looks Like," *Washington Post*, January 7, 2015, http://www .washingtonpost.com/news/innovations/wp/2015/01/07/take-note-republicans -and-democrats-this-is-what-a-pro-innovation-platform-looks-like.

5. Joshua D. Wright, "D.C.'s Cab Rules Should Put Consumers First," *Washington Post*, September 6, 2013, http://www.washingtonpost.com/opinions/has-the-dc-cab -commission-forgotten-who-it-serves/2013/09/06/cb3d0c18-15a6-11e3-be6e -dc6ae8a5b3a8_story.html; Andrew Vila and Kevin Gardner, "Bringing out the Regulatory Wheel Clamps for Uber," *Wall Street Journal*, September 28, 2015, http://www.wsj.com/articles/bringing-out-the-regulatory-wheel-clamps-for-uber -1443385825.

6. Joe Mullin, "Airbnb Gets Subpoena Demand for Data on All 15,000 NYC-Area Hosts," *Ars Technica*, October 7, 2013, http://arstechnica.com/tech-policy/2013/10 /airbnb-gets-subpoena-demand-for-all-data-on-all-15000-nyc-area-hosts.

7. Larry Downes and Paul Nunes, "Regulating 23andMe to Death Won't Stop the New Age of Genetic Testing," *Wired*, January 1, 2014, http://www.wired.com/opinion /2014/01/the-fda-may-win-the-battle-this-holiday-season-but-23andme-will-win -the-war.

8. Adam Thierer, "The Internet of Things and Wearable Technology: Addressing Privacy and Security Concerns without Derailing Innovation," *Richmond Journal of Law and Technology* 21, no. 6 (2015), http://papers.ssrn.com/sol3/papers.cfm ?abstract_id=2494382.

9. Adam Thierer and Ryan Hagemann, "Removing Roadblocks to Intelligent Vehicles and Driverless Cars" (Mercatus Working Paper, Mercatus Center at George Mason University, Arlington, VA, September 17, 2014), http://mercatus.org/publication /removing-roadblocks-intelligent-vehicles-and-driverless-cars.

10. Jerry Brito, Eli Dourado, and Adam Thierer, "Federal Aviation Administration: Unmanned Aircraft System Test Site Program Docket No: FAA-2013-0061" (Public Interest Comment, Mercatus Center at George Mason University, Arlington, VA, April 23, 2013), http://mercatus.org/publication/federal-aviation -administration-unmanned-aircraft-system-test-site-program; Eli Dourado, "The Next Internet-Like Platform for Innovation? Airspace. (Think Drones)," *Wired*, April 23, 2013, http://www.wired.com/opinion/2013/04/then-internet-now

-airspace-dont-stifle-innovation-on-the-next-great-platform; Adam Thierer, "Filing to FAA on Drones & 'Model Aircraft,'" *Technology Liberation Front*, September 23, 2014, http://techliberation.com/2014/09/23/filing-to-faa-on -drones-model-aircraft.

11.   Jerry Brito and Andrea Castillo, *Bitcoin: A Primer for Policymakers* (Arlington, VA: Mercatus Center at George Mason University, August 19, 2013), http://mercatus.org /publication/bitcoin-primer-policymakers.

12.   Adam Thierer, "The Right to Try, 3D Printing, the Costs of Technological Control & the Future of the FDA," *Technology Liberation Front*, August 10, 2015, http://techliberation.com/2015/08/10/the-right-to-try-3d-printing-the-costs-of -technological-control-the-future-of-the-fda.

13.   Adam Thierer, "Problems with Precautionary Principle-Minded Tech Regulation & a Federal Robotics Commission," *Medium*, September 22, 2014, https://medium.com /@AdamThierer/problems-with-precautionary-principle-minded-tech-regulation -a-federal-robotics-commission-c71f6f20d8bd.

14.   Richard Williams, Robert Graboyes, and Adam Thierer, "US Medical Devices: Choices and Consequences" (Arlington, VA: Mercatus Center at George Mason University, October 21, 2015), http://mercatus.org/publication/us-medical-devices -choices-and-consequences.

15.   Wendell Wallach, *A Dangerous Master: How to Keep Technology from Slipping beyond Our Control* (New York: Basic Books, 2015), 28–9.

16.   See http://mercatus.org/adam-thierer.

17.   Adam Thierer, "Tech Policy Threat Matrix," *Technology Liberation Front*, September 24, 2015, http://techliberation.com/2015/09/24/tech-policy-threat-matrix.

CHAPTER I
WHY PERMISSIONLESS INNOVATION MATTERS

1.   Adam Thierer, "The Media Cornucopia," *City Journal* (Spring 2007), http://www.city -journal.org/html/17_2_media.html.

2.   See Shawn Dubravac, *Digital Destiny: How the New Age of Data Will Transform the Way We Work, Live, and Communicate* (Washington, DC: Regnery, 2015), 182. ("Since the days of the ancient poets and playwrights, one characteristic has defined entertainment for mankind: scarcity.")

3.   Taylor Owen, *Disruptive Power: The Crisis of the State in the Digital Age* (Oxford: Oxford University Press, 2015), 29. ("Digital information, and the forms of behavior which it allows, are unbound. Communications are no longer constrained by the linearity of print of the hierarchy of the 20th century, existing instead in fluid networks. They are emboldened by new attributes, such as anonymity and constant change.")

4.   World Economic Forum, *Deep Shift: Technology Tipping Points and Societal Impact* (Geneva, Switzerland: September 2015), 3, http://www3.weforum.org/docs/WEF _GAC15_Technological_Tipping_Points_report_2015.pdf.

5.   Richard R. Nelson and Sidney G. Winter, *An Evolutionary Theory of Economic Change* (Cambridge, MA: Belknap Press, 1982), 131. ("The attempt to develop an effective new combination ordinarily involves a substantial amount of trial-and-error search, in which obstacles to effective performance are detected, diagnosed, and solved.")

6.   Daniel Castro and Alan McQuinn, "The Privacy Panic Cycle: A Guide to Public Fears about New Technologies," Information Technology and Innovation Foundation, September 10, 2015, 28, http://www.itif.org/publications/2015/09/10/privacy -panic-cycle-guide-public-fears-about-new-technologies. ("Policymakers should not get caught up in the panics that follow in the wake of new technologies, and they should not allow hypothetical, speculative, or unverified claims to color the policies they put in place. Similarly, they should not allow unsubstantiated claims put forth by privacy fundamentalists to derail legitimate public sector efforts to use technology to improve society.")

7.   Alex Rosenblat, Tamara Kneese, and Danah Boyd, "Understanding Intelligent Systems," Data & Society Research Institute, October 8, 2014, 4, http://papers.ssrn .com/sol3/papers.cfm?abstract_id=2537535. ("When innovative technology, sys-tems, or products are developed, they tend to disrupt not only familiar ways of doing things, but also wreak temporary havoc on the laws and policies designed to regulate their predecessors.")

8.   Vinton Cerf, "Keep the Internet Open," *New York Times*, May 24, 2012, http://www .nytimes.com/2012/05/25/opinion/keep-the-internet-open.html. The term "permission-less innovation" is of recent but uncertain origin. It has been a popular term in Silicon Valley and has often been heard in discussions about technology policy since the rise of the commercial Internet in the mid-1990s. The term is also related to another popular Silicon Valley saying, "It's easier to ask forgiveness than it is to get permission." That say-ing is also of uncertain origin, although it is often attributed to Grace M. Hopper, a com-puter scientist who was a rear admiral in the United States Navy. See Diane Hamblen, "Only the Limits of Our Imagination: An Exclusive Interview with RADM Grace M. Hopper," *Ships Ahoy*, July 1986, http://web.archive.org/web/20090114165606 /http://www.chips.navy.mil/archives/86_jul/interview.html.

9.   Downes, "Take Note Republicans and Democrats."

10.   Michael Nelson, "Six Myths of Innovation Policy," The European Institute, July 2013, http://www.europeaninstitute.org/EA-July-2013/perspectives-six-myths-of -innovation-policy.html. ("On Capitol Hill and in Brussels, there seems to be a belief that if only governments adopt the right tax policies, adequately fund R&D, enforce patents and copyrights, and support manufacturing, innovative, then start-ups will pop up everywhere and supercharge economic growth. Unfortunately, that misses an underlying problem: In many parts of the U.S. and Europe, innovation is not really welcome. It is misunderstood and even feared.")

11.   Donald J. Boudreaux, "Deirdre McCloskey and Economists' Ideas about Ideas," *Online Library of Liberty*, July 2014, http://oll.libertyfund.org/pages/mccloskey; Fred Smith, "We're in a Cultural War between the Forces of Economic Dynamism and Stasis," *Forbes*, August 5, 2013, http://www.forbes.com/sites/fredsmith/2013 /08/05/were-in-a-cultural-war-between-the-forces-of-economic-dynamism-and -stasis.

12.   Deirdre N. McCloskey, *The Bourgeois Virtues: Ethics for an Age of Commerce* (Chicago: University of Chicago Press, 2006); Deirdre N. McCloskey, *Bourgeois Dignity: Why Economics Can't Explain the Modern World* (Chicago: University of Chicago Press, 2010).

13.   Deirdre McCloskey, "Bourgeois Dignity: A Revolution in Rhetoric," *Cato Unbound*, October 4, 2010, http://www.cato-unbound.org/2010/10/04/deirdre-mccloskey /bourgeois-dignity-revolution-rhetoric.

14.   Donald J. Boudreaux, "Executive Summary," in *What America's Decline in Economic Freedom Means for Entrepreneurship and Prosperity*, ed. Donald J. Boudreaux

(Canada: Fraser Institute, 2015), 16, http://www.fraserinstitute.org/uploadedFiles
/fraser-ca/Content/research-news/research/publications/what-americas-decline
-in-economic-freedom-means-for-entrepreneurship-and-prosperity.pdf.
("McCloskey's work is showing that the change in rhetoric and ethics encouraged
individuals to enter commercial life. Ethics, attitudes, and norms are an aspect of
the institutional environment—called the 'informal institutions'—and thus, when the
institutional environment becomes more favorable to the entrepreneurial environment, there would be increase in entrepreneurial activity.")

15. Randall Holcombe, "Entrepreneurship and Economic Growth," *Quarterly Journal of
Austrian Economics* 1, no. 2 (Summer 1998): 58, http://mises.org/journals/qjae/pdf
/qjae1_2_3.pdf. ("When entrepreneurship is seen as the engine of growth, the empha-
sis shifts toward the creation of an environment within which opportunities for entrepreneurial activity are created, and successful entrepreneurship is rewarded.")

16. Joel Mokyr, *Lever of Riches: Technological Creativity and Economic Progress* (New
York: Oxford University Press, 1990), 182.

17. Mokyr, *Lever of Riches*, 12. ("[E]conomic and social institutions have to encourage
potential innovators by presenting them with the right incentive structure."); Bret
Swanson, "More Disruption, Please," *TechPolicyDaily*, August 20, 2014, http://www
.techpolicydaily.com/technology/disruption-please/#sthash.PVUNga9N.dpuf. ("To
reignite economic growth, we need a broad commitment to an open economy and
robust entrepreneurship.")

18. Adam Thierer, "Embracing a Culture of Permissionless Innovation," *Cato Online
Forum*, November 2014, http://www.cato.org/publications/cato-online-forum
/embracing-culture-permissionless-innovation.

19. Mokyr, *Lever of Riches*, 16.

20. Kenneth Cukier and Viktor Mayer-Schönberger, "The Financial Bonanza of Big Data,"
Wall Street Journal, March 7, 2013, http://online.wsj.com/article/
SB10001424127887324178904578343120139164986.html.

21. Software & Information Industry Association, "Data-Driven Innovation, A Guide for
Policymakers: Understanding and Enabling the Economic and Social Value of Data,"
May 2013, http://siia.net/index.php?option=com_content&view=article&id=1293
:data-driven-innovation&catid=163:public-policy-articles&Itemid=1411.

22. Joe Weinman, "How Customer Intimacy Is Evolving to Collective Intimacy, Thanks to
Big Data," *Forbes*, June 4, 2013, http://www.forbes.com/sites/joeweinman/2013
/06/04/how-customer-intimacy-is-evolving-to-collective-intimcy-thanks-to-big
-data.

23. OECD, *Data-Driven Innovation: Big Data for Growth and Well-Being*, October 6,
2015, http://www.oecd-ilibrary.org/science-and-technology/data-driven
-innovation_9789264229358-en.

24. Michael Mandel, "Beyond Goods and Services: The (Unmeasured) Rise of the Data-
Driven Economy" (Policy Memo, Progressive Policy Institute, October 2012), http://
www.progressivepolicy.org/wp-content/uploads/2012/10/10.2012-Mandel_Beyond
-Goods-and-Services_The-Unmeasured-Rise-of-the-Data-Driven-Economy.pdf.

25. White House, *Big Data: Seizing Opportunities, Preserving Values* (May 2014), 5,
https://www.whitehouse.gov/sites/default/files/docs/big_data_privacy_report
_may_1_2014.pdf. ("Used well, big data analysis can boost economic productivity,
drive improved consumer and government services, thwart terrorists, and save lives.")

26. Federal Trade Commission, *Protecting Consumer Privacy in an Era of Rapid Change: A Proposed Framework for Businesses and Policymakers* (Washington, DC: Federal Trade Commission, 2010), http://www.ftc.gov/os/2010/12/101201privacyreport.pdf.

27. John Manoogian III, "How Free Apps Can Make More Money Than Paid Apps," *Tech Crunch*, August 26, 2012, http://techcrunch.com/2012/08/26/how-free-apps-can-make-more-money-than-paid-apps.

28. Christopher Mims, "Hats off to Web Advertising. No, Really," *Wall Street Journal*, July 6, 2015, http://www.wsj.com/articles/where-would-we-be-without-internet-ads-1436120809?mod=ST1.

29. Amy O'Leary, "An App That Saved 10,000 Lives," *New York Times*, October 5, 2013, http://bits.blogs.nytimes.com/2013/10/05/how-to-save-10000-lives-with-an-app-flatter-doctors.

30. A study commissioned by the Direct Marketing Association, John Deighton of Harvard Business School, and Peter Johnson of Columbia University found that data-driven marketing added $156 billion in revenue to the US economy and fueled more than 675,000 jobs in 2012. See John Deighton and Peter A. Johnson, "The Value of Data: Consequences for Insight, Innovation & Efficiency in the U.S. Economy" (2013), http://ddminstitute.thedma.org/#valueofdata. Major reports from economic consultancies Gartner and McKinsey Global Institute have also documented significant consumer benefits from big data across multiple sectors. See Gartner, "Gartner Says Big Data Will Drive $28 Billion of IT Spending in 2012," October 17, 2012, http://www.gartner.com/newsroom/id/2200815; James Manyika, Michael Chui, Brad Brown, Jacques Bughin, Richard Dobbs, Charles Roxburgh, and Angela Hung Byers, "Big Data: The Next Frontier for Innovation, Competition, and Productivity," McKinsey & Co., May 2011, 97–106, http://www.mckinsey.com/insights/business_technology/big_data_the_next_frontier_for_innovation.

31. Adam Thierer, "A Status Update on the Development of Voluntary Do-Not-Track Standards" (Testimony before the Senate Committee on Commerce, Science, and Transportation, April 24, 2013), http://mercatus.org/publication/status-update-development-voluntary-do-not-track-standards.

32. Adam Thierer, "Relax and Learn to Love Big Data," *US News and World Report*, September 16, 2013, http://www.usnews.com/opinion/blogs/economic-intelligence/2013/09/16/big-data-collection-has-many-benefits-for-internet-users.

33. L. Gordon Crovitz, "WeHelpedBuildThat.com," *Wall Street Journal*, July 29, 2012, http://online.wsj.com/article/SB10000872396390443931404577555073157895692.html.

34. "Notable & Quotable: Milton Friedman," *Wall Street Journal*, October 6, 2015, http://www.wsj.com/articles/notable-quotable-milton-friedman-1444169267. ("One of the great mistakes is to judge policies and programs by their intentions rather than their results. We all know a famous road that is paved with good intentions.")

35. Russell Roberts, "Getting the Most out of Life: The Concept of Opportunity Cost," Library of Economics and Liberty, February 5, 2007, http://www.econlib.org/library/Columns/y2007/Robertsopportunitycost.html. ("Opportunity cost is what you have to give up to get something.")

36. Frédéric Bastiat, *What Is Seen and What Is Not Seen* (Indianapolis, IN: Liberty Fund, 1848, 1955), http://www.econlib.org/library/Bastiat/basEss1.html.

37. Daniel O'Connor of the Computer and Communications Industry Association argues

that the Internet "moves markets closer to the 'perfect competition' end of the spectrum," by minimizing barriers to entry, increasing the mobility of labor and capital, expanding information flows, minimizing transaction costs, and maximizing the overall number of buyers and sellers. See Daniel O'Connor, "Rent Seeking and the Internet Economy (Part 1): Why Is the Internet So Frequently the Target of Rent Seekers?," *DisCo blog*, August 15, 2013, http://www.project-disco.org/competition /081513-rent-seeking-and-the-internet-economy-part-1-why-is-the-internet-so -frequently-the-target-of-rent-seekers.

38.   Shane Greenstein, *How the Internet Became Commercial: Innovation, Privatization, and the Birth of a New Network* (Princeton, NJ: Princeton University Press, 2015).

39.   Adam Thierer, "The Greatest of All Internet Laws Turns 15," *Forbes*, May 8, 2011, http://www.forbes.com/sites/adamthierer/2011/05/08/the-greatest-of-all-internet -laws-turns-15.

40.   David Post, "A Bit of Internet History, or How Two Members of Congress Helped Create a Trillion or So Dollars of Value," *Volokh Conspiracy*, August 27, 2015, https:// www.washingtonpost.com/news/volokh-conspiracy/wp/2015/08/27/a-bit-of -internet-history-or-how-two-members-of-congress-helped-create-a-trillion-or-so -dollars-of-value. ("Yet it is impossible to imagine what the Internet ecosystem would look like today without it. Virtually every successful online venture that emerged after 1996—including all the usual suspects, viz. Google, Facebook, Tumblr, Twitter, Reddit, Craigslist, YouTube, Instagram, eBay, Amazon—relies in large part (or entirely) on content provided by their users, who number in the hundreds of millions, or billions.")

41.   White House, *The Framework for Global Electronic Commerce* (July 1997), http://clinton4.nara.gov/WH/New/Commerce.

42.   Adam Thierer, "15 Years On, President Clinton's 5 Principles for Internet Policy Remain the Perfect Paradigm," *Forbes*, February 12, 2012, http://www.forbes.com /sites/adamthierer/2012/02/12/15-years-on-president-clintons-5-principles-for -internet-policy-remain-the-perfect-paradigm.

43.   White House, *Framework for Global Electronic Commerce*.

44.   Ibid.

45.   Ibid.

46.   Ibid.

47.   See Larry Downes, "How Europe Can Create Its Own Silicon Valley," *Harvard Business Review*, June 11, 2015, https://hbr.org/2015/06/how-europe-can-create-its -own-silicon-valley.

48.   Maureen K. Ohlhausen, "The Internet of Things and the FTC: Does Innovation Require Intervention?" (Remarks before the US Chamber of Commerce, Washington, DC, October 18, 2013), https://www.ftc.gov/public-statements/2013 /10/internet-things-ftc-does-innovation-require-intervention-0.

49.   Om Malik, "Will Industrial Internet Create More Jobs? GE Thinks Yes," *GigaOm*, October 8, 2013, http://gigaom.com/2013/10/08/will-industrial-internet-create -more-jobs-ge-thinks-yes.

50.   Adam Thierer, Jerry Brito, and Eli Dourado, "Technology Policy: A Look Ahead," *Technology Liberation Front*, May 12, 2014, http://techliberation.com/2014/05/12 /technology-policy-a-look-ahead.

51. Marc Andreessen, "Why Software Is Eating the World," *Wall Street Journal*, August 20, 2011, http://www.wsj.com/articles/ SB10001424053111903480904576512250915629460.

52. Tony Fadell, "Nest CEO Tony Fadell on the Future of the Internet," *Wall Street Journal*, April 26, 2015, http://www.wsj.com/articles/nest-ceo-tony-fadell-on-the-future-of -the-internet-1430104501. ("Tomorrow's Internet will be everywhere and in every- thing. . . . In many ways, the Internet of the future will feel different from the Internet we know today. Instead of seeking it out, we'll be surrounded by it. And instead of extracting data from it, we'll be fed a constant stream of curated, personalized infor- mation to help us solve problems and live better—and live better together.")

53. Chris Anderson, *Makers: The New Industrial Revolution* (New York: Crown Business, 2012), 17.

54. Quoted in Christopher Mims, "A New Dawn for Breast Pumps and Other Products," *Wall Street Journal*, March 22, 2015, http://www.wsj.com/articles/a-new-dawn-for -gadgets-1427065972?mod=LS1&ref=/news/technology.

55. Michael Mandel, "Can the Internet of Everything Bring Back the High-Growth Economy?" (Policy Memo, Progressive Policy Institute, Washington, DC, September 2013), 9, http://www.progressivepolicy.org/2013/09/can-the-internet-of -everything-bring-back-the-high-growth-economy. ("Now we are at the next stage of the Internet Revolution, where the physical world gets connected to data, people, and processes. No one can predict the ultimate course of innovative technologies, but it appears that the Internet of Everything has the potential to help revive the high-growth economy.")

56. Bret Swanson, "The Immersive Internet: Public Policy in a Hundred-Billion Device World," US Chamber of Commerce Foundation, September 22, 2015, http://www .uschamberfoundation.org/article/immersive-internet-public-policy-hundred -billion-device-world.

57. Ian G. Smith, ed., *The Internet of Things 2012—New Horizons* (Halifax, UK: Internet of Things European Research Cluster, 2012), 29–31.

58. Dave Evans, "The Internet of Things: How the Next Evolution of the Internet Is Changing Everything" (Cisco White Paper, Cisco Systems, Inc., San Jose, CA, April 2011), 2, http:// www.cisco.com/web/about/ac79/docs/innov/IoT_IBSG_0411FINAL.pdf.

59. Steve Lohr, "A Messenger for the Internet of Things," *New York Times*, April 25, 2013, http://bits.blogs.nytimes.com/2013/04/25/a-messenger-for-the-internet-of -things.

60. See Adam Thierer and Andrea Castillo, "Projecting the Growth and Economic Impact of the Internet of Things" (Research Summary, Mercatus Center at George Mason University, Arlington, VA, June 15, 2015), http://mercatus.org/publication /projecting-growth-and-economic-impact-internet-things.

61. James Manyika, Michael Chui, Peter Bisson, Jonathan Woetzel, Richard Dobbs, Jacques Bughin, and Dan Aharon, "Unlocking the Potential of the Internet of Things," McKinsey Global Institute, June 2015, http://www.mckinsey.com/insights /business_technology/the_internet_of_things_the_value_of_digitizing_the _physical_world.

62. Antony Savvas, "Internet of Things Market Will Be Worth Almost $9 Trillion," *CNME*, October 6, 2013, http://www.cnmeonline.com/news/internet-of-things-market-will -be-worth-almost-9-trillion.

63. Joseph Bradley, Joel Barbier, and Doug Handler, *Embracing the Internet of Everything to Capture Your Share of $14.4 Trillion* (San Jose, CA: Cisco, 2013), http://www.cisco.com/web/about/ac79/docs/innov/IoE_Economy.pdf.

64. Zeynep Tufekci, "Why 'Smart' Objects May Be a Dumb Idea," *New York Times*, August 10, 2015, http://www.nytimes.com/2015/08/11/opinion/zeynep-tufekci-why -smart-objects-may-be-a-dumb-idea.html.

65. Federal Trade Commission, *The Internet of Things: Privacy and Security in a Connected World* (2015), http://www.ftc.gov/system/files/documents/reports /federal-trade-commission-staff-report-november-2013-workshop-entitled -internet-things-privacy/150127iotrpt.pdf.

66. See generally Bruce Schneier, "Will Giving the Internet Eyes and Ears Mean the End of Privacy?," *Guardian*, May 16, 2013, http://www.guardian.co.uk/technology/2013 /may/16/internet-of-things-privacy-google; Mike Wheatley, "Big Brother's Big Data: Why We Must Fear the Internet of Things," *Silicon Angle*, January 10, 2013, http://siliconangle.com/blog/2013/01/10/big-brothers-big-data-why-we-must-fear -the-internet-of-things.

67. Adam Thierer, "How Not to Strangle the Internet of Things," *Politico*, June 2015, http://www.politico.com/agenda/story/2015/06/internet-of-things-regulation -000124; Giulio Coraggio, "Fear Cannot Stop the Internet of Things!," *IoT Law*, August 6, 2015, http://iotlaw.net/2015/08/06/fear-cannot-stop-the-internet-of -things. ("Any technological revolution has brought some disruption and inevitably some mistakes. However, this is not the reason for stopping progress.")

68. Adam Thierer, "Uncle Sam Wants Your Fitbit," *Reason*, May 2015, https://reason .com/archives/2015/04/09/uncle-sam-wants-your-fitbit.

69. Thierer, "The Internet of Things and Wearable Technology"; Adam Thierer, "The Connected World: Examining the Internet of Things" (Testimony before the Senate Committee on Commerce, Science, and Transportation, February 11, 2015), http:// mercatus.org/publication/connected-world-examining-internet-things.

70. Eli Dourado, "The Third Industrial Revolution Has Only Just Begun," *EliDourado.com*, October 10, 2012, http://elidourado.com/blog/the-third-industrial-revolution -has-only-just-begun.

71. Robert Graboyes, "Fortress and Frontier in American Health Care" (Mercatus Research, Mercatus Center at George Mason University, Arlington, VA, October 20, 2014), http://mercatus.org/publication/fortress-and-frontier-american-health-care.

72. Peter W. Huber, *The Cure in the Code: How 20th Century Law Is Undermining 21st Century Medicine* (New York: Basic Books, 2013).

73. Joseph V. Gulfo, *Innovation Breakdown: How the FDA and Wall Street Cripple Medical Advances* (Franklin, TN: Post Hill Press, 2014), 45–6.

74. April Dembrosky, "Play This Video Game and Call Me in the Morning," *NPR*, August 17, 2015, http://www.npr.org/sections/health-shots/2015/08/17/432004332/play -this-video-game-and-call-me-in-the-morning.

75. Vinod Khosla, "Fireside Chat with Google Cofounders, Larry Page and Sergey Brin," *Khosla Adventures* website, July 3, 2014, http://www.khoslaventures.com/fireside -chat-with-google-co-founders-larry-page-and-sergey-brin.

76. Israel Kirzner, an economist associated with the Austrian school of economics, spoke of "the shortsightedness of those who, not recognizing the open-ended character of entrepreneurial discovery, repeatedly fall into the trap of forecasting

the future against the background of today's expectations rather than against the unknowable background of tomorrow's discoveries." Israel Kirzner, *Discovery and the Capitalist Process* (Chicago: University of Chicago Press, 1985), xi.

77.   Mark Buchanan, "Is Innovation Over?," *Bloomberg View*, December 11, 2014, http://www.bloombergview.com/articles/2014-12-11/is-innovation-over. ("In such matters, we're as clueless about what might be possible as physical scientists were about electricity and chemistry in 1700. This would suggest that there's plenty of profound innovation yet to be done.")

78.   L. Gordon Crovitz, "Drones Cleared for Takeoff," *Wall Street Journal*, March 16, 2014, http://www.wsj.com/news/articles/SB10001424052702304914904579441052310129582.

CHAPTER II
SAVING PROGRESS FROM THE TECHNOCRATS

1.   Virginia Postrel, *The Future and Its Enemies* (New York: The Free Press, 1998), xv.

2.   Ibid., xiv.

3.   Ibid., 7–8.

4.   Robert D. Atkinson, *The Past and Future of America's Economy* (Cheltenham, UK: Edward Elgar, 2004), 201 [emphasis added].

5.   Adam Thierer, "Robert Graboyes on What the Internet Can Teach Us about Health Care Innovation," *Technology Liberation Front*, November 10, 2014, http://techliberation.com/2014/11/10/robert-graboyes-on-what-the-internet-can-teach-us-about-health-care-innovation.

6.   Graboyes, "Fortress and Frontier."

7.   Adam Thierer, "Thinking about Innovation Policy Debates: 4 Related Paradigms," *Technology Liberation Front*, November 11, 2014, http://techliberation.com/2014/11/11/thinking-about-innovation-policy-debates-4-related-paradigms.

8.   Scott Berkun, "The Ten Myths of Innovation: The Best Summary," *ScottBerkun.com*, last updated July 7, 2013, http://scottberkun.com/2013/ten-myths-of-innnovation.

9.   Dennis Baron, *A Better Pencil: Readers, Writers, and the Digital Revolution* (Oxford, UK: Oxford University Press, 2009), 12, (noting that "the shock of the new often brings out critics eager to warn us away").

10.   Aaron Wildavsky, *Searching for Safety* (New Brunswick, CT: Transaction Books, 1988), 54. ("A lot of misplaced nostalgia goes into the (mis)perception that all old, handcrafted items are safer than the new and mass-produced.")

11.   Postrel, *The Future and Its Enemies*, xv.

12.   See Adam Thierer, "Technopanics, Threat Inflation, and the Danger of an Information Technology Precautionary Principle," *Minnesota Journal of Law, Science & Technology* 14, no. 1 (2013): 312–50.

13.   Postrel, *The Future and Its Enemies*, 216.

14.   Ibid., 19.

15. Frank Furedi, "Precautionary Culture and the Rise of Probabilistic Risk Assessment," *Erasmus Law Review* 2, no. 2 (2009), 215. ("Worse-case thinking encourages society to adopt fear as of one of the dominant principles around which the public, its government, and institutions should organise their life. It institutionalises insecurity and fosters a mood of confusion and powerlessness. Through popularising the belief that worst cases are normal, it incites people to feel defenceless and vulnerable to a wide range of future threats. In all but name it constitutes an invitation to terror.")

16. This section adapted from Thierer, "Technopanics," 352-79.

17. As Steven Horwitz and Jack Knych observe, "[F]ailure drives change. While success is the engine that accelerates us toward our goals, it is failure that steers us toward the most valuable goals possible. Once failure is recognized as being just as important as success in the market process, it should be clear that the goal of a society should be to create an environment that not only allows people to succeed freely but to fail freely as well." Steven Horwitz and Jack Knych, "The Importance of Failure," *Freeman* 61, no. 9 (November 2011), http://www.fee.org/the_freeman /detail/the-importance-of-failure#axzz2ZnNlpqHQ.

18. James Bessen, *Learning by Doing: The Real Connection between Innovation, Wages, and Wealth* (New Haven, CT: Yale University Press, 2015), 50. ("Major new technologies become 'revolutionary' only after a long process of learning by doing and incremental improvement. Having the breakthrough idea is not enough. But learning through experience and experimentation is expensive and slow. Experimentation involves a search for productive techniques: testing and eliminating bad techniques in order to find good ones. This means that workers and equipment typically operate for extended periods at low levels of productivity using poor techniques and are able to eliminate those poor practices only when they find something better.")

19. Samuel Beckett, *Worstward Ho* (1983).

20. As quoted in Nathan Furr, "How Failure Taught Edison to Repeatedly Innovate," *Forbes*, June 9, 2011, http://www.forbes.com/sites/nathanfurr/2011/06/09/how -failure-taught-edison-to-repeatedly-innovate.

21. Wildavsky, *Searching for Safety*, 38.

22. Thierer, "Technopanics," 309-86.

23. Cass R. Sunstein, *Laws of Fear: Beyond the Precautionary Principle* (Cambridge, UK: Cambridge University Press, 2005). ("The Precautionary Principle takes many forms. But in all of them, the animating idea is that regulators should take steps to protect against potential harms, even if causal chains are unclear and even if we do not know that those harms will come to fruition.")

24. John Frank Weaver, "We Need to Pass Legislation on Artificial Intelligence Early and Often," *Slate*, September 12, 2014, http://www.slate.com/blogs/future_tense /2014/09/12/we_need_to_pass_artificial_intelligence_laws_early_and_often. html. See also Wallach, *Dangerous Master*, 72. (Wallach argues for more "upstream governance" or "more control over the way that potentially harmful technologies are developed or introduced into the larger society. Upstream management is certainly better than introducing regulations downstream, after a technology is deeply entrenched, or something major has already gone wrong.")

25. Henk van den Belt, "Debating the Precautionary Principle: 'Guilty until Proven Innocent' or 'Innocent until Proven Guilty'?," *Plant Physiology* 132 (2003): 1124.

26. Steve Clarke, "Future Technologies, Dystopic Futures and the Precautionary Principle," *Ethics and Information Technology* 7 (2005): 121.

27. Jonathan H. Adler, "The Problems with Precaution: A Principle without Principle," *The American*, May 25, 2011, http://www.american.com/archive/2011/may/the -problems-with-precaution-a-principle-without-principle.

28. van den Belt, "Debating the Precautionary Principle," 1125. ("[A] risk-free world is not a real option. Thus, a consistent application of the [precautionary principle] would in the final analysis stifle all innovation.")

29. Bruce Schneier, "Worst-Case Thinking," *Schneier on Security*, May 13, 2010, https:// www.schneier.com/blog/archives/2010/05/worst-case_thin.html.

30. Thierer, "How Not to Strangle."

31. Schneier, "Worst-Case Thinking." ("There's a certain blindness that comes from worst-case thinking. An extension of the precautionary principle, it involves imagining the worst possible outcome and then acting as if it were a certainty. It substitutes imagination for thinking, speculation for risk analysis, and fear for reason. It fosters powerlessness and vulnerability and magnifies social paralysis.")

32. Adam Thierer, "Who Really Believes in 'Permissionless Innovation'?," *Technology Liberation Front*, March 4, 2013, http://techliberation.com/2013/03/04/who-really -believes-in-permissionless-innovation.

33. Eli Dourado, "'Permissionless Innovation' Offline as Well as On," *Umlaut*, February 6, 2013, http://theumlaut.com/2013/02/06/permissionless-innovation-of-line-as-well -as-on. ("Advocates of the Internet are right to extol the permissionless innovation model—but they are wrong to believe that it need be unique to the Internet. We can legalize innovation in the physical world, too. All it takes is a recognition that real-world innovators should not have to ask permission either.")

34. Stefan H. Thomke, *Experimentation Matters: Unlocking the Potential of New Technologies for Innovation* (Boston, MA: Harvard Business Review Press, 2003), 5. ("Indeed, at the heart of every company's ability to innovate lies a process of experimentation that enables the organization to create and evaluate new ideas and concepts for products, services, business models, or strategies.")

35. See Paul Ohm, "The Myth of the Superuser: Fear, Risk, and Harm Online," *University of California-Davis Law Review* 41 (2008): 1327–402.

36. See, for example, Schneier, "Giving the Internet Eyes and Ears"; Wheatley, "Big Brother's Big Data"; Sarah A. Downey, "Google Glass Cons: How the Camera-Embedded Eyeglasses Could Shatter Privacy," *Variety*, July 17, 2013, http://variety .com/2013/biz/news/google-glass-cons-how-the-camera-embedded-eyeglasses -could-shatter-privacy-1200563731.

37. Roel Pieterman, "Introduction: The Many Facets of Precautionary Logic," *Erasmus Law Review* 2, no. 2 (2009), at 100. ("Whereas people in the 20th century embraced modern utopias, in the 21st century we seem to focus on post-modern dystopias.")

38. This section adapted from Thierer, "Technopanics," 332–47.

39. Ibid., 311.

40. See, for example, Michael Shermer, *The Believing Brain: From Ghosts and Gods to Politics and Conspiracies—How We Construct Beliefs and Reinforce Them as Truths* (New York: Times Books, 2011), 274–75; Bruce Schneier, *Liars & Outliers: Enabling*

the Trust That Society Needs to Thrive (Indianapolis, IN: John Wiley & Sons, Inc., 2012), 203.

41. Furedi, "Precautionary Culture," 205. ("The shift towards possibilistic thinking is driven by a powerful sense of cultural pessimism about knowing and an intense feeling of apprehension about the unknown. The cumulative outcome of this sensibility is the routinisation of the expectation of worst possible outcomes. The principal question posed by possibilistic thinking, 'what can possibly go wrong', continually invites the answer 'everything'. The connection between possibilistic and worse-case thinking is self-consciously promoted by the advocates of this approach.")

42. See Shermer, *Believing Brain*, 136, 275. ("Negativity bias: the tendency to pay closer attention and give more weight to negative events, beliefs, and information than to positive.")

43. Steven Pinker, *The Blank Slate: The Modern Denial of Human Nature* (New York: Penguin Books, 2002), 232.

44. Clive Thompson, *Smarter Than You Think: How Technology Is Changing Our Minds for the Better* (New York: Penguin Press, 2013), 283.

45. Adam Thierer, "Why Do We Always Sell the Next Generation Short?," *Forbes*, January 8, 2012, http://www.forbes.com/sites/adamthierer/2012/01/08/why-do-we-always-sell-the-next-generation-short.

46. Jason Feifer, "The Internet Is Not Harming You. Here's What's Harmful: Fearmongering about the Internet," *Fast Company*, November 2014, http://www.fastcompany.com/3036428/fear-and-loathing-of-silicon-valley. ("Falsely romanticizing the past allows us to think that we stand at a threshold as some last vestige of better, tech-disconnected humans. The truth is that as culture evolves our priorities change as well.")

47. See generally Thierer, "Technopanics," 335. ("Excessive nostalgia can help explain skepticism about many forms of technological change. It can even result in calls for restrictions on technology."); Matt Ridley, *The Rational Optimist: How Prosperity Evolves* (New York: Harper Collins, 2010), 292. ("There has probably never been a generation since the Paleolithic that did not deplore the fecklessness of the next and worship a golden memory of the past.")

48. Shermer, *Believing Brain*, 275.

49. Bryan Caplan, *Myth of the Rational Voter: Why Democracies Choose Bad Policies* (Princeton, NJ: Princeton University Press, 2007), 44.

50. Steven Johnson, "We're Living the Dream; We Just Don't Realize It," *CNN Opinion*, November 24, 2014, http://www.cnn.com/2012/11/24/opinion/johnson-progress-overlooked/index.html?c=weekend-homepage-t&page=2.

51. Mike Masnick, "Hacking Society: It's Time to Measure the Unmeasurable," *TechDirt*, April 27, 2012, https://www.techdirt.com/blog/innovation/articles/20120425/01215118644/hacking-society-its-time-to-measure-unmeasurable.shtml.

52. Adam Thierer, "Sarkozy, Facebook, Moral Panics & the Third-Person Effect Hypothesis," *Technology Liberation Front*, May 29, 2011, http://techliberation.com/2011/05/29/sarkozy-facebook-moral-panics-the-third-person-effect-hypothesis.

53. Erich Goode and Nachman Ben-Yehuda, *Moral Panics: The Social Construction of Deviance* (Malden, MA: Blackwell Publishing, 2009), 122. ("Whenever the question

'What is to be done?' is asked concerning behavior deemed threatening, someone puts forth the suggestion, 'There ought to be a law.' If laws already exist addressing the threatening behavior, moral entrepreneurs will call for stiffer penalties or a law-enforcement crack-down. Legislation and law enforcement are two of the most obvious and widely resorted to efforts to crush a putative threat during a moral panic."); Furedi, "Precautionary Culture," 214. ("Possibilistic thinking succeeds in transmitting the philosophy of fear entrepreneurs in a coherent form. This form of thinking successfully captures and expresses the dominant mood of cultural pessimism. In the name of directing the public's attention to its worst fears, it adopts a cavalier stance towards the authority of knowledge and of evidence.")

54. See Wendy McElroy, "Destroying Childhood to Save Children," *Freeman*, December 6, 2011, http://www.thefreemanonline.org/headline/destroying -childhood-to-save-children.

55. Adam Thierer, "Achieving Internet Order without Law," *Forbes*, June 24, 2012, http:// www.forbes.com/sites/adamthierer/2012/06/24/achieving-internet-order -without-law.

56. Giandomenico Majone, "What Price Safety? The Precautionary Principle and Its Policy Implications," in Risk *Regulation in the European Union: Between Enlargement and Internationalization*, ed. Giandomenico Majone (Florence, Italy: European University Institute, Robert Schuman Centre for Advanced Studies, 2003), 49. ("[T]he precautionary principle has a legitimate but limited role to play in risk regulation whenever there is an imminent danger of irreversible damage, and/or knowledge of causal processes is too limited to bring about a consensus of scientific opinion.")

57. See generally Sunstein, *Laws of Fear*, 109–28; Cass R. Sunstein, "The Catastrophic Harm Precautionary Principle," *Issues in Legal Scholarship*, Article 3, (2007), http:// papers.ssrn.com/sol3/papers.cfm?abstract_id=2532598.

58. This section adapted from Thierer, "Technopanics," 356–64.

59. John Morrall and James Broughel, "The Role of Regulatory Impact Analysis in Federal Rulemaking," Mercatus Center at George Mason University, April 10, 2014, http://mercatus.org/publication/role-regulatory-impact-analysis-federal -rulemaking.

60. See Susan E. Dudley and Jerry Brito, *Regulation: A Primer*, 2nd ed. (Arlington, VA: Mercatus Center at George Mason University, 2012), 97–8. ("The cost of a regulation is the opportunity cost—whatever desirable things society gives up in order to get the good things the regulation produces. The opportunity cost of alternative approaches is the appropriate measure of costs. This measure should reflect the benefits foregone when a particular action is selected and should include the change in consumer and producer surplus."); Jerry Ellig and Patrick A. McLaughlin, "The Quality and Use of Regulatory Analysis in 2008," *Risk Analysis* 32, no. 855 (2012).

61. Sunstein, *Laws of Fear*, 115. ("[C]osts matter as such. The extent of precautions cannot reasonably be divorced from their expense.")

62. Ibid. ("[U]se of the [Anti-Catastrophe Principle] should be closely attentive to the idea of cost-effectiveness, which requires regulators to choose the least costly means of achieving their ends.")

63. Sunstein, *Laws of Fear*, 114.

64. Frank B. Cross, "Paradoxical Perils of the Precautionary Principle," *Washington and Lee Law Review* 53, no. 1 (1996): 924.

65. Joel Mokyr, Chris Vickers, and Nicolas L. Ziebarth, "The History of Technological Anxiety and the Future of Economic Growth: Is This Time Different?" *Journal of Economic Perspectives* 29, no. 3 (Summer 2015): 31–50, http://www.ingentaconnect .com/content/aea/jep/2015/00000029/00000003/art00002;jsessionid =58w6sj0v1f6vm.alexandra.

66. Thierer, "Technopanics," 361.

67. Witherspoon Council on Ethics and the Integrity of Science, "The Threat of Human Cloning: Ethics, Recent Developments, and the Case for Action," *New Atlantis* 46 (Summer 2015), http://www.thenewatlantis.com/publications/number-46-summer -2015.

68. Wallach, *Dangerous Master*, 13. ("The power to alter the genome, and most specifically the human genome, signals a major inflection point in the history of humanity.")

69. These issues are thoroughly explored in Joel Garreau, *Radical Evolution: The Promise and Peril of Enhancing Our Minds, Our Bodies—And What It Means to Be Human* (New York: Broadway Books, 2005).

70. Wallach, *Dangerous Master*, 8. ("A juggernaut of change in the form of genetic engi-neering, mood- and character-altering drugs, nanotechnology, and advanced forms of artificial intelligence threaten to redesign our minds and bodies and redefine what it means to be human.")

71. Glen Martin, "'Biohackers' Mining Their Own Bodies' Data," *SF Gate*, June 28, 2012, http://www.sfgate.com/health/article/Biohackers-mining-their-own-bodies-data -3668230.php; Jim McLauchlin, "The Future of Bionic Humans: What's Next in Bio-Hacking?," *LiveScience*, June 18, 2013, http://www.livescience.com/37507 -biohacking-james-rollins.html.

72. Carolyn Y. Johnson, "As Synthetic Biology Becomes Affordable, Amateur Labs Thrive," *Boston Globe*, September 16, 2008, http://tech.mit.edu/V128/N39/biohack.html.

73. Keiron Monks, "Forget Wearable Tech: Embeddable Implants Are Already Here," *CNN*, April 9, 2014, http://www.cnn.com/2014/04/08/tech/forget-wearable -tech-embeddable-implants.

74. Ben Popper, "Cyborg America: Inside the Strange New World of Basement Body Hackers," *Verge*, August 8, 2012, http://www.theverge.com/2012/8/8/3177438 /cyborg-america-biohackers-grinders-body-hackers.

75. Thomke, *Experimentation Matters*, 4.

76. Ibid., 1.

77. Mokyr, Vickers, and Ziebarth, "History of Technological Anxiety," 31, http://www .ingentaconnect.com/content/aea/jep/2015/00000029/00000003/art00002 ;jsessionid=58w6sj0v1f6vm.alexandra.

CHAPTER III
WHY THIS CLASH OF VISIONS MATTERS

1.   For an overview, see Adam Thierer, "The Case for Internet Optimism, Part 1: Saving the Net from Its Detractors," in *The Next Digital Decade: Essays on the Future of the Internet*, ed. Berin Szoka and Adam Marcus (Washington, DC: Tech Freedom, 2010), 57–87, http://papers.ssrn.com/sol3/papers.cfm?abstract_id=1751044. For a concise critique of "humanist" technological criticism, see Andrew McAfee, "Who Are the Humanists, and Why Do They Dislike Technology So Much?," *Financial Times*, July 7, 2015, http://blogs.ft.com/andrew-mcafee/2015/07/07/who-are-the-humanists -and-why-do-they-dislike-technology-so-much.

2.   James Fallows, "The 50 Greatest Breakthroughs since the Wheel," *Atlantic*, November 2013, 65. See also Mokyr, Vickers, and Ziebarth, "History of Technological Anxiety," 31, http://www.ingentaconnect.com/content/aea/jep/2015/00000029 /00000003/art00002;jsessionid=58w6sj0v1f6vm.alexandra. ("Technology is widely considered the main source of economic progress, but it has also generated cultural anxiety throughout history.")

3.   Garreau, *Radical Evolution*.

4.   Ibid., 130.

5.   Ibid., 95.

6.   Ibid., 108.

7.   See Adam Thierer, "Are You an Internet Optimist or Pessimist? The Great Debate over Technology's Impact on Society," *Technology Liberation Front*, January 31, 2010, http://techliberation.com/2010/01/31/are-you-an-internet-optimist-or -pessimist-the-great-debate-over-technology%E2%80%99s-impact-on-society.

8.   For an overview of these thinkers and their theories, see Christopher May, ed., *Key Thinkers for the Information Society* (London: Routledge, 2003); Carl Mitcham, *Thinking through Technology: The Path between Engineering and Philosophy* (Chicago: University of Chicago Press, 1994), 39–61.

9.   Jacques Ellul, *La Technique ou L'enjeu du Siècle* (1954). Ellul's book was later trans-lated into English: Jacques Ellul, *The Technological Society* (New York: Vintage Books, 1964). See also Doug Hill, "Jacques Ellul, Technology Doomsdayer before His Time," *Boston Globe*, July 8, 2015, http://www.bostonglobe.com/ideas/2012/07/07 /jacques-ellul-conference/1BVZp8uEiGKoeXAmkDJpeO/story.html.

10. Lewis Mumford, *Technics and Civilization* (London: Routledge & Sons, 1934); Lewis Mumford, *Technics and Human Development* (New York: Harcourt Brace Jovanovich, 1966).

11. Neil Postman, *Technopoly: The Surrender of Culture to Technology* (New York: Vintage Books, 1992), 52, xii.

12. Nick Carr, *The Shallows: What the Internet Is Doing to Our Brains* (New York: W.W. Norton & Co., 2010).

13. Andrew Keen, *The Cult of the Amateur: How Today's Internet Is Killing Our Culture* (New York: Doubleday, 2007).

14. Lee Siegel, *Against the Machine: Being Human in the Age of the Electronic Mob* (New York: Random House, 2008).

15. Mark Helprin, *Digital Barbarism: A Writer's Manifesto* (New York: Harper Collins, 2009).

16. Wallach, *Dangerous Master.*

17. Ellul, *Technological Society*, 4.

18. Wallach, *Dangerous Master*, 13. ("Slowing down the accelerating adoption of technology should be done as a responsible means to ensure basic human safety and to support broadly shared values.")

19. David Auerbach, "It's OK to Be a Luddite," *Slate*, September 9, 2015, http://www .slate.com/articles/technology/bitwise/2015/09/luddism_today_there_s_an _important_place_for_it_really.single.html.

20. Evgeny Morozov, *To Save Everything, Click Here: The Folly of Technological Solutionism* (New York: PublicAffairs, 2013). Morozov's argument mimics the linguistic analysis of the term "technology" that the historian Leo Marx set forth in essays such as "Does Improved Technology Mean Progress?," *Technology Review* (January 1987): 33–41; and "Technology: The Emergence of a Hazardous Concept," *Technology and Culture* 51, No. 3 (July 2010): 561–77. Marx worried about "treating these inanimate objects—machines—as causal agents" and "invest[ing] the concept of technology with agency."

21. Ibid.

22. Martin Ford, *Rise of the Robots: Technology and the Threat of a Jobless Future* (New York: Basic Books, 2015).

23. Wallach, *Dangerous Master.*

24. Thomas P. Keenan, *Techno Creep: The Surrender of Privacy and the Capitalization of Intimacy* (New York: Greystone Books, 2014).

25. Philip N. Howard, *Pax Technica: How the Internet of Things May Set Us Free or Lock Us Up* (New Haven, CT: Yale University Press, 2015); Evan Selinger and Brett Frischmann, "Will the Internet of Things Result in Predictable People?," *Guardian*, August 10, 2015, http://www.theguardian.com/technology/2015/aug/10/internet -of-things-predictable-people.

26. Almost every book by the techno-critics cited previously contains an allusion to the *Terminator* movies and fears about a robot apocalypse of some sort. See also Ben Austen, "The Terminator Scenario: Are We Giving Our Machines Too Much Power?," *Popular Science*, January 13, 2011, http://www.popsci.com/technology/article /2010-12/terminator-scenario; John Markoff and Claire Cain Miller, "As Robotics Advances, Worries of Killer Robots Rise," *New York Times*, June 16, 2014, http:// www.nytimes.com/2014/06/17/upshot/danger-robots-working.html?_r=0&abt =0002&abg=1.

27. See, for example, Slavoj Žižek, "A Litmus Test for Humanistic Technology Critics," *MetaReader*, July 12, 2015, http://www.metareader.org/post/a-litmus-test-for -humanistic-technology-critics.html.

28. This section adapted from Adam Thierer, "A Net Skeptic's Conservative Manifesto," *Reason*, July 2013, http://reason.com/archives/2013/06/26/a-net-skeptics -conservative-manifesto; Thierer, "Internet Optimist or Pessimist?"; Thierer, "Case for Internet Optimism," 57–87.

29. Adam Thierer, "Muddling Through: How We Learn to Cope with Technological Change," *Medium*, June 30, 2014, https://medium.com/tech-liberation/muddling -through-how-we-learn-to-cope-with-technological-change-6282d0d342a6.

30. James Surowiecki, "Epic Fails of the Startup World," *New Yorker*, May 19, 2014, http://www.newyorker.com/magazine/2014/05/19/epic-fails-of-the-startup-world.

31. Ridley, *Rational Optimist*.

32. Herman Kahn and Anthony Wiener, *The Year 2000: A Framework for Speculation on the Next Thirty-Three Years* (New York: Macmillan, 1967).

33. Julian Simon, *The Ultimate Resource 2* (Princeton, NJ: Princeton University Press, 1996). See also Paul Dragos Aligica, *Prophecies of Doom and Scenarios of Progress: Herman Kahn, Julian Simon, and the Prospective Imagination* (New York: The Continuum International Publishing Group, 2007).

34. F. A. Hayek, *The Constitution of Liberty* (London: Routledge, 1960, 1990).

35. Ithiel de Sola Pool, *Technologies of Freedom: On Free Speech in an Electronic Age* (Cambridge, MA: Harvard University Press, 1983).

36. Lynne Kiesling, *Power Up: The Framework for a New Era of UK Energy Distribution* (London: Adam Smith Institute), 27, http://www.adamsmith.org/news/press -release-create-an-uber-for-electricity-by-deregulating-power-supply-argues-new -report. ("One of the most important reasons why an environment for permission-less innovation is valuable is because it enables the experimentation and learning that can mitigate the knowledge problem. Neither regulators nor other market par-ticipants have access to the knowledge influencing individual decisions made about production or consumption. In dynamic markets with diffuse private knowledge, neither entrepreneurs nor policy makers can know a priori which goods and services will succeed with consumers and at what prices.")

37. Thomke, *Experimentation Matters*, 7. ("Innovators make progress through iterative experimentation that is guided by some insight where a solution might lie.")

38. Sofia Ranchordás, "Does Sharing Mean Caring? Regulating Innovation in the Sharing Economy," *Minnesota Journal of Law, Science & Technology* 16, no. 1 (2015): 14. ("Innovation is a broad concept that can be defined differently depending on the context and field in question.")

39. See generally Adam Thierer, "Defining 'Technology,'" *Technology Liberation Front*, April 29, 2014, http://techliberation.com/2014/04/29/defining-technology. As a leading textbook on the philosophy of technology has noted, "'Technology' refers to many different concepts and phenomena, and it is therefore impossible to give a clear-cut definition of what is to be understood by the term." Jan Kyrre Berg Olsen, Stig Andur Pedersen, Vincent F. Hendricks, eds., *A Companion to the Philosophy of Technology* (Blackwell Publishing, 2009), 1. For a more extensive historical survey of how "technology" has been defined over time, see Mitcham, *Thinking through Technology*, 137–60.

40. OECD, *The Measurement of Scientific and Technological Activities: Guidelines for Collecting and Interpreting Innovation Data: Oslo Manual*, 3rd ed., prepared by the Working Party of National Experts on Scientific and Technology Indicators, OECD, (Paris: 2005), 46, http://www.uis.unesco.org/Library/Documents /OECDOsloManual05_en.pdf.

41. Ibid.

42. W. Brian Arthur, *The Nature of Technology: What It Is and How It Evolves* (New York: Free Press, 2009), 90.

43. Ibid., 164.

44. Robert D. Atkinson and Stephen J. Ezell, *Innovation Economics: The Race for Global Advantage* (New Haven, CT: Yale University Press, 2012), 8.

45. Ranchordás, 10.

46. Frank Furedi, "Precautionary Culture," 216. ("By all objective accounts, it is difficult to explain why Western societies should feel so overwhelmed by the condition of vulnerability. Compared with the past, people living in Western societies have less familiarity with physical pain, suffering, debilitating disease, poverty, and death than previously. Western societies enjoy what is by historical standards a high level of stability and relative prosperity. . . . And yet despite an unprecedented level of stability and prosperity, contemporary culture continually communicates the idea that humanity is confronted by powerful destructive forces that threaten our everyday existence.")

47. Robert Bryce, *Smaller Faster Lighter Denser Cheaper: How Innovation Keeps Proving the Catastrophists Wrong* (New York: Public Affairs, 2014), xxi–xxii.

48. Aki Ito, "Six Things Technology Has Made Insanely Cheap," *Bloomberg Business*, February 5, 2015, http://www.bloomberg.com/news/articles/2015-02-05/six-things -technology-has-made-insanely-cheap.

49. Lynne Kiesling, "Technological Change, Culture, and a "Social License to Operate," *Knowledge Problem*, July 7, 2015, http://knowledgeproblem.com/2015/07/07 /technological-change-culture-and-a-social-license-to-operate. ("Producers create new products and services, make old ones obsolete, and create and destroy profits and industries in the process, all to the better on average over time.")

50. Brink Lindsey, "Why Growth Is Getting Harder" (Policy Analysis No. 737, Cato Institute, October 8, 2013), 11, http://www.cato.org/publications/policy-analysis /why-growth-getting-harder.

51. Arti Rai, Stuart Graham, and Mark Doms, "Patent Reform: Unleashing Innovation, Promoting Economic Growth, and Producing High-Paying Jobs" (White Paper, US Department of Commerce, April 13, 2010), 1, 2–3, http://2010-2014.commerce.gov /sites/default/files/documents/migrated/Patent_Reform-paper.pdf.

52. Yasmina Reem Limam and Stephen M. Miller, "Explaining Economic Growth: Factor Accumulation, Total Factor Productivity Growth, and Production Efficiency Improvement" (2003), 10, https://faculty.unlv.edu/smiller/EFFICIENCY _PRODUCTIVITY_PAPER.pdf. ("In Africa and the West, technological progress accounts respectively for 17 and 30 percent of total output growth."); Scott L. Baier, Gerald P. Dwyer Jr., and Robert Tamura, "How Important Are Capital and Total Factor Productivity for Economic Growth?," *Economic Inquiry* 44, no. 1 (2006): 23–49, http://onlinelibrary.wiley.com/doi/10.1093/ei/cbj003/abstract. ("TFP accounts for about 34% of the average growth of output per worker in the Western Countries and 26% in Southern Europe and the NICs. Other regions have less, negligible, and even negative growth of TFP. These negative growth rates are consistent with the importance of institutional changes and conflicts.")

53. Diego A. Comin and Martí Mestieri Ferrer, "If Technology Has Arrived Everywhere, Why Has Income Diverged?" (NBER Working Paper No. 19010, May 2013), http:// www.wipo.int/edocs/mdocs/mdocs/en/wipo_ip_econ_ge_2_14/wipo_ip_econ _ge_2_14_ref_comin.pdf. ("[D]ifferences in technology diffusion patterns account for a major part of the evolution of the world income distribution over the last two centuries. In particular, differences in the evolution of adoption margins in Western and non-Western countries account for around 80% of the Great Divergence.") This is generally consistent with the findings of the study cited above by the Commerce Department. See Robert E. Hall and Charles I. Jones, "Why Do Some Countries Produce So Much More Output Than Others?," *Quarterly Journal of Economics* 114 (1999).

54. Joseph Schumpeter, *Capitalism, Socialism and Democracy* (New York: Harper Perennial, 1942, 2008), 84.

55. Jerry Ellig, "Introduction," in *Dynamic Competition and Public Policy: Technology, Innovation, and Antitrust Issues*, ed. Jerry Ellig (Cambridge: Cambridge University Press, 2001), 6. The work of economist Israel Kirzner is also directly relevant to modern innovation policy. Kirzner identified entrepreneurship as the driving force within the economy and he explained how both producers and consumers can be entrepreneurs, seeking out entrepreneurial opportunities as they process market-place information. See Israel Kirzner, *Competition and Entrepreneurship* (Chicago: University of Chicago Press, 1973); Kirzner, *Discovery and the Capitalist Process*.

56. J. Gregory Sidak and David J. Teece, "Dynamic Competition in Antitrust Law," *Journal of Competition Law & Economics* 5 (2009): 603. ("The adjective 'dynamic' is a shorthand descriptor for a variety of rigorously competitive activities such as sig-nificant product differentiation and rapid response to change, whether from inno-vation or simply from new market opportunities ensuing from changes in taste or other forces of disequilibrium. Dynamic competition is, in fact, more intuitive and much closer to today's everyday view of competition than is the stylized notion of static competition routinely depicted in textbooks.")

57. Adam Thierer, "Of 'Tech Titans' and Schumpeter's Vision," *Forbes*, August 22, 2011, http://www.forbes.com/sites/adamthierer/2011/08/22/of-tech-titans-and -schumpeters-vision.

58. Howard A. Shelanski, "Information, Innovation, and Competition Policy for the Internet," *University of Pennsylvania Law Review* 161 (2013): 1684–5. ("If there is any single force that best characterizes digital platform markets, it is probably the inten-sive and continuous investment in research and development to improve existing products and develop new platforms and applications. It is easy to find examples of companies quickly rising and falling on the Internet. . . . The key point is that it is rare to find a significant digital product or service that stays the same from day to day.")

59. "Schumpeterian competition is primarily about active, risk-taking decision mak-ers who seek to change their parameters," note economists Jerry Ellig and Daniel Lin. "It is about continually destroying the old economic structure from within and replacing it with a new one." Jerry Ellig and Daniel Lin, "A Taxonomy of Dynamic Competition Theories," in *Dynamic Competition and Public Policy*, ed. Jerry Ellig (Cambridge: Cambridge University Press, 2001), 18–19.

60. Thierer, "Of Tech Titans."

61. Paul Dragos Aligica and Vlad Tarko, *Capitalist Alternatives Models, Taxonomies, and Scenarios* (London: Routledge, 2015), 90. ("Part of the reason why adaptation was so difficult was that the company had a large infrastructure focused on film photog-raphy that was made largely obsolete. In other words, precisely the same structure that created its economy of scale efficiency made it more vulnerable to an unex-pected disruption! What used to be a very large barrier to entry to competitors, and, hence, the key to its large market share and profits, now became a huge liability as it was very costly to change that structure and re-allocate that capital in due time.")

62. Victor Keegan, "Will MySpace Ever Lose Its Monopoly?," *Guardian*, February 7, 2007, http://www.guardian.co.uk/technology/2007/feb/08/business.comment. ("John Barrett of TechNewsWorld claims that MySpace is well on the way to becoming what economists call a 'natural monopoly.' Users have invested so much social capital in putting up data about themselves it is not worth their changing

sites, especially since every new user that MySpace attracts adds to its value as a network of interacting people.")

63. Brian Stelter, "News Corporation Sells MySpace for $35 Million," *New York Times*, June 29, 2011, http://mediadecoder.blogs.nytimes.com/2011/06/29/news-corp -sells-myspace-to-specific-media-for-35-million.

64. Sam Grobart and Ian Austen, "The BlackBerry, Trying to Avoid the Hall of Fallen Giants," *New York Times*, January 28, 2012, http://www.nytimes.com/2012/01/29 /business/blackberry-aiming-to-avoid-the-hall-of-fallen-giants.html. ("Palm Pilots were dazzling when they first appeared: all of your contacts, calendars and notes in one slim, pocket-size device. A touch screen, which required a stylus, made navigation easy. And you could add software, bought through an online store. Want a Zagat guide to go along with your personal data? No problem. In later years, Palm even added telephone features, creating a compelling, all-in-one gadget. Despite boardroom dramas that affected the company's name and its ownership, Palm's reputation as a source of innovative hardware and software endured until Jan. 9, 2007. Why that date? That's when Apple introduced the iPhone.")

65. Jason Perlow, "Love Stinks: The Worst Mergers in the History of the Technology Industry," *ZDNet*, February 11, 2012, http://www.zdnet.com/photos/love-stinks-the -worst-mergers-in-the-history-of-the-technology-industry/6344256?seq=3&tag =photo-frame;get-photo-roto.

66. Holman W. Jenkins Jr., "Game over for BlackBerry?," *Wall Street Journal*, January 6, 2012, http://online.wsj.com/article/ SB10001424052970203513604577144614178603068.html?mod=WSJ_Opinion _LEFTTopOpinion.

67. Grobart and Austen, "BlackBerry."

68. Ibid.

69. In December 2006, Palm CEO Ed Colligan summarily dismissed the idea that a traditional personal computing company could compete in the smartphone business. "We've learned and struggled for a few years here figuring out how to make a decent phone," he said. "PC guys are not going to just figure this out. They're not going to just walk in." In January 2007, Microsoft CEO Steve Ballmer laughed off the prospect of an expensive smartphone without a keyboard having a chance in the marketplace: "Five hundred dollars? Fully subsidized? With a plan? I said that's the most expensive phone in the world and it doesn't appeal to business customers because it doesn't have a keyboard, which makes it not a very good e-mail machine." John Paczkowski, "Apple: How Do You Say 'Eat My Dust' in Finnish?," *All Things D*, November 11, 2009, http://allthingsd.com/20091111/nokia-apple. In March 2007, computing industry pundit John C. Dvorak argued that "Apple should pull the plug on the iPhone" since "there is no likelihood that Apple can be successful in a business this competitive." John C. Dvorak, "Apple Should Pull the Plug on the iPhone," *Wall Street Journal: Market Watch*, March 28, 2007, http://www.marketwatch.com/story/apple-should-pull-the-plug -on-the-iphone. Dvorak believed the mobile handset business was already locked up by the era's major players. ("This is not an emerging business. In fact it's gone so far that it's in the process of consolidation with probably two players dominating everything, Nokia Corp. and Motorola Inc.")

70. Stan Schroeder, "Nokia's Profits Fall, Its Smartphone Business Weakens," *Mashable*, January 27, 2011, http://mashable.com/2011/01/27/nokias-profits-fall; Anton Troianovski and Arild Moen, "Nokia Crisis Deepens, Shares Plunge," *Wall Street Journal*, April 11, 2012, http://online.wsj.com/article/ SB10001424052702304356604577337452563544904.html.

71. Horace Dediu, "The Fate of Mobile Phone Brands," *Asymco*, August 2, 2011, http://www.asymco.com/2011/08/08/the-fate-of-mobile-phone-brands.

72. Daron Acemoglu and James A. Robinson, *Why Nations Fail: The Origins of Power, Prosperity, and Poverty* (New York: Crown Business, 2012).

73. James Bailey and Diana Thomas, "Regulating Away Competition: The Effect of Regulation on Entrepreneurship and Employment" (Mercatus Working Paper, Mercatus Center at George Mason University, Arlington, VA, September 9, 2015), http://mercatus.org/publication/regulating-away-competition-effect-regulation -entrepreneurship-and-employment; Patrick McLaughlin and Robert Greene, "The Unintended Consequences of Federal Regulatory Accumulation" (Mercatus Working Paper, Mercatus Center at George Mason University, Arlington, VA, May 8, 2014), http://mercatus.org/publication/unintended-consequences-federal -regulatory-accumulation.

74. This section adapted from Adam Thierer, "Europe's Choice on Innovation," *Technology Liberation Front*, December 3, 2014, http://techliberation .com/2014/12/03/europes-choice-on-innovation; Adam Thierer, "How Attitudes about Risk & Failure Affect Innovation on Either Side of the Atlantic," *Technology Liberation Front*, June 19, 2015, http://techliberation.com/2015/06/19/how -attitudes-about-risk-failure-affect-innovation-on-either-side-of-the-atlantic.

75. James B. Stewart, "A Fearless Culture Fuels U.S. Tech Giants," *New York Times*, June 19, 2015, http://www.nytimes.com/2015/06/19/business/the-american-way-of-tech -and-europes.html.

76. Stephen Ezell and Philipp Marxgut, "Comparing American and European Innovation Cultures," in *Shaping the Future: Economic, Social, and Political Dimensions of Innovation* (Austrian Council for Research and Technology Development, August 2015), 193, http://www2.itif.org/2015-comparing-american-european-innovation -cultures.pdf. ("[C]ultural aspects have a significant impact on innovation and inform how entrepreneurial countries, organizations, and people can be. The United States maintains the world's most vibrant innovation culture, where risk and failure are broadly tolerated, inquiry and discussion are encouraged, and the government's role in business plays a less prominent role. . . . [T]here are elements in the European innovation culture that need improvement: a simpler regulatory environment, a broader availability of risk capital, and more tolerance of risk and change being criti- cally important.")

77. Mims, "Hats Off." ("[W]ithout ads, there would be no Gmail, no Facebook, no count- less other services on which we all rely every day.")

78. Josh Lerner, "The Impact of Privacy Policy Changes on Venture Capital Investment in Online Advertising Companies," *Analysis Group*, February 13, 2012, 1–2, http://www.analysisgroup.com/news-and-events/news/affiliate-joshua-lerner-studies -the-effect-of-privacy-policies-on-venture-capital-and-innovation. ("[T]he EU e-Privacy Directive, which regulates the electronic collection and use of personal data in the EU more tightly than in other countries, has reduced VC investment in EU-based businesses that lend themselves to the use of such data. . . . We find that VC [venture capitalist] investment in online advertising companies decreased sig- nificantly in the EU relative to the US after passage of the EU e-Privacy Directive. Our results suggest that the EU e-Privacy Directive has led to an incremental decrease in investment in EU-based online advertising companies of approximately $249 million over the approximately eight-and-a-half years from passage through the end of 2010. When paired with the findings of the enhanced effects of VC

investment relative to corporate investment, this may be the equivalent of approximately $750 million to $1 billion in traditional R&D investment.")

79. Matt Moffett, "New Entrepreneurs Find Pain in Spain," *Wall Street Journal*, November 27, 2014, http://www.wsj.com/articles/new-entrepreneurs-find-pain-in-spain-1417133197.

80. Anna Prior, "How Fear Can Derail an Entrepreneur," *Wall Street Journal*, August 24, 2015, http://www.wsj.com/articles/how-fear-can-derail-an-entrepreneur-1440381701. (Quoting Philipp K. Berger, "There's a huge difference between the U.S. culture and the German culture. In the U.S., it seems to be a lot more acceptable to fail. It's the 'fail and stand up' culture. It's accepted to some degree as part of the normal part of the entrepreneurial process. That's different in Germany. There's more of a stigmatization of a failed entrepreneur, so that drives more fear.")

81. Matti Huuhtanen, "Why Europe Isn't Creating Any Googles or Facebooks," *Washington Post*, September 22, 2015, http://www.washingtonpost.com/business/technology/why-europe-isnt-creating-any-googles-or-facebooks/2015/09/22/ddb3e9f2-611c-11e5-8475-781cc9851652_story.html. ("The European Union's . . . 28-nation bloc is, above all, lacking in the risk-taking culture and financial networks needed to grow Internet startups into globally dominant companies.")

82. Quoted in Ibid.

83. Stewart, "Fearless Culture."

84. Ibid.

85. Daniel Castro and Alan McQuinn, "How and When Regulators Should Intervene," *Information Technology and Innovation Foundation Reports*, February 2015, 2, http://www.itif.org/publications/how-and-when-regulators-should-intervene.

86. James Pethokoukis, "Why Does the US Generate More Fast-Growing Tech Startups than Europe?," *AEI Ideas*, July 10, 2015, https://www.aei.org/publication/why-does-the-us-generate-more-fast-growing-tech-startups-than-europe.

87. Barry Jaruzelski, "The Top Innovators and Spenders, 2013," *Strategy&*, accessed on October 15, 2014, http://www.strategyand.pwc.com/global/home/what-we-think/global-innovation-1000/top-innovators-spenders.

88. Larry Downes, "Europe's Innovation Deficit Isn't Disappearing Any Time Soon," *Washington Post*, June 8, 2015, http://www.washingtonpost.com/blogs/innovations/wp/2015/06/08/europes-innovation-deficit-isnt-disappearing-any-time-soon.

89. Based on market capitalization data for Amazon, Apple, eBay, Facebook, Google, and Yahoo as of September 2015. Retrieved from Yahoo! Finance, http://finance.yahoo.com. See also Scott Austin, Chris Canipe, and Sarah Slobin, "The Billion Dollar Startup Club," *Wall Street Journal*, September 2015, http://graphics.wsj.com/billion-dollar-club; Manish Madhvani, et al., "European Unicorns: Do They Have Legs?" *GP Bullhound*, 2015, http://www.gpbullhound.com/wp-content/uploads/2015/06/GP-Bullhound-Research-Billion-Dollar-Companies-2015.pdf.

90. Quoted in Stewart, "Fearless Culture."

91. Tom Fairless and Stephen Fidler, "Europe Wants the World to Embrace Its Internet Rules," *Wall Street Journal*, February 24, 2015, http://www.wsj.com/articles/europe-wants-the-world-to-embrace-its-data-privacy-rules-1424821453.

92. Downes, "How Europe Can Create." ("Europeans—or anyone else—could leverage those mistakes to gain competitive advantage in the global digital market, at

an economic cost far lower than building campuses and seeding investment. But they'll have to learn to appreciate in the first place the profound role regulation (or the lack of it) plays in the creation of economic value in the Internet economy.")

93. Kelly Couturier, "How Europe Is Going After Amazon, Google and Other U.S. Tech Giants," *New York Times*, July 16, 2015, http://www.nytimes.com/interactive/2015/04/13/technology/How-Europe-Is-Going-After-U.S.-Tech-Giants.html.

94. Sam Schechner, "Uber Meets Its Match in France," *Wall Street Journal*, September 18, 2015, http://www.wsj.com/articles/uber-meets-its-match-in-france-1442592333.

95. Romain Dillet, "Uber France Leaders Arrested for Running Illegal Taxi Company," *TechCrunch*, June 29, 2015, http://techcrunch.com/2015/06/29/uber-france-leaders-arrested-for-running-illegal-taxi-company.

96. Dan Primack, "Uber Downloads in France Hit All-Time High after Strike," *Fortune*, June 30, 2015, http://fortune.com/2015/06/30/uber-downloads-in-france-hit-all-time-high-after-strike.

97. Tom Fairless, "Europe Looks to Tame Web's Economic Risks," *Wall Street Journal*, April 23, 2015, http://www.wsj.com/articles/eu-considers-creating-powerful-regulator-to-oversee-web-platforms-1429795918.

98. See Thierer, "Risk & Failure."

99. Mike Elgan, "Why Europe's Regulatory War against Silicon Valley Will Backfire," *eWeek*, April 14, 2015, http://www.eweek.com/cloud/why-europes-regulatory-war-against-silicon-valley-will-backfire.html.

100. This section adapted from Adam Thierer, "Global Innovation Arbitrage: Commercial Drones & Sharing Economy Edition," *Technology Liberation Front*, December 9, 2014, http://techliberation.com/2014/12/09/global-innovation-arbitrage-commercial-drones-sharing-economy-edition; Adam Thierer, "Global Innovation Arbitrage: Genetic Testing Edition," *Technology Liberation Front*, December 12, 2014, http://techliberation.com/2014/12/12/global-innovation-arbitrage-genetic-testing-edition.

101. "When Software Eats the Physical World, Startups Bump Up against Regulations: A Conversation with a16z's Ted Ullyot," *Andreessen Horowitz blog*, accessed April 22, 2015, http://a16z.com/2015/04/22/ted-ullyot-policy-regulatory-affairs.

102. Marc Andreessen, "Turn Detroit into Drone Valley," *Politico*, June 15, 2014, http://www.politico.com/magazine/story/2014/06/turn-detroit-into-drone-valley-107853.html#ixzz3LQf5XIiD. ("Entrepreneurs can take advantage of the difference between opportunities in different regions, where innovation in a particular domain of interest may be restricted in one region, allowed and encouraged in another, or completely legal in still another.")

103. Quoted in Adam Thierer, "What Cory Booker Gets about Innovation Policy," *Technology Liberation Front*, February 16, 2015, http://techliberation.com/2015/02/16/what-cory-booker-gets-about-innovation-policy.

104. Jack Nicas and Greg Bensinger, "Amazon: U.S. Is Blocking Its Testing of Drones," *Wall Street Journal*, December 8, 2014, http://www.wsj.com/articles/amazon-warns-it-will-move-drone-research-abroad-1418076981.

105. Quoted in Ibid.

106. Alan McQuinn, "Commercial Drone Companies Fly Away from FAA Regulations, Go Abroad," *Inside Sources*, September 30, 2014, http://www.insidesources.com/commercial-drone-companies-fly-away-from-faa-regulations-go-abroad.

107. Andrew Trotman, "Amazon Threatens US Government over Drone Testing," *Telegraph*, December 9, 2014, http://www.telegraph.co.uk/finance/newsbysector /mediatechnologyandtelecoms/electronics/11281531/Amazon-threatens-US -government-over-drone-testing.html.

108. Martin Anderson, "Google Sees UK as Prime Market For Self-Driving Cars Due to 'Non-regulatory Approach,'" December 14, 2015, https://thestack.com/world/2015 /12/14/google-sees-uk-as-prime-market-for-self-driving-cars-due-to-non -regulatory-approach.

109. Mark Scott, "Britain Offers Itself as a Proving Ground," *New York Times Bits*, June 10, 2015, http://bits.blogs.nytimes.com/2015/06/10/britain-offers-itself-as-a-proving -ground.

110. Stephanie M. Lee, "23andMe's Health DNA Kits Now For Sale in U.K., Still Blocked in U.S.," *SF Gate*, December 2, 2014, http://blog.sfgate.com/techchron/2014/12/02 /23andmes-health-dna-kits-now-for-sale-in-u-k-still-blocked-in-u-s.

111. Matthew Herper, "What 23andMe's FDA Approval Means for the Future of Genomics," *Forbes*, February 20, 2015, http://www.forbes.com/sites /matthewherper/2015/02/20/what-23andmes-fda-approval-means-for-the-future -of-genomics/#179c26257293.

112. Jessica Firger, "U.K. Approves Sales of 23andMe Genetic Test Banned in U.S.," *CBS News*, December 3, 2014, http://www.cbsnews.com/news/23-and-me-genetic-test -uk-approves-sale-banned-in-us.

113. Christopher Koopman, Matthew Mitchell, and Adam Thierer, "The Sharing Economy and Consumer Protection Regulation: The Case for Policy Change" (Mercatus Working Paper, Mercatus Center at George Mason University, Arlington, VA, December 8, 2014), 18–19, http://mercatus.org/publication/sharing-economy-and -consumer-protection-regulation-case-policy-change.

114. Debbie Wosskow, *Unlocking the Sharing Economy: Independent Review*, November 2014, https://www.gov.uk/government/uploads/system/uploads/attachment _data/file/378291/bis-14-1227-unlocking-the-sharing-economy-an-independent -review.pdf.

115. Ibid. [emphasis added].

116. Some critics deride this sort of jurisdictional competition or worry about the implications for efforts to control technological innovation globally. See Wallach, *Dangerous Master*, 8. ("There is the risk that developers will simply move to those countries that place the least restrictions on their research. Government leaders desirous of repealing economic benefits as torchbearers in new fields will embrace areas of research that are controversial in other regions.")

117. Quoted in Thierer, "Cory Booker."

118. Jerry Brito, "Domestic Drones Are Coming Your Way," *Reason.com*, March 11, 2013, http://reason.com/archives/2013/03/11/domestic-drones-are-coming-your-way.

119. Farhad Manjoo, "Giving the Drone Industry the Leeway to Innovate," *New York Times*, February 4, 2015, http://techliberation.com/2015/02/04/permissionless -innovation-commercial-drones.

120. Scott Pham, "When Journalism Becomes a Game of Drones," *Mashable*, July 28, 2013, http://mashable.com/2013/07/28/game-of-drones-journalism.

121. Quoted in Thierer, "Cory Booker."

122. Association for Unmanned Vehicle Systems International, *Economic Impact of Unmanned Aircraft Systems Integration in the United States*, March 2013, http://www.auvsi.org/auvsiresources/economicreport.

123. Alistair Barr and Greg Bensinger, "Google Is Testing Delivery Drone System," *Wall Street Journal*, August 29, 2014, http://online.wsj.com/articles/google-reveals -delivery-drone-project-1409274480; Thomas Claburn, "Google Has Plans for Titan Drones," *Information Week*, April 15, 2014, http://www.informationweek.com /mobile/mobile-devices/google-has-plans-for-titan-drones/d/d-id/1204456.

124. Harrison Weber, "Amazon Seeks Approval to Test Drone Deliveries in 30 Minutes or Less," *Venture Beat*, July 11, 2014, http://venturebeat.com/2014/07/11/amazon -seeks-approval-to-test-prime-air-drone-deliveries-in-30-minutes-or-less.

125. Issie Lapowsky, "Facebook Lays Out Its Roadmap for Creating Internet-Connected Drones," *Wired*, September 23, 2014, http://www.wired.com/2014/09 /facebook-drones-2.

126. Sally French, "Drones vs. Driverless Cars: A Tale of Two Robotics Policies," *Marketwatch*, September 24, 2015, http://www.marketwatch.com/story/drones-vs -driverless-cars-a-tale-of-two-robotics-policies-2015-09-24.

127. Keith Laing, "Feds Miss Deadline to Legalize Drones," *The Hill*, October 1, 2015, http://thehill.com/policy/transportation/255638-feds-miss-deadline-to-legalize-drones.

128. Candice Bernd, "The Coming Domestic Drone Wars," *Truthout*, September 19, 2013, http://www.truth-out.org/news/item/18951-the-coming-domestic-drone-wars; Anne Einsenberg, "Preflight Turbulence for Commercial Drones," *New York Times*, September 7, 2013, http://www.nytimes.com/2013/09/08/business/preflight -turbulence-for-commercial-drones.html?pagewanted=all&_r=1&.

129. "Unmanned Aircraft System Test Site Program," 78 Fed. Reg. 12259 (February 22, 2013).

130. Keith Laing, "Sen. Markey Files Bill to Protect Privacy in Commercial Drone Use," *The Hill*, November 4, 2013, http://thehill.com/blogs/transportation-report /aviation/189208-sen-markey-files-bill-to-protect-privacy-in-commercial.

131. Lisa Cornwell, "States Consider Regulation of Drones in US Skies," *AP*, August 6, 2013, http://bigstory.ap.org/article/states-consider-regulation-drones-us-skies; Timm Herdt, "California Drone Bill Would Restrict Civilian Use," *Huffington Post*, May 1, 2013, http://www.huffingtonpost.com/2013/05/01/california-drone-bill_n_3191468.html.

132. White House, "Promoting Economic Competitiveness While Safeguarding Privacy, Civil Rights, and Civil Liberties in Domestic Use of Unmanned Aircraft Systems," February 15, 2015, https://www.whitehouse.gov/the-press-office/2015/02/15 /presidential-memorandum-promoting-economic-competitiveness-while-safegua.

133. Dourado, "Next Internet-Like Platform?"

134. Cynthia Love, Sean Lawson, and Avery Holton, "News from Above: First Amendment Implications of the Federal Aviation Administration Ban on Commercial Drones" (Mercatus Working Paper, Mercatus Center at George Mason University, Arlington, VA, September 19, 2014), http://mercatus.org/publication/news-above-first -amendment-implications-federal-aviation-administration-ban-commercial.

135. Kenneth Anderson, "Domestic Drone Regulation for Safety and Privacy," *Volokh Conspiracy*, September 8, 2013, http://www.volokh.com/2013/09/08/domestic -drone-regulation-safety-privacy.

136. John Villasenor, "Who Is at Fault When a Driverless Car Gets in an Accident?," *Atlantic*, April 25, 2014, http://www.theatlantic.com/business/archive/2014/04/who-is-at-fault -when-a-driverless-car-gets-in-an-accident/361250. ("[W]hen confronted with new, often complex, questions involving products liability, courts have generally gotten things right. . . . Products liability law has been highly adaptive to the many new tech- nologies that have emerged in recent decades, and it will be quite capable of adapt- ing to emerging autonomous vehicle technologies as the need arises.")

137. Manjoo, "Leeway to Innovate." ("Imposing broad limitations on drone use now would be squashing a promising new area of innovation just as it's getting started, and before we've seen many of the potential uses.")

138. Jerry Brito, Eli Dourado, and Adam Thierer, *Comments of the Mercatus Center to Federal Aviation Administration in the Matter of Unmanned Aircraft System Test Site Program*, Docket No: FAA-2013-0061, April 23, 2013, http://mercatus.org /publication/federal-aviation-administration-unmanned-aircraft-system-test -site-program; Dourado, "Next Internet-Like Platform?"

139. Jack Nicas, "Regulation Clips Wings of U.S. Drone Makers," *Wall Street Journal*, October 5, 2014, http://www.wsj.com/articles/regulation-clips-wings-of-u-s-drone -makers-1412546849. ("[M]any U.S. drone entrepreneurs are finding it hard to get off the ground, even as rivals in Europe, Canada, Australia and China are taking off.")

CHAPTER IV
HOW WE ADAPT TO TECHNOLOGICAL CHANGE

1. Garreau, *Radical Evolution*, 149.

2. Arthur Herman, *The Idea of Decline in Western History* (New York: The Free Press, 1997), 442.

3. Daniel Gardner, *The Science of Fear: How the Culture of Fear Manipulates Your Brain*, (New York: Plume, 2009), 140–41. ("As strange as it sounds, we want to believe the expert predicting a dark future is exactly right, because knowing that the future will be dark is less tormenting than suspecting it. Certainty is always preferable to uncertainty, even when what's certain is disaster.")

4. Dan Gardner, *Future Babble: Why Expert Predictions Are Next to Worthless, and You Can Do Better* (New York: Dutton, 2011), 140–41.

5. Garreau, *Radical Evolution*, 148.

6. Ibid., 13.

7. Ibid., 95.

8. Ibid., 154.

9. John Seely Brown and Paul Duguid, "A Response to Bill Joy and the Doom-and-Gloom Technofuturists," reprinted in *AAAS Science and Technology Policy Yearbook 2001*, ed. Albert H. Teich, Stephen D. Nelson, Celia McEnaney, and Stephen J. Lita (American Association for the Advancement of Science, 2001), 79, 82–3.

10. See, for example, my exchange with philosopher Michael Sacasas: Michael Sacasas, "A Reply to Adam Thierer," *Frailest Thing*, April 4, 2014, http://thefrailestthing.com /2014/04/04/a-reply-to-adam-thierer.

11. Maureen K. Ohlhausen, "The Internet of Everything: Data, Networks & Opportunities," speech before the US Chamber of Commerce Foundation,

September 22, 2015, 5, https://www.ftc.gov/public-statements/2015/09/internet
-everything-data-networks-opportunities. ("[I]nnovation can, and will, be unnerving
or unsettling. By its very nature, innovation changes things. Change is uncomfortable. That is why, as long as there has been innovation, there have been detractors
and doomsayers.")

12. Jack Shafer, "Digital Native Calms the Anxious Masses," *Slate*, September 13, 2010,
     http://www.slate.com/articles/news_and_politics/press_box/2010/09/digital
     _native_calms_the_anxious_masses.html. ("Cultures tend to assimilate and normal-
     ize new technology in ways the fretful never anticipate.")

13. This section adapted from Thierer, "Technopanics," 309–86; Thierer, "Muddling Through."

14. Garreau, *Radical Evolution*, 209. ("Prevail's trick is that it embraces uncertainty.
     Even in the face of unprecedented threats, it displays a faith that the ragged human
     convoy of divergent perceptions, piqued honor, posturing, insecurity and humor
     will wend its way to glory. It puts a shocking premium of Faulkner's hope that man
     will prevail 'because he has a soul, a spirit capable of compassion and sacrifice and
     endurance.'")

15. Andrew Zolli and Ann Marie Healy, *Resilience: Why Things Bounce Back* (New York:
     Free Press, 2012), 7.

16. Ibid., 7–8 [emphasis in original].

17. See, for example, Michael Sacasas, "10 Points of Unsolicited Advice for Tech
     Writers," *Frailest Thing*, March 30, 2014, http://thefrailestthing.com/2014/03/30
     /10-points-of-unsolicited-advice-for-technology-writers. ("Do not cite apparent his-
     torical parallels to contemporary concerns about technology as if they invalidated
     those concerns. That people before us experienced similar problems does not mean
     that they magically cease being problems today.")

18. Adrienne LaFrance, "In 1858, People Said the Telegraph Was 'Too Fast for the Truth,'"
     Atlantic, July 28, 2014, http://www.theatlantic.com/technology/archive/2014/07/in
     -1858-people-said-the-telegraph-was-too-fast-for-the-truth/375171.

19. Quoted in Ibid.

20. Keith Collins, "OK, Glass, Don't Make Me Look Stupid," *Slate*, May 14, 2013, http://
     www.slate.com/articles/technology/future_tense/2013/05/google_glass_social
     _norms_will_it_be_too_awkward_to_use_in_public.html.

21. Ibid.

22. "'Kodak Fiends' at Newport," *New York Times*, August 18, 1899.

23. Samuel D. Warren and Louis D. Brandeis, "The Right to Privacy," *Harvard Law Review*
     4 (1890): 193.

24. Ibid., 195.

25. Castro and McQuinn, "The Privacy Panic Cycle," 13.

26. Quoted in Ibid., 15.

27. S. J. Diamond, "What's behind the Fuss over Caller ID," *Los Angeles Times*, June
     15, 1990, http://articles.latimes.com/1990-06-15/business/fi-370_1_caller-id-units;
     Matthew L. Wald, "Caller ID Reaches out a Bit Too Far," *New York Times*, February 2,
     1995, http://www.nytimes.com/1995/02/02/nyregion/caller-id-reaches-out-a-bit
     -too-far.html.

28. Electronic Privacy Information Center, "Caller ID," accessed December 12, 2015, http://epic.org/privacy/caller_id.

29. Mark Baard, "RFID: Sign of the (End) Times?," *Wired*, June 6, 2006, http://www.wired.com/science/discoveries/news/2006/06/70308.

30. Declan McCullagh, "Don't Regulate RFID—Yet," *CNET News*, April 30, 2004, http://news.cnet.com/Don%27t%20regulate%20RFID--yet/2010-1039_3-5327719.html.

31. See generally Jerry Brito, "Relax, Don't Do It: Why RFID Privacy Concerns Are Exaggerated and Legislation Is Premature," *UCLA Journal of Law & Technology* 8 (Fall 2004) (discussing how most fears concerning RFID use are exaggerated).

32. Zhi Zhang, "Networked RFID Systems for the Internet of Things," doctoral thesis, KTH School of Information and Communication Technology Stockholm, Sweden, May 2013, http://www.diva-portal.org/smash/get/diva2:613266/FULLTEXT01.

33. See Adam Thierer, "Lessons from the Gmail Privacy Scare of 2004," *Technology Liberation Front*, March 25, 2011, http://techliberation.com/2011/03/25/lessons-from-the-gmail-privacy-scare-of-2004.

34. Letter from Chris Jay Hoofnagle et al. to Bill Lockyer, Attorney General (May 3, 2004), http://epic.org/privacy/gmail/agltr5_3_04.html.

35. Dante D'Orazio, "Gmail Now Has 425 Million Active Users," *Verge*, June 28, 2012, http://www.theverge.com/2012/6/28/3123643/gmail-425-million-total-users.

36. See Kashmir Hill, "Apple and Google to Be the Whipping Boys for Location Privacy," *Forbes*, April, 26, 2011, http://www.forbes.com/sites/kashmirhill/2011/04/26/apple-and-google-to-be-the-whipping-boys-for-location-privacy.

37. Brian X. Chen, "Why and How Apple Is Collecting Your iPhone Location Data," *Wired: Gadget Lab*, April 21, 2011, http://www.wired.com/gadgetlab/2011/04/apple-iphone-tracking (explaining how and why Apple uses location data, but pointing out that there was no known reason to keep phones' entire location history in an unencrypted file on the device).

38. See Adam Thierer, "Apple, the iPhone and a Locational Privacy Techno-Panic," *Forbes*, May 1, 2011, http://www.forbes.com/sites/adamthierer/2011/05/01/apple-the-iphone-and-a-locational-privacy-techno-panic.

39. Rahul Patel, "Where Is Wearable Tech Headed?," *GigaOm*, September 28, 2013, http://gigaom.com/2013/09/28/where-is-wearable-tech-headed.

40. David Evans, "The Future of Wearable Technology: Smaller, Cheaper, Faster, and Truly Personal Computing," *LinkedIn*, October 24, 2013, http://www.linkedin.com/today/post/article/20131024145405-122323-the-future-of-wearable-technology-smaller-cheaper-faster-and-truly-personal-computing.

41. BI Intelligence, "The Wearables Report: Growth Trends, Consumer Attitudes, and Why Smartwatches Will Dominate," *Business Insider*, July 27, 2015, http://www.businessinsider.com/the-wearable-computing-market-report-bii-2015-7#ixzz3hBgqr6Cf.

42. Max Knoblauch, "The History of Wearable Tech, from the Casino to the Consumer," *Mashable*, May 13, 2014, http://mashable.com/2014/05/13/wearable-technology-history.

43. Dara Kerr, "Fitbit Rules 50 Percent of the World's Wearable Market," *CNET*, May 21, 2014, http://www.cnet.com/news/fitbit-rules-50-percent-of-the-worlds-wearable-market.

44. Stacey Higginbotham, "You Call Google Glass Wearable Tech? Heapsylon Makes Sensor-Rich Fabric," *GigaOm*, May 16, 2013, http://gigaom.com/2013/05/16/you -call-google-glass-wearable-tech-heapsylon-makes-sensor-rich-fabric.

45. Nathan Olivarez-Giles, "WebMD Relaunches iPhone App as a Hub for Fitness Data," *Wall Street Journal*, June 16, 2014, http://blogs.wsj.com/personal-technology/2014 /06/16/webmd-relaunches-iphone-app-as-a-hub-for-fitness-data.

46. ABI Research, "Disposable Wireless Sensor Market Shows Signs of Life—Healthcare Shipments to Reach 5 Million in 2018," May 3, 2013, http://www.abiresearch.com /press/disposable-wireless-sensor-market-shows-signs-of-l.

47. Jessica Glazer, "Psst! Wearable Devices Could Make Big Tech Leaps, into Your Ear," *NPR All Tech Considered*, April 29, 2014, http://www.npr.org/blogs /alltechconsidered/2014/04/23/306171641/psst-wearable-devices-could-make-big -tech-leaps-into-your-ear.

48. Kia Makarechi, "Move over, Google Glass; Here Come Google Contact Lenses," *Vanity Fair*, April 22, 2014, http://www.vanityfair.com/online/daily/2014/04/google -contact-lenses; Lance Ulanoff, "Google Smart Contact Lenses Move Closer to Reality," *Mashable*, April 21, 2014, http://mashable.com/2014/04/21/google-smart -contact-lenses-patents/#:eyJzljoidCIsImkiOiJfbXBtazRkemRvdWttcXQ4byJ9.

49. "Woven Electronics: An Uncommon Thread," *Economist*, March 8, 2014, http:// www.economist.com/news/technology-quarterly/21598328-conductive-fibres -lighter-aircraft-electric-knickers-flexible-filaments.

50. Eric Topol, *The Creative Destruction of Medicine: How the Digital Revolution Will Create Better Health Care* (New York: Basic Books, 2012).

51. Matthew Panzarino, "Disney Gets into Wearable Tech with the MagicBand," *Next Web*, May 29, 2013, http://thenextweb.com/insider/2013/05/29/disney-goes-into -wearable-tech-with-the-magic-band.

52. Thierer, "Internet of Things and Wearable Technology," 28–31.

53. Hayley Tsukayama, "Wearable Tech Such as Google Glass, Galaxy Gear Raises Alarms for Privacy Advocates," *Washington Post*, September 30, 2013, http://www .washingtonpost.com/business/technology/wearable-technology-raise-privacy -concerns/2013/09/30/0a81a960-2493-11e3-ad0d-b7c8d2a594b9_story.html.

54. Matt Hamblen, "UL Creating Standard for Wearable Privacy and Security," *Computerworld*, October 13, 2015, http://www.computerworld.com/article/2991331 /security/ul-creating-standard-for-wearable-privacy-and-security.html.

55. Larry Downes, "A Rational Response to the Privacy 'Crisis'" (Policy Analysis No. 716, Cato Institute, January 7, 2013), 10. (Downes has observed that, "after the initial panic, we almost always embrace the service that once violated our visceral sense of privacy."); Mike Masnick, "Moral Panics and How 'The Kids These Days' Adapt: From Facebook 'Permanence' to Snapchat's 'Impermanence,'" *TechDirt*, August 31, 2015, https://www.techdirt.com/articles/20150826/17101432074/moral-panics-how-kids -these-days-adapt-facebook-permanence-to-snapchats-impermanence.shtml. ("But it's important to note that everything adapts. Kids adapt. New services adapt. Societal norms and culture adapt. And things don't turn into some dystopian nightmare that some worry about. So many people look at these new services and react with outrage because they're different, and because they're different and will create different kinds of experiences, they must be bad. But history has shown that people are pretty damn resilient, and are pretty good at figuring out how to do things in a way that best suits them. And some will fail. And some will make mistakes. But it's hardly a crisis deserv-

ing of a moral panic. These things seem to take care of themselves pretty well.")

56. Postrel, *Future and Its Enemies*, 214.

57. This section adapted from Thierer, "Muddling Through"; Adam Thierer, Anne Hobson, Christopher Koopman, and Chris Kuiper, "How the Internet, the Sharing Economy & Reputation Feedback Mechanisms Solve the 'Lemons Problem'" (Mercatus Working Paper, Mercatus Center at George Mason University, Arlington, VA, May 2015), 11–24, http://mercatus.org/publication/how-internet-sharing -economy-and-reputational-feedback-mechanisms-solve-lemons-problem.

58. Castro and McQuinn, "The Privacy Panic Cycle," 28.

59. Cass Sunstein, "Social Norms and Social Roles," *Columbia Law Review* 96 (1996): 914.

60. Sunstein, "Social Norms and Social Roles."

61. Ibid.

62. Cristina Bicchieri, *The Grammar of Society: The Nature and Dynamics of Social Norms* (Cambridge: Cambridge University Press, 2006), 175.

63. Ibid., ix.

64. "We feel guilt when we have undertaken or attained something which, though desired by the elemental driving forces within us, we know to be incompatible with the official norms of our group—incompatible, that is, if we seek its realization." Helmut Schoeck, *Envy: A Theory of Social Behaviour* (Indianapolis, IN: Liberty Fund, 1966, 1987), 90.

65. Martha C. White, "Hang up and Eat: Give up Your Cell Phone and Restaurant Discounts Your Meal," *NBC News.com*, August 16, 2012, http://www.nbcnews.com /business/hang-eat-give-your-cell-phone-restaurant-discounts-your-meal-946635.

66. Elie Ayrouth, "Phone Stacking—Is This the Next Phone Etiquette Dining Trend?," *Food Beast*, January 6, 2012, http://foodbeast.com/content/2012/01/06/phone -stacking-is-this-gem-of-social-engineering-the-next-dining-trend.

67. Parents Television Council, http://www.parentstv.org/PTC/awards/main.asp.

68. Electronic Privacy Information Center, "About EPIC," http://epic.org/epic/about .html.

69. Privacy Rights Clearinghouse, "Fact Sheets," https://www.privacyrights.org/privacy -rights-fact-sheets.

70. Nicole A. Ozer, "It's Time to Demand Our dotRights!," ACLU of Northern California, November 18, 2009, https://www.aclunc.org/blog/its-time-demand-our-dotrights.

71. Glenn Reynolds, *An Army of Davids: How Markets and Technology Empower Ordinary People to Beat Big Media, Big Government and Other Goliaths* (Nashville, TN: Thomas Nelson, Inc., 2006).

72. Dan Gillmor, *We the Media* (Sebastopol, CA: O'Reilly Media, 2004), xii.

73. Yochai Benkler, *The Wealth of Networks: How Social Production Transforms Markets and Freedom* (New Haven, CT: Yale University Press, 2006), 11.

74. Joe Silver, "Shamed on Twitter, Corporations Do an About-face," *Ars Technica*, April 21, 2014, http://arstechnica.com/business/2014/04/shamed-on-twitter -corporations-do-an-about-face. ("[A] properly placed tweet can be a powerful weapon for consumers to combat corporate malfeasance.")

75. W. M. Elofson and John A. Woods, eds. *Writings and Speeches of Edmund Burke*, Vol. IX (Oxford: Oxford University Press, 1996), 242.

76. Vamien McKalin, "Augmented Reality vs. Virtual Reality: What Are the Differences and Similarities?," *Tech Times*, April 6, 2015, http://www.techtimes.com/articles /5078/20140406/augmented-reality-vs-virtual-reality-what-are-the -differences-and-similarities.htm.

77. Daniel Terdiman, "VR and Augmented Reality Will Soon Be Worth $150 Billion. Here Are the Major Players," *Fast Company*, October 13, 2015, http://www.fastcompany .com/3052209/tech-forecast/vr-and-augmented-reality-will-soon-be-worth-150 -billion-here-are-the-major-pla.

78. Jonathan Strickland, "How Virtual Reality Works," *How Stuff Works*, June 29, 2007, http://electronics.howstuffworks.com/gadgets/other-gadgets/virtual-reality.htm.

79. Ben Popper, "Can an Augmented Reality Headset Change the Way We Work?," *Verge*, September 22, 2015, http://www.theverge.com/2015/9/22/9370931/daqri -augmented-reality-headset-interview-video.

80. Lea Winerman, "A Virtual Cure," *Monitor on Psychology* (July/August 2005), http://www.apa.org/monitor/julaug05/cure.aspx.

81. Peter Graham, "Doctors Could Use VR to Explore the Body," *VR Focus*, August 23, 2015, http://vrfocus.com/archives/20415/doctors-could-use-vr-to-explore-the-body.

82. John Gaudiosi, "Here's Why Hospitals Are Using Virtual Reality to Train Staff," *Fortune*, August 17, 2015, http://fortune.com/2015/08/17/virtual-reality-hospitals.

83. Michelle Roberts, "Virtual Arm Eases Phantom-Limb Pain," *BBC*, February 26, 2014, http://www.bbc.com/news/health-26327457.

84. Alice Truong, "An Entrepreneur Is Using Virtual-Reality Headsets to Cure Vision Disorder," *Quartz*, August 27, 2015, http://qz.com/489048/an-entrepreneur-is -using-virtual-reality-headsets-to-try-to-cure-vision-disorders.

85. "Controlling Pain without Drugs," *Firsthand Technology*, last accessed October 13, 2015, http://www.firsthand.com/portfolio/pain.html.

86. David Quaid, "Bring Virtual Reality Field Trips to Your School with Google Expeditions," *Google for Education*, September 28, 2015, http://googleforeducation .blogspot.com/2015/09/bring-virtual-reality-field-trips-to-your-school-with-Google -Expeditions.html.

87. Ellen Gamerman, "A Look at the Museum of the Future," *Wall Street Journal*, October 15, 2015, http://www.wsj.com/articles/a-look-at-the-museum-of-the -future-1444940447.

88. Alison E. Berman, "Put Down the Textbook: How VR Is Reimagining Classroom Education," *SingularityHUB*, September 2, 2015, http://singularityhub.com/2015/09 /02/put-down-the-textbook-how-vr-is-reimagining-classroom-education.

89. Jason Lynch, "Embracing the Future, Discovery Goes All-In on Virtual Reality," *AdWeek*, August 27, 2015, http://www.adweek.com/news/television/embracing -future-discovery-goes-all-virtual-reality-166580.

90. Adrian Slobin, "Virtual Reality Is the Next Frontier for Retail," *Advertising Age*, August 24, 2015, http://adage.com/article/digitalnext/virtual-reality-frontier-retail /300061.

91. Omar Mouallem, "Real Estate Video Gaming Brings Floor Plans to Life," *Globe and Mail*, August 21, 2015, http://www.theglobeandmail.com/life/home-and-garden /real-estate/real-estate-video-gaming-brings-floor-plans-to-life/article26054805.

92. Brian Steinburg, "ABC News Brings Virtual Reality to Its Reporting," *Variety*, September 16, 2015, http://variety.com/2015/tv/news/abc-news-virtual-reality -syria-1201594907.

93. Leo King, "Ford, Where Virtual Reality Is Already Manufacturing Reality," *Forbes*, May 3, 2014, http://www.forbes.com/sites/leoking/2014/05/03/ford-where-virtual -reality-is-already-manufacturing-reality.

94. Matt Shaw, "What You See Is What You Get: Oculus Rift's Virtual Reality Architecture App," *Architizer*, September 14, 2014, http://architizer.com/blog/what -you-see-is-what-you-will-get-oculus-rifts-architecture-app.

95. Liz Gannes, "Narrative—Formerly Known as Memoto—Launches Life-Logging Camera, Raises $3M," *All Things D*, October 3, 2013, http://allthingsd.com/20131003 /narrative-formerly-known-as-memoto-launches-life-logging-camera-raises-3m; Clive Thompson, "Googling Yourself Takes on a Whole New Meaning," *New York Times*, August 30, 2013, http://mobile.nytimes.com/2013/09/01/magazine /googling-yourself-takes-on-a-whole-new-meaning.html?pagewanted=5&_r =0&hpw=&.

96. See generally "Every Step You Take," *Economist*, November 16, 2013, http://www .economist.com/news/leaders/21589862-cameras-become-ubiquitous-and-able -identify-people-more-safeguards-privacy-will-be.

CHAPTER V
WHAT ISSUES PROMPT PRECAUTIONARY THINKING AND POLICY TODAY?

1. Emmanuel G. Mesthene, "The Social Impact of Technological Change," in *Philosophy of Technology: The Technological Condition—An Anthology*, ed. Robert C. Scharff and Val Dusek (Malden, MA: Blackwell Publishing, 2003), 619. ("[W]e must not blink at the fact that technology does indeed destroy some values. It creates a million possibilities, heretofore undreamed of, but it also makes impossible some others heretofore enjoyed. . . . Some values are unquestionably bygone. To try to restore them is futile, and simply to deplore their loss is sterile. But it is perfectly human to regret them.")

2. Garreau, *Radical Evolution*, 229–30. ("Science works by making mistakes. We shouldn't torture ourselves with hypotheticals. Minimize the actual problems that arise.")

3. Schneier, "Worst-Case Thinking."

4. This section adapted from Adam Thierer, "Edith Ramirez's 'Big Data' Speech: Privacy Concerns Prompt Precautionary Principle Thinking," *Technology Liberation Front*, August 29, 2013, http://techliberation.com/2013/08/29/edith-ramirezs-big-data -speech-privacy-concerns-prompt-precautionary-principle-thinking; Adam Thierer, "A Framework for Benefit-Cost Analysis in Digital Privacy Debates," *George Mason University Law Review* 20, no. 4 (Summer 2013): 1066–69.

5. Edith Ramirez, "The Privacy Challenges of Big Data: A View from the Lifeguard's Chair," August 19, 2013, http://www.ftc.gov/speeches/ramirez/130819bigdataaspen .pdf.

6. Ibid., 4.

7.   Ibid., 6.

8.   Ryan Calo, "Digital Market Manipulation," *George Washington Law Review* 82 (2014): 999, http://papers.ssrn.com/sol3/papers.cfm?abstract_id=2309703. See also David Talbot, "Data Discrimination Means the Poor May Experience a Different Internet," *MIT Technology Review*, October 9, 2013, http://www.technologyreview .com/news/520131/data-discrimination-means-the-poor-may-experience-a -different-internet.

9.   See Anita L. Allen, "Coercing Privacy," *William & Mary Law Review* 40 (1999): 723; Mark MacCarthy, "New Directions in Privacy: Disclosure, Unfairness and Externalities," *I/S: A Journal of Law and Policy for the Information Society* 6 (2011): 443. ("The idea is that individual choice in this area would lead, in a piecemeal fashion, to the erosion of privacy protections that are the foundation of the democratic regime, which is the heart of our political system. Individuals are making an assessment—at least implicitly—of the advantages and disadvantages to them of sharing information. They are determining that information sharing is, on balance, a net gain for them. But the aggregate effect of these decisions is to erode the expectation of privacy and also the role of privacy in fostering self-development, personhood, and other values that underlie the liberal way of life. In this way, individual choices are not sufficient to justify information practices that collectively undermine widely shared public values" [footnote omitted].)

10.   Siva Vaidhyanathan, *The Googlization of Everything (And Why We Should Worry)* (Berkeley, CA: University of California Press, 2011), 83.

11.   Ibid., 84.

12.   Ibid.

13.   Ibid., 89.

14.   Ibid.

15.   Sunstein, *Laws of Fear*, 125. ("Government ought to treat its citizens with respect; it should not treat them as objects to be channeled in government's preferred directions.")

16.   Benjamin R. Sachs, "Comment: Consumerism and Information Privacy: How Upton Sinclair Can Again Save Us from Ourselves," *Virginia Law Review* 95 (2009): 223–26 (arguing that regulation is needed due to the complexity of the information economy and the limits of consumer competence).

17.   See Thierer, "Benefit-Cost Analysis," 1055–105.

18.   Calo, "Digital Market Manipulation," 38.

19.   Ibid.

20.   Thomas M. Lenard and Paul H. Rubin, *The Big Data Revolution: Privacy Considerations* (Washington, DC: Technology Policy Institute, December 2013), 24, http://www.techpolicyinstitute.org/files/lenard_rubin _thebigdatarevolutionprivacyconsiderations.pdf.

21.   Wildavsky, *Searching for Safety*, 38.

22.   Ibid., 92.

23.   Mayer-Schönberger and Cukier, *Big Data*.

24.   Ohlhausen, "Internet of Things."

25.   Ibid.

26. Downes, "Rational Response," 10. ("[A]fter the initial panic, we almost always embrace the service that once violated our visceral sense of privacy."); Adam Thierer, "On 'Creepiness' as the Standard of Review in Privacy Debates," *Technology Liberation Front*, December 13, 2011, http://techliberation.com/2011/12/13 /on-creepiness-as-the-standard-of-review-in-privacy-debates.

27. Castro and McQuinn, "The Privacy Panic Cycle," 28.

28. This section adapted from Thierer, "Technopanics"; Adam Thierer, "Do We Need a Ministry of Truth for the Internet?," *Forbes*, January 29, 2012, http://www .forbes.com/sites/adamthierer/2012/01/29/do-we-need-a-ministry-of-truth-for -the-internet; Adam Thierer, "Morozov's Algorithmic Auditing Proposal: A Few Questions," *Technology Liberation Front*, November 19, 2012, http://techliberation .com/2012/11/19/morozovs-algorithmic-auditing-proposal-a-few-questions.

29. Robert Corn-Revere, "New Age Comstockery," *CommLaw Conspectus* 4 (1996): 183–84 (analyzing the application of the Communications Decency Act to the Internet).

30. Mike Godwin, *Cyber Rights: Defending Free Speech in the Digital Age*, rev. ed. (Cambridge, MA: MIT Press, 2003), 259.

31. Alice E. Marwick, "To Catch a Predator? The MySpace Moral Panic," *First Monday*, June 2, 2008, http://firstmonday.org/htbin/cgiwrap/bin/ojs/index.php/fm/article /view/2152/1966.

32. Emily Steel and Julia Angwin, "MySpace Receives More Pressure to Limit Children's Access to Site," *Wall Street Journal*, June 23, 2006, B3.

33. Adam Thierer, "Social Networking and Age Verification: Many Hard Questions; No Easy Solutions" (*PFF Progress on Point* No. 14.5, Progress & Freedom Foundation, Washington, DC, March 21, 2007), http://papers.ssrn.com/sol3/papers.cfm ?abstract_id=976936.

34. Adam Thierer, "Would Your Favorite Website Be Banned by DOPA?," *Technology Liberation Front*, March 10, 2007, http://techliberation.com/2007/03/10/would -your-favorite-website-be-banned-by-dopa.

35. Deleting Online Predators Act, H.R. 5319, 109th Cong. (2006). See also Adam Thierer, "The Middleman Isn't the Problem," *Philly.com*, May 31, 2006, http://articles.philly .com/2006-05-31/news/25400396_1_web-sites-social-networking-block-access.

36. 152 Cong. Rec. 16231 (2006) (referring the bill to the Senate Committee on Commerce, Science, and Transportation); 152 Cong. Rec. 16040 (2006) (House vote).

37. 153 Cong. Rec. 4559 (2007) (introducing the bill into the House and referring it to the Committee on Energy and Commerce).

38. The North Carolina bill, as enacted, no longer included the prior access-restriction language. See S. 132, 2007 Gen. Assemb., Reg. Sess. (N.C. 2007) (enacted).

39. See Danah Michele Boyd, "Taken out of Context: American Teen Sociality in Networked Publics" (unpublished PhD diss., University of California, Berkeley, 2008), 266, http://www.danah.org/papers/TakenOutOfContext.pdf.

40. Ibid.

41. Samantha Craven, et al., "Sexual Grooming of Children: Review of Literature and Theoretical Considerations," *Journal of Sexual Aggression* 12 (2006): 289 (describing a study in which 45 percent of a sample of convicted child sex offenders had employed sexual grooming behaviors, but also noting that this type of offender

may be less likely to be reported, identified, and convicted than more aggressive offenders).

42. Gardner, *Science of Fear*, 185–86 (stating that earlier unfounded statistics estimated 50,000 to 75,000 children were kidnapped each year, when in fact, each year only about 115 "stereotypical kidnappings" [defined as "[a] stranger or slight acquaintance takes or detains a child for ransom or with the intention of keeping him or her, or kills the child"] occur in the United States).

43. Lenore Skenazy, *Free-Range Kids: Giving Our Children the Freedom We Had without Going Nuts with Worry* (San Francisco, CA: Jossey-Bass, 2009), 16.

44. Office of Juvenile Justice and Delinquency Prevention, US Department of Justice, *The Crime of Family Abduction: A Child's and Parent's Perspective* (Washington, DC: US Department of Justice, 2010), i, https://www.ncjrs.gov/pdffiles1/ojjdp/229933 .pdf.

45. See generally Adam Thierer, *Parental Controls & Online Child Protection: A Survey of Tools and Methods* (Washington, DC: Progress & Freedom Foundation, 2009), http://www.pff.org/parentalcontrols.

46. Family Online Safety Institute, "Initiatives: Broadband Responsibility Awareness Campaign," http://www.fosi.org/initiatives/broadband-responsibility-awareness -campaign.html.

47. Family Online Safety Institute, *Broadband Responsibility: A Blueprint for Safe & Responsible Online Use*, http://www.fosi.org/images/stories/resources/fosi-brac -book-electronic-version.pdf.

48. See Adam Thierer, "The Constructive Way to Combat Online Hate Speech: Thoughts on 'Viral Hate' by Foxman & Wolf," *Technology Liberation Front*, June 24, 2013, http://techliberation.com/2013/06/24/the-constructive-way-to-combat -online-hate-speech-thoughts-on-viral-hate-by-foxman-wolf.

49. Alexander Tsesis, "Dignity and Speech: The Regulation of Hate Speech in a Democracy," *Wake Forest Law Review* 44 (2009).

50. Sean McElwee, "The Case for Censoring Hate Speech," *AlterNet*, July 12, 2013, http://www.alternet.org/civil-liberties/case-censoring-hate-speech.

51. Evgeny Morozov, "Warning: This Site Contains Conspiracy Theories," *Slate*, January 23, 2012, http://www.slate.com/articles/technology/future_tense/2012/01/anti _vaccine_activists_9_11_deniers_and_google_s_social_search_.single.html.

52. Ibid.

53. Ibid.

54. Ibid.

55. Evgeny Morozov, "You Can't Say That on the Internet," *New York Times*, November 16, 2012, http://www.nytimes.com/2012/11/18/opinion/sunday/you-cant-say-that -on-the-internet.html?pagewanted=all&_r=3&.

56. Ibid.

57. This section partially adapted from Thierer, "Internet Order without Law." The author wishes to thank Andrea Castillo for major contributions to this section.

58. See Richard A. Serrano, "Cyber Attacks Seen as a Growing Threat," *Los Angeles Times*, February 11, 2011, A18. ("[T]he potential for the next Pearl Harbor could very well be a cyber attack.")

59. Harry Raduege, "Deterring Attackers in Cyberspace," *The Hill*, September 23, 2011, 11, http://thehill.com/opinion/op-ed/183429-deterring-attackers-in-cyberspace.

60. Kurt Nimmo, "Former CIA Official Predicts Cyber 9/11," *InfoWars.com*, August 4, 2011, http://www.infowars.com/former-cia-official-predicts-cyber-911.

61. Rodney Brown, "Cyber Bombs: Data-Security Sector Hopes Adoption Won't Require a 'Pearl Harbor' Moment," *Innovation Report*, October 26, 2011, 10, http://digital .masshightech.com/launch.aspx?referral=other&pnum=&refresh=6t0M1Sr380Rf& EID=1c256165-396b-454f-bc92-a7780169a876&skip=; Craig Spiezle, "Defusing the Internet of Things Time Bomb," *TechCrunch*, August 11, 2015, http://techcrunch. com/2015/08/10/defusing-the-internet-of-things-time-bomb.

62. "Morning Edition: Cybersecurity Bill: Vital Need or Just More Rules?," *NPR*, March 22, 2012, http://www.npr.org/templates/transcript/transcript.php?storyId=149099866.

63. Jerry Brito and Tate Watkins, "Loving the Cyber Bomb? The Dangers of Threat Inflation in Cybersecurity Policy" (Mercatus Working Paper No. 11-24, Mercatus Center at George Mason University, Arlington, VA, 2011).

64. Jane K. Cramer and A. Trevor Thrall, "Introduction: Understanding Threat Inflation," in *American Foreign Policy and the Politics of Fear: Threat Inflation Since 9/11*, ed. A. Trevor Thrall and Jane K. Cramer (London: Routledge, 2009), 1.

65. Tufekci, "Dumb Idea"; Byron Acohido, "Hackers Take Control of Internet Appliances," *USA Today*, October 15, 2013, http://www.usatoday.com/story/cybertruth /2013/10/15/hackers-taking-control-of-internet-appliances/2986395.

66. Ed Markey, *Tracking & Hacking: Security & Privacy Gaps Put American Drivers at Risk*, US Senate, February 2015, http://www.markey.senate.gov/imo/media/doc /2015-02-06_MarkeyReport-Tracking_Hacking_CarSecurity%202.pdf.

67. Ed Markey, "Markey, Blumenthal to Introduce Legislation to Protect Drivers from Auto Security and Privacy Vulnerabilities with Standards and 'Cyber Dashboard,'" press release, February 11, 2015, http://www.markey.senate.gov/news/press -releases/markey-blumenthal-to-introduce-legislation-to-protect-drivers-from -auto-security-and-privacy-vulnerabilities-with-standards-and-cyber-dashboard.

68. Andrea Castillo, "How CISA Threatens Both Privacy and Cybersecurity," *Reason*, May 10, 2015, https://reason.com/archives/2015/05/10/why-cisa-wont-improve -cybersecurity.

69. Eli Dourado and Andrea Castillo, "Poor Federal Cybersecurity Reveals Weakness of Technocratic Approach" (Mercatus Working Paper, Mercatus Center at George Mason University, Arlington, VA, June 22, 2015), http://mercatus.org/publication /poor-federal-cybersecurity-reveals-weakness-technocratic-approach.

70. Eli Dourado, "Internet Security without Law: How Security Providers Create Online Order" (Mercatus Working Paper No. 12-19, Mercatus Center at George Mason University, Arlington, VA, June 19, 2012), http://mercatus.org/publication /internet-security-without-law-how-service-providers-create-order-online.

71. Ibid.

72. Charlie Miller, "The Legitimate Vulnerability Market: Inside the Secretive World of 0-day Exploit Sales," *Independent Security Evaluators*, May 6, 2007, http://www .econinfosec.org/archive/weis2007/papers/29.pdf.

73.   Andrea Castillo, "The Economics of Software-Vulnerability Sales: Can the Feds Encourage 'Pro-social' Hacking?," *Reason*, August 11, 2015, https://reason.com /archives/2015/08/11/economics-of-the-zero-day-sales-market.

74.   Roger Grimes, "The Cyber Crime Tide Is Turning," *Infoworld*, August 9, 2011, http://www.pcworld.com/article/237647/the_cyber_crime_tide_is_turning.html.

75.   Dourado, "Internet Security."

76.   Anthony D. Glosson, "Active Defense: An Overview of the Debate and a Way Forward" (Mercatus Working Paper, Mercatus Center at George Mason University, Arlington, VA, August 10, 2015), http://mercatus.org/publication/active-defense -overview-debate-and-way-forward-guardians-of-peace-hackers-cybersecurity.

77.   http://stopbadware.org.

78.   https://www.iamthecavalry.org.

79.   Andrea Castillo, "The Government's Latest Attempt to Stop Hackers Will Only Make Cybersecurity Worse," *Reason*, July 28, 2015, https://reason.com/archives/2015 /07/28/gov-ploy-to-stop-hackers-will-backfire.

80.   Russell Brandom, "The US is Rewriting its Controversial Zero-Day Export Policy," *Verge*, July 29, 2015, http://www.theverge.com/2015/7/29/9068665/wassenaar -export-zero-day-revisions-department-of-commerce.

81.   Dourado, "Internet Security."

82.   Ibid.

83.   Glosson, "Active Defense."

84.   Dourado, "Internet Security."

85.   Dourado, "Internet Security."

86.   Future of Privacy Forum, "Best Practices," http://www.futureofprivacy.org /resources/best-practices/.

87.   See http://www.staysafeonline.org/ncsam and http://www.staysafeonline.org /data-privacy-day.

88.   Glosson, "Active Defense," 22. ("The precautionary principle is especially inadvisable in the dynamic realm of tech policy, and until the ostensible harms of active defense materialize, the law should facilitate maximum innovation in the network security field.")

89.   Postrel, *Future and Its Enemies*, 199.

90.   Ibid., 202.

91.   See Future of Privacy Forum, "Connected Cars Project," accessed October 16, 2015, http://www.futureofprivacy.org/connectedcars; Auto Alliance, "Automakers Believe That Strong Consumer Data Privacy Protections Are Essential to Maintaining the Trust of Our Customers," accessed October 16, 2015, http://www.autoalliance.org/ automotiveprivacy. See also Future of Privacy Forum, "Comments of the Future of Privacy Forum on Connected Smart Technologies in Advance of the FTC 'Internet of Things' Workshop," May 31, 2013, http://www.futureofprivacy.org /wp-content/uploads/FPF-Comments-Regarding-Internet-of-Things.pdf.

92.   Adam Thierer, "Don't Panic over Looming Cybersecurity Threats," *Forbes*, August 7, 2011, http://www.forbes.com/sites/adamthierer/2011/08/07/dont-panic-over -looming-cybersecurity-threats.

93. Thierer and Hagemann, "Removing Roadblocks."

94. Eno Center for Transportation, *Preparing a Nation for Autonomous Vehicles: Opportunities, Barriers and Policy Recommendations* (Washington, DC: October 2013), 17, https://www.enotrans.org/wp-content/uploads/wpsc/downloadables /AV-paper.pdf.

95. Ibid., 3.

96. Ibid., 3-4.

97. Ibid., 3.

98. Adrienne LaFrance, "Self-Driving Cars Could Save 300,000 Lives per Decade in America," *Atlantic*, September 29, 2015, http://www.theatlantic.com/technology /archive/2015/09/self-driving-cars-could-save-300000-lives-per-decade-in -america/407956.

99. Morgan Stanley, "Autonomous Cars: Self-Driving the New Auto Industry Paradigm," *Morgan Stanley Research*, November 6, 2013, http://www.morganstanley.com /public/11152013.html.

100. Kevin Roose, "Driving Should Be Illegal," *Fusion*, October 5, 2015, http://fusion.net /story/207965/driving-should-be-illegal.

101. Patrick Lin, "The Ethics of Saving Lives with Autonomous Cars Are Far Murkier Than You Think," *Wired*, July 30, 2013, http://www.wired.com/opinion/2013/07/the -surprising-ethics-of-robot-cars.

102. Claire Cain Miller, "When Driverless Cars Break the Law," *New York Times*, May 13, 2014, http://www.nytimes.com/2014/05/14/upshot/when-driverless-cars-break -the-law.html?_r=0.

103. Keith Kirkpatrick, "The Moral Challenges of Driverless Cars," *Communications of the ACM* 58, no. 8 (August 2015), http://cacm.acm.org/magazines/2015/8/189836 -the-moral-challenges-of-driverless-cars/fulltext. For a response to those concerns, see Adam Thierer, "On the Line between Technology Ethics vs. Technology Policy," *Technology Liberation Front*, August 1, 2013, http://techliberation.com /2013/08/01/on-the-line-between-technology-ethics-vs-technology-policy; Adam Thierer, "Making Sure the 'Trolley Problem' Doesn't Derail Life-Saving Innovation," *Technology Liberation Front*, January 13, 2015, http://techliberation.com/2015/01/13 /making-sure-the-trolley-problem-doesnt-derail-life-saving-innovation.

104. Ryan Hagemman, "Autonomous Vehicles under Attack: Cyber Dashboard Standards and Class Action Lawsuits," *Technology Liberation Front*, March 14, 2015, http://techliberation.com/2015/03/14/autonomous-vehicles-under-attack-cyber -dashboard-standards-and-class-action-lawsuits.

105. Adam Thierer, "Don't Hit the (Techno-)Panic Button on Connected Car Hacking & IoT Security," *Technology Liberation Front*, February 10, 2015, http://techliberation .com/2015/02/10/dont-hit-the-techno-panic-button-on-connected-car-hacking -iot-security.

106. Mike Ramsey, "Regulators Have Hands Full with Tesla's Plan for Hands-Free Driving," *Wall Street Journal*, March 27, 2015, http://www.wsj.com/articles /regulators-have-hands-full-with-teslas-plan-for-hands-free-driving-1427484220. Similarly, Carlos Ghosn, chief executive of Renault SA and Nissan Motor Co., said in a summer 2015 interview that "[a]ll these technologies will move much faster than

the regulator." Quoted in Orr Hirschauge, "Are Driverless Cars Safer Cars?," *Wall Street Journal*, August 14, 2015, http://www.wsj.com/articles/are-driverless-cars-safer-cars-1439544601.

107.   John Villasenor, "Products Liability and Driverless Cars: Issues and Guiding Principles for Legislation" (Washington, DC: Brookings Institution Research Paper, April 24, 2014), http://www.brookings.edu/research/papers/2014/04/products-liability-driverless-cars-villasenor.

108.   Derek Thompson, "A World without Work," *Atlantic*, July/August 2015, http://www.theatlantic.com/magazine/archive/2015/07/world-without-work/395294.

109.   Mark J. Perry, "Schumpeterian Creative Destruction—The Rise of Uber and the Great Taxicab Collapse," *AEI Ideas*, September 2, 2015, http://www.aei.org/publication/schumpeterian-creative-destruction-the-rise-of-uber-and-the-great-taxicab-collapose.

110.   Steven Hill, "The Future of Work in the Uber Economy," *Moyers & Company*, July 27, 2015, http://billmoyers.com/2015/07/27/the-future-of-work-in-the-uber-economy; Douglas Macmillian, "Sharing Economy Workers Need 'Safety Net,' U.S. Senator Says," *Wall Street Journal*, June 8, 2015, http://blogs.wsj.com/digits/2015/06/08/sharing-economy-workers-need-government-safety-net-u-s-senator-says.

111.   Rory Cellan-Jones, "Robots on the Rise," *BBC News*, July 2, 2015, http://www.bbc.com/news/technology-33360744.

112.   Ford, *Rise of the Robots*.

113.   David H. Autor, "Why Are There Still So Many Jobs? The History and Future of Workplace Automation," *Journal of Economic Perspectives* 29, no. 3 (Summer 2015): 3, http://www.ingentaconnect.com/content/aea/jep/2015/00000029/00000003/art00001;jsessionid=58w6sj0v1f6vm.alexandra.

114.   Mokyr, Vickers, and Ziebarth, "History of Technological Anxiety," 45. ("Discussions of how technology may affect labor demand are often focused on existing jobs, which can offer insights about which occupations may suffer the greatest dislocation, but offer much less insight about the emergence of as-yet-nonexistent occupations of the future.")

115.   Ibid., 36. ("In the end, the fears of the Luddites that machinery would impoverish workers were not realized, and the main reason is well understood. The mechanization of the early 19th century could only replace a limited number of human activities. At the same time, technological change increased the demand for other types of labor that were complementary to the capital goods embodied in the new technologies. This increased demand for labor included such obvious jobs as mechanics to fix the new machines, but it extended to jobs for supervisors to oversee the new factory system and accountants to manage enterprises operating on an unprecedented scale. More importantly, technological progress also took the form of product innovation, and thus created entirely new sectors for the economy, a development that was essentially missed in the discussions of economists of this time.")

116.   Ian Stewart, Debapratim De, and Alex Cole, *Technology and People: The Great Job-Creating Machine* (London: Deloitte LLP, December 2014), 9, http://www2.deloitte.com/content/dam/Deloitte/uk/Documents/about-deloitte/deloitte-uk-technology-and-people.pdf.

117.   Ibid., 10. (They continue on to note that "[m]achines will take on more repetitive and laborious tasks, but seem no closer to eliminating the need for human labour than at any time in the last 150 years. It is not hard to think of pressing, unmet needs

even in the rich world: the care of the elderly and the frail, lifetime education and retraining, health care, physical and mental well-being.")

118. Katie Allen, "Technology Has Created More Jobs Than It Has Destroyed, Says 140 Years of Data," *Guardian*, August 14, 2015, http://www.theguardian.com/business /2015/aug/17/technology-created-more-jobs-than-destroyed-140-years-data-census.

119. Autor, "Still So Many Jobs?," 4.

120. Ibid., 5. ("[J]ournalists and even expert commentators tend to overstate the extent of machine substitution for human labor and ignore the strong complementarities between automation and labor that increase productivity, raise earnings, and augment demand for labor.")

121. Marc Andreessen, "This Is Probably a Good Time to Say That I Don't Believe Robots Will Eat All the Jobs ...," *Marc Andreessen blog*, June 13, 2014, http://blog.pmarca. com/2014/06/13/this-is-probably-a-good-time-to-say-that-i-dont-believe-robots -will-eat-all-the-jobs.

122. Colin Lewis, "Study—Robots Are Not Taking Jobs," *Roboteconomics*, September 16, 2015, http://robotenomics.com/2015/09/16/study-robots-are-not-taking-jobs.

123. Ibid.

124. Glassdoor, "25 Highest Paying Jobs In Demand," *Glassdoor Blog*, February 17, 2015, http://www.glassdoor.com/blog/highest-paying-jobs-demand.

125. John Tschetter, "An Evaluation of BLS' Projections of 1980 Industry Employment," *Monthly Labor Review*, August 1984, http://www.bls.gov/opub/mlr/1984/08 /art3full.pdf.

126. Bessen, *Learning by Doing*, 223.

127. Ohlhausen, "Internet of Everything," 5. ("But if the past 200 years of innovation have any lesson, it is this: society has repeatedly and quickly integrated and greatly benefited from innovation.")

128. Mandel, "High-Growth Economy?," 9.

129. Mokyr, *Lever of Riches*, 261. ("The continuous obsolescence of specific, nonmalleable assets, both physical and human, is the price a society pays for sustained progress.")

130. Antone Gonsalves, "Apple Remote-Mobile Device Management Patent Raises Red Flags," *Macworld*, September 2, 2013, http://www.macworld.com.au/news/apple -remote-mobile-device-management-patent-raises-red-flags-106254.

131. This section condensed from Christopher Koopman, Matthew Mitchell, and Adam Thierer, filing before the Federal Trade Commission workshop on "The 'Sharing' Economy: Issues Facing Platforms, Participants, and Regulators," May 26, 2015, http://mercatus.org/publication/sharing-economy-issues-facing-platforms -participants-and-regulators; Koopman, Mitchell, and Thierer, "Sharing Economy and Consumer Protection Regulation," 529–45.

132. Ranchordás, "Does Sharing Mean Caring?," 4. ("One decade ago, sharing economy practices would have been unthinkable, not only because we were living in more prosperous times, but also because we would not have conceived of engaging in such transactions with strangers, not to mention unlicensed strangers that play taxi drivers in their spare time.")

133. Vila and Gardner, "Regulatory Wheel Clamps."

134. See, for example, Rachel Boston, "The Sharing Economy Lacks a Shared Definition," *Fast Company*, November 21, 2013, http://www.fastcoexist.com/3022028/the-sharing-economy-lacks-a-shared-definition. It may be helpful to think of a sharing economy as a special case of a "two-sided" or "platform" market. It is special because it typically employs technology to bring together large numbers of buyers and large numbers of sellers. For more on platform markets, see Alex Tabarrok, "Jean Tirole and Platform Markets," *Marginal Revolution*, October 13, 2014, http://marginalrevolution.com/marginalrevolution/2014/10/tirole-and-platform-markets.html. See also Stewart Dompe and Adam Smith, "Regulation of Platform Markets in Transportation" (Mercatus on Policy, Mercatus Center at George Mason University, Arlington, VA, October 27, 2014), http://mercatus.org/publication/regulation-platform-markets-transportation.

135. Dara Kerr, "'Sharing Economy' Apps to Boom with Their Lure of Cheap and Easy," *CNet*, April 14, 2015, http://www.cnet.com/news/sharing-economy-expected-to-boom-customers-say-it-makes-life-cheap-and-easy.

136. Federal Trade Commission, "FTC to Examine Competition, Consumer Protection, and Economic Issues Raised by the Sharing Economy at June Workshop," press release, April 17, 2015, https://www.ftc.gov/news-events/press-releases/2015/04/ftc-examine-competition-consumer-protection-economic-issues.

137. See Koopman, Mitchell, and Thierer, "Sharing Economy and Consumer Protection Regulation."

138. Daniel M. Rothschild, "How Uber and Airbnb Resurrect 'Dead Capital,'" *Umlaut*, April 9, 2014, http://theumlaut.com/2014/04/09/how-uber-and-airbnb-resurrect-dead-capital. On the broader concept of "dead capital," see Hernando De Soto, *The Mystery of Capital Why Capitalism Succeeds in the West and Fails Everywhere Else*, 1st ed. (New York: Basic Books, 2000).

139. Alex Howard, "How Digital Platforms Like LinkedIn, Uber and TaskRabbit Are Changing the On-Demand Economy," July 13, 2015, http://www.huffingtonpost.com/entry/online-talent-platforms_55a03545e4b0b8145f72ccf6. (Highlighting the findings of new report by the McKinsey Global Institute: "McKinsey's research suggests that the long-term effects of digital talent marketplaces could shorten the length of time that people are unemployed and provide more opportunities for freelance workers.")

140. Thierer, Hobson, Koopman, and Kuiper, "The 'Lemons Problem.'" See also Alex Tabarrok and Tyler Cowen, "The End of Asymmetric Information?," *Cato Unbound*, April 6, 2015, http://www.cato-unbound.org/2015/04/06/alex-tabarrok-tyler-cowen/end-asymmetric-information.

141. Michael Farren, "Ending the Uber Wars: How to Solve a Special Interest Nightmare," *Fiscal Times*, August 11, 2015, http://mercatus.org/expert_commentary/ending-uber-wars-how-solve-special-interest-nightmare.

142. Michael Farren, "No Permission Slips Needed," *US News and World Report*, June 22, 2015, http://www.usnews.com/opinion/economic-intelligence/2015/06/22/sharing-economy-innovators-shouldnt-be-shackled-by-rules-for-a-bygone-era.

143. Adam Thierer, "Curbing the New Corporate Power," *Boston Review*, May 5, 2015, http://bostonreview.net/forum/curbing-new-corporate-power/adam-thierer-adam-thierer-response-curbing-new-corporate-power.

144. PricewaterhouseCoopers, "Customer Intelligence Series: The Sharing Economy," April 18, 2015, 16, http://www.pwc.com/us/en/industry/entertainment-media/publications/consumer-intelligence-series/assets/pwc-cis-sharing-economy.pdf.

CHAPTER VI
A BLUEPRINT FOR PRESERVING PERMISSIONLESS INNOVATION

1. This section adapted from Thierer, "Technopanics," 352–68.

2. Mokyr, *Lever of Riches*, 16.

3. Larry Downes, "Fewer, Faster, Smarter," *Democracy: A Journal of Ideas* 38 (Fall 2015), http://www.democracyjournal.org/38/fewer-faster-smarter.php?page=all. ("As the technology revolution proceeds, the concept of government may return to its pre-industrial roots, setting the most basic rules of the economy and standing by as regulator of last resort when markets fail for some or all consumers over an extended period of time. Even then, the solution may simply be to tweak the incentives to encourage better behavior, rather than more full-fledged—and usually ill-fated—micromanagement of fast-changing industries.")

4. Postrel, *Future and Its Enemies*, 212 [emphasis in original].

5. Ibid.

6. Ibid., 213.

7. Geoffrey A. Manne and Joshua D. Wright, eds., *Competition Policy and Patent Law under Uncertainty: Regulating Innovation* (Cambridge: Cambridge University Press, 2011), 1.

8. Ohlhausen, "Internet of Everything," 6. ("[R]egulators face a fundamental knowledge problem that limits the effective reach of regulation. A regulator must acquire knowledge about the present state and future trends of the industry being regulated. The more prescriptive the regulation, and the more complex the industry, the more detailed knowledge the regulator must collect. But, regulators simply cannot gather all the information relevant to every problem. Such information is widely distributed and therefore very expensive to collect. Even when a regulator manages to collect information, it quickly becomes out of date as a regulated industry continues to evolve. Obsolete data is a particular concern for regulators of fast-changing technological fields like the Internet of Things. This knowledge problem means that centralized problem solving cannot make full use of the available knowledge about a problem. Therefore, centralized regulation generally offers worse solutions when compared to distributed or emergent constraints such as social norms.")

9. Nathan Rosenberg, *Exploring the Black Box: Technology, Economics, and History* (Cambridge: Cambridge University Press, 1994), 92–3. ("This uncertainty, by which we mean an inability to predict the outcome of the search process, or to predetermine the most efficient path to some particular goal, has a very important implication: the activity cannot be planned. No person, or group of persons, is clever enough to plan the outcome of the search process, in the sense of identifying a particular innovation target and moving in a predetermined way to its realization—as one might read a road map and plan the most efficient route to a historical monument.")

10. Ohlhausen, "Internet of Things," 3–4. See also Ohlhausen, "Internet of Everything," 12. ("Over the past two centuries, humankind has proven its ability to transform innovation into widespread prosperity. Fueled by supportive social attitudes and free market institutions, businesses have been the engines of this prosperity. Regulators who don't want to stall these engines of innovation should remember the long history of beneficial innovation, remain humble about what they can know and accomplish, focus on addressing real consumer harm, and apply tools appropriate to the harms that do arise.")

11. Larry Downes, "Happy Birthday to Moore's Law," *Washington Post*, April 16, 2015, http://www.washingtonpost.com/blogs/innovations/wp/2015/04/16/happy -birthday-to-moores-law; Dan Tynan, "Moore's Law: 50 Years Old and Still Going Strong," *Yahoo! Tech*, April 17, 2015, https://www.yahoo.com/tech/moores-law-50 -years-old-and-still-going-strong-116599978474.html.

12. "Definition of Moore's Law," *PC Magazine Encyclopedia*, http://www.pcmag.com /encyclopedia_term/0,,t=&i=47229,00.asp. See also Bret Swanson, *Moore's Law at 50: The Performance and Prospects of the Exponential Economy* (Washington, DC: American Enterprise Institute, November 2014) http://www.aei.org/publication /moores-law-at-50-the-performance-and-prospects-of-the-exponential-economy.

13. This section adapted from Adam Thierer, "Sunsetting Technology Regulation: Applying Moore's Law to Washington," *Forbes*, March 25, 2012, http://www.forbes .com/sites/adamthierer/2012/03/25/sunsetting-technology-regulation-applying -moores-law-to-washington.

14. Larry Downes, *The Laws of Disruption: Harnessing the New Forces That Govern Life and Business in the Digital Age* (New York: Basic Books, 2009), 2.

15. Unsurprisingly, technology critics are more worried about this "pacing problem." See, for example, Wallach, *Dangerous Master*, 60. ("The faster the rate of change, the more difficult it becomes to effectively monitor and regulate emerging technologies. Indeed, as the pace of technological development quickens, legal and ethical mechanisms for their oversight are bogging down. This has been referred to as the pacing problem: The growing gap between the time technologies are deployed and the time effective means are enacted to ensure public safety.")

16. Ibid., 2–3. In a similar sense, Andy Grove, former CEO of Intel, once reportedly said that "high tech runs three-times faster than normal businesses. And the government runs three-times slower than normal businesses. So we have a nine-times gap." Lillian Cunningham, "Google's Eric Schmidt Expounds on His Senate Testimony," *Washington Post*, October 1, 2011, http://www.washingtonpost.com/national /on-leadership/googles-eric-schmidt-expounds-on-his-senate-testimony /2011/09/30/gIQAPyVgCL_story.html.

17. Jonathan Askin, "A Remedy to Clueless Tech Lawyers," *Venture Beat*, November 13, 2013, http://venturebeat.com/2013/11/13/a-remedy-to-clueless-tech-lawyers.

18. Ibid.

19. Ibid.

20. Downes, *Laws of Disruption*, 272. ("Lawmakers have also too often heeded the siren call to do something, anything, to prove that digital life is not a lawless frontier," he says. "But legislating ahead of the technology helps no one and often leaves behind rules that trap those who were doing nothing wrong.")

21. Ibid., 60.

22. Ranchordás, "Does Sharing Mean Caring?," 37.

23. Jack Nicas, "Amazon Says FAA Approval to Test Delivery Drones Already Obsolete," *Wall Street Journal*, March 25, 2015, http://www.wsj.com/articles/amazon-says -its-approval-to-test-delivery-drones-already-obsolete-1427219327.

24. Ramsey, "Regulators Have Hands Full." (Quoting Carl Tobias, a product liability law professor at the University of Richmond, commenting on self-driving technology: "Technology is always running ahead of the law, but in this case, it is running way ahead of the law.")

25. See Ranchordás, "Does Sharing Mean Caring?"

26. Joshua Barajas, "FDA Regulation Can't Keep Pace with New Mobile Health Apps," *PBS NewsHour*, July 7, 2014, http://www.pbs.org/newshour/rundown/fda -regulation-unable-keep-pace-new-mobile-health-apps.

27. Ranchordás, "Does Sharing Mean Caring?," 39. ("Regulators can increase flexibility of regulations to accompany the pace of innovation both by including a sunset clause—which predetermines their expiry at the end of a certain period—or by experimenting with new rules. . . . Terminating regulations by employing sunset clauses or by experimenting on a small-scale can be useful to ensure that rules keep up with the changes in technology and society.")

28. Ranchordás, "Does Sharing Mean Caring?," 10–11. ("The regulation of innovation in the sharing economy is particularly complex because it is unclear whether these practices fit within existing legal frameworks that apply to equivalent commercial practices and should play by the same rules, whether these practices should remain to a great extent unregulated, or whether these practices should benefit from less demanding regulations.")

29. Koopman, Mitchell, and Thierer, "Sharing Economy and Consumer Protection Regulation," 18–19, http://mercatus.org/publication/sharing-economy-and -consumer-protection-regulation-case-policy-change.

30. Marsali Hancock, et al., "From Safety to Literacy: Digital Citizenship in the 21st Century," *Threshold Magazine* (Summer 2009): 4.

31. Anne Collier, "'Delete Day': Students Putting Messages That Matter Online," *NetFamilyNews.org*, May 6, 2011, http://www.netfamilynews.org/?p=30376.

32. Anne Collier, "From Users to Citizens: How to Make Digital Citizenship Relevant," *NetFamilyNews.org*, November 16, 2009, http://www.netfamilynews.org/2009/11 /from-users-to-citizen-how-to-make.html; Larry Magid, "We Need to Rethink Online Safety," *Huffington Post*, January 22, 2010, http://www.huffingtonpost.com /larry-magid/we-need-to-rethink-online_b_433421.html; Nancy Willard, *Comprehensive Layered Approach to Address Digital Citizenship and Youth Risk Online* (Eugene, OR: Center for Safe & Responsible Internet Use, November 2008), http://csriu.org/PDFs/yrocomprehensiveapproach.pdf; ConnectSafely.org, *Online Safety 3.0: Empowering and Protecting Youth*, http://www.connectsafely.org /Commentaries-Staff/online-safety-30-empowering-and-protecting-youth.html.

33. Anne Collier, "A Definition of Digital Literacy & Citizenship," *NetFamilyNews.org*, September 15, 2009, www.netfamilynews.org/2009/09/definition-of-digital -literacy.html.

34. White House, *Big Data*, 64.

35. Ibid.

36. Ibid.

37. Larry Magid, "Digital Citizenship and Media Literacy Beat Tracking Laws and Monitoring," *SafeKids.com*, August 29, 2011, http://www.safekids.com/2011/08/29 /digital-literacy-critical-thinking-accomplish-more-than-monitoring-tracking-laws.

38. Ibid.

39. *Volunteer Privacy Educators Program*, Fordham Center on Law and Information Policy, October 16, 2013, http://law.fordham.edu/center-on-law-and-information -policy/30317.htm.

40. Fordham Center on Law and Information Policy, *Fordham CLIP Volunteer Privacy Educators Program* (2013), http://law.fordham.edu/assets/CLIP/2013_CLIP_VPE _Complete.pdf.

41. See Adam Thierer, *Public Interest Comment on Federal Trade Commission Report, Protecting Consumer Privacy in an Era of Rapid Change* (Arlington, VA: Mercatus Center at George Mason University, 2011), 9, http://mercatus.org/sites/default/files /public-interest-comment-on-protecting-consumer-privacy-do-not-track -proceeding.pdf. ("[S]ome companies appear to be competing on privacy. . . . [O]ne company offers an Internet search service . . . as being . . . more privacy -sensitive. . . . [I]n response to Google's decision to change its privacy policies . . . Microsoft encouraged consumers to switch to Microsoft's more privacy-protective products and services.")

42. Federal Trade Commission, "Strategic Plan for Fiscal Years 2009 to 2014" (Washington, DC: 2009), 4, http://www.ftc.gov/opp/gpra/spfy09fy14.pdf. ("Most FTC law enforcement initiatives include a consumer and/or business education component aimed at preventing consumer injury and unlawful business practices, and mitigating financial losses. From time to time, the agency conducts pre-emptive consumer and business education campaigns to raise awareness of new or emerging marketplace issues that have the potential to cause harm. The agency creatively uses new technologies and private and public partnerships to reach new and underserved audiences, particularly those who may not seek information directly from the FTC.")

43. OnGuard Online, http://www.onguardonline.gov.

44. The FTC's YouTube page, https://www.youtube.com/user/FTCvideos.

45. FCC Smartphone Security Checker, http://www.fcc.gov/smartphone-security, accessed October 31, 2014.

46. David Hoffman, "What's One Way Organizations Can Be More Accountable? Privacy Education," *Privacy Perspectives*, April 2, 2013, https://www.privacyassociation.org /privacy_perspectives/post/whats_one_way_organizations_can_be_more _accountable_educate_educate_educate.

47. See http://www.smokeybear.com and http://en.wikipedia.org/wiki/Smokey_the _Bear.

48. http://en.wikipedia.org/wiki/Woodsy_Owl.

49. http://mcgruff.org.

50. http://www.nhtsa.dot.gov/portal/site/nhtsa/menuitem .cda13865569778598fcb6010dba046a0.

51. Ira S. Rubinstein, "Regulating Privacy by Design," *Berkeley Technology Law Journal* 26 (2011), 1409; Peter Schaar, "Privacy by Design," *Identity in the Information Society* 3 (2010), 267.

52. Ann Cavoukian, "2011: The Decade of Privacy by Design Starts Now," *ITBusiness*, January 15, 2011, http://blogs.itbusiness.ca/2011/01/2011-the-decade-of-privacy-by -design-starts-now.

53. Ibid.

54. Alexandra Deschamps-Sonsino, "Designing Security into the Internet of Things," *GigaOm*, October 3, 2013, http://gigaom.com/2013/10/03/designing-security-into -the-internet-of-things.

55. Andrew Clearwater, "The Evolving Privacy Profession: Analysing History and Prospects," *Data Protection Law & Policy* (October 2013): 13. ("The outlook for privacy professionals has never been better. The growth of privacy challenges will continue to support the need for privacy expertise.")

56. Kenneth A. Bamberger and Deirdre K. Mulligan, "New Governance Chief Privacy Officers, and the Corporate Management of Information Privacy in the United States: An Initial Inquiry," *Law & Public Policy* 33, no. 477 (2011).

57. International Association for Privacy Professionals, "About the IAPP," https://www.privacyassociation.org/about_iapp.

58. Kenneth A. Bamberger and Deirdre K. Mulligan, "Privacy on the Books and on the Ground," *Stanford Law Review* 63 (2011): 260.

59. See generally Thierer, *Parental Controls*.

60. Thierer, "Achieving Internet Order."

61. See generally Adam Thierer, "Can We Adapt to the Internet of Things?," *Privacy Perspectives*, IAPP, June 19, 2013, https://www.privacyassociation.org/privacy_perspectives/post/can_we_adapt_to_the_internet_of_things.

62. Bamberger and Mulligan, "Privacy on the Books," 247.

63. Ibid.

64. Ibid.

65. Ibid.

66. Mark Fleming, "What Is 3D Printing? An Overview," *3D Printer*, accessed December 14, 2015, http://www.3dprinter.net/reference/what-is-3d-printing.

67. See Imran Ali, "The Future of Work: From Bits to Atoms," *GigaOm*, February 10, 2010, http://gigaom.com/2010/02/10/the-future-of-work-from-bits-to-atoms; www.3ders.org, "3D Printing Basics," http://www.3ders.org/3d-printing-basics.html.

68. Louis Columbus, "2015 Roundup of 3D Printing Market Forecasts and Estimates," *Forbes*, March 31, 2015, http://www.forbes.com/sites/louiscolumbus/2015/03/31/2015-roundup-of-3d-printing-market-forecasts-and-estimates.

69. John Biggs, "Gartner Estimates Home 3D Printer Shipments Will Grow 49% This Year," *TechCrunch*, October 3, 2013, http://techcrunch.com/2013/10/03/gartner-estimates-home-3d-printer-shipments-will-grow-49-this-year.

70. Gartner, "Gartner Says Worldwide Shipments of 3D Printers to Reach More Than 490,000 in 2016," press release, September 29, 2015, http://www.gartner.com/newsroom/id/3139118.

71. T. J. McCue, "$4.1 Billion Industry Forecast in Crazy 3D Printing Stock Market," *Forbes*, July 30, 2015, http://www.forbes.com/sites/tjmccue/2015/07/30/4-1-billion-industry-forecast-in-crazy-3d-printing-stock-market.

72. Brian Proffitt, "How We'll 3D-Print the Internet of Things," *ReadWrite*, October 2, 2013, http://readwrite.com/2013/10/02/3d-printing-internet-of-things#awesm=~oj7KcYZXH93jxD.

73. Data provided to author from *Shapeways*. On file with author.

74. Esther Dyson, "3D Fantasies," *Project Syndicate*, July 24, 2013, http://www.project-syndicate.org/commentary/how-3d-printing-will-change-the-world-by-esther-dyson.

75. Proffitt, "How We'll 3D-Print."

76. Alexander Howard, "6 Amazing 3D-Printed Body Parts That Changed Patients' Lives," *Huffington Post*, October 9, 2015, http://www.huffingtonpost.com /entry/3d-printed-body-parts_560ed88ce4b076812701f9b7; Jerome Groopman, "Print Thyself," *New Yorker*, November 24, 2014, http://www.newyorker.com /magazine/2014/11/24/print-thyself.

77. "3-D Printed Device Helps Children with Rare Breathing Disorder," *Voice of America*, May 3, 2015, http://learningenglish.voanews.com/content/three-d-printed -device-rare-breathing-disorder/2744108.html.

78. Mike Murphy, "Doctors Have Implanted a 3D-Printed Ribcage in an Actual Human Being," *Quartz*, September 11, 2015, http://qz.com/500409/doctors-have-implanted -a-3d-printed-ribcage-in-an-actual-human-being.

79. Sara Breselor, "Man Saves Wife's Sight by 3D Printing Her Tumor," *Make*, January 14, 2015, http://makezine.com/2015/01/14/hands-on-health-care.

80. Andrea Chang, "With Ingenuity and a 3-D Printer, Group Changes Lives," *Los Angeles Times*, April 25, 2014, http://www.latimes.com/business/la-fi-c1-3d -printing-prosthetics-20140425-m-story.html.

81. See http://enablingthefuture.org/about.

82. Robert Graboyes, "How to Print Yourself a New Hand," *CNN*, October 24, 2014, http://www.cnn.com/2014/10/24/opinion/graboyes-3-d-printer-prosthetics.

83. Thierer, "Right to Try."

84. Giulio Coraggio, "Top 3 Legal Issues of 3D Printing!," *Technology's Legal Edge*, September 7, 2015, http://www.technologyslegaledge.com/2015/09/07/top-3 -legal-issues-of-3d-printing.

85. See Deven R. Desai and Gerard N. Magliocca, "3D Printers: The Next Intellectual Property Game Changer," *Philly.com*, October 21, 2013, http://www.philly.com /philly/news/science/3D_printers_The_next_intellectual_property_game_changer. html; Matt Schruers, "3D Printing: Sorry, This Seat Is Reserved," *DisCo (Disruptive Competition)*, February 14, 2013, http://www.project-disco.org/intellectual -property/021413-3d-printing-sorry-this-seat-is-reserved.

86. Dara Kerr, "3D-Printed Guns May Face Regulations, Bans in New York," *CNet.com*, June 13, 2013, http://news.cnet.com/8301-11386_3-57589294-76/3d-printed-guns -may-face-regulations-bans-in-new-york.

87. Wildavsky, *Searching for Safety*, 183. ("Regulation, because it deals with the general rather than with the particular, necessarily results in forbidding some actions that might be beneficial. Regulators cannot devise specifications sufficiently broad to serve as guidelines for every contingency without also limiting some actions that might increase safety. Because regulation is anticipatory, regulators frequently guess wrong about which things are dangerous; therefore, they compensate by blanket prohibitions.")

88. Philip K. Howard, "Radically Simplify Law," Cato Institute, *Cato Online Forum*, http://www.cato.org/publications/cato-online-forum/radically-simplify-law.

89. de Sola Pool, *Technologies of Freedom*, 231.

90. Richard Epstein, *Simple Rules for a Complex World* (Cambridge, MA: Harvard University Press, 1995).

91. See Villasenor, "Products Liability and Driverless Cars," 7–14.

92. Villasenor, "Who Is at Fault?"

93. Peter Fleischer, "Privacy-Litigation: Get Ready for an Avalanche in Europe," *Peter Fleischer: Privacy . . . ?*, October 26, 2012, http://peterfleischer.blogspot.com/2012 /10/privacy-litigation-get-ready-for.html?m=1.

94. Ibid. ("Within hours of any newspaper headline [accurate or not] alleging any sort of privacy mistake, a race begins among privacy class action lawyers to find a plaintiff and file a class action. Most of these class actions are soon dismissed, or settled as nuisance suits, because most of them fail to be able to demonstrate any 'harm' from the alleged privacy breach. But a small percentage of privacy class actions do result in large transfers of money, first and foremost to the class action lawyers themselves, which is enough to keep the wheels of the litigation-machine turning.")

95. Antone Gonsalves, "Courts Widening View of Data Breach Damages, Lawyers Say," *CSO Online*, October 29, 2012, http://www.csoonline.com/article/720128/courts -widening-view-of-data-breach-damages-lawyers-say.

96. For example, in October 2012, the web analytics company KISSmetrics agreed to settle a class action lawsuit associated with its use of "supercookies," which tracked users online without sufficient notice or choice being given beforehand. The firm agreed to pay each consumer who was part of the suit $2,500. See Wendy Davis, "KISSmetrics Settles Supercookies Lawsuit," *Online Media Daily*, October 19, 2012, http://www.mediapost.com/publications/article/185581/kissmetrics-settles -supercookies-lawsuit.html#ixzz2A306a5mq.

97. See, for example, Va. Code Ann. § 18.2-130 Peeping or spying into dwelling or enclosure.

98. See J. Howard Beales III, "The FTC's Use of Unfairness Authority: Its Rise, Fall, and Resurrection," Federal Trade Commission, June 2003, http://www.ftc.gov /speeches/beales/unfair0603.shtm; J. Thomas Rosch, "Deceptive and Unfair Acts and Practices Principles: Evolution and Convergence," speech at the California State Bar, Los Angeles, CA, May 18, 2007, http://www.ftc.gov/speeches/rosch /070518evolutionandconvergence.pdf; Andrew Serwin, "The Federal Trade Commission and Privacy: Defining Enforcement and Encouraging the Adoption of Best Practices," *San Diego Law Review* 48 (Summer 2011).

99. 15 U.S.C. § 45(a).

100. Federal Trade Commission, *Policy Statement on Unfairness*, 104 F.T.C. 949, 1070 (1984) 15 U.S.C. § 45.

101. Ibid.

102. FTC, *Protecting Consumer Privacy in an Era of Rapid Change: Recommendations for Businesses and Policymakers* (Washington, DC: Federal Trade Commission, 2012), i–ii, http://ftc.gov/os/2012/03/120326privacyreport.pdf.

103. See, for example, Health Insurance Portability and Accountability Act (HIPAA) of 1996, Pub. L. 104-191, 110 Stat. 1936 (1996).

104. See, for example, Truth in Lending Act, 15 U.S.C. §§ 1601-1667(f) (2006); Fair Credit Reporting Act of 1970, 15 U.S.C. §§ 1681-1681(u) (2006).

105. See, for example, Children's Online Privacy Protection Act (COPPA) of 1998, 15 U.S.C. § 6501 (2006).

106. Christopher Wolf, "Targeted Enforcement and Shared Lawmaking Authority as Catalysts for Data Protection" (BNA Privacy and Security Law Report, October 25,

2010), 3, http://www.justice.gov.il/NR/rdonlyres/8D438C53-82C8-4F25-99F8
-E3039D40E4E4/26451/Consumer_WOLFDataProtectionandPrivacyCommissioners
.pdf. ("At the state level, legislatures have become the proving grounds for new
statutory approaches to privacy regulation. Some of these developments include
the enactment of data security breach notification laws . . . as well as highly detailed
data security laws, enacted largely in response to data breaches. This partnership
has resulted in a set of robust standards for the protection of personal data.")

107.   Thierer, *Parental Controls*, 19, 41–42.

108.   Ibid., 22.

109.   For a debate about these proposals, see John Palfrey and Adam Thierer, "Dialogue:
The Future of Online Obscenity and Social Networks," *Ars Technica*, March 5, 2009,
http://arstechnica.com/tech-policy/news/2009/03/a-friendly-exchange-about-the
-future-of-online-liability.ars.

110.   See generally Saul Levmore and Martha C. Nussbaum, eds., *The Offensive Internet:
Speech, Privacy, and Reputation* (Cambridge, MA: Harvard University Press, 2010).

111.   Thierer, "Greatest of All Internet Laws."

112.   Joe Kennedy, "An Ever-Growing Jungle: Rethinking the U.S. Regulatory Process,"
International Economy (Spring 2015), http://www.itif.org/publications/2015/06/22
/ever-growing-jungle-rethinking-us-regulatory-process. ("It is true that the benefits
of regulation are often hard to measure. But that is not a license for bad regulation.
Agencies need to be diligent in making sure that the benefits of new rules exceed
the costs and disclosing the major assumptions behind their analysis.")

113.   This section adapted from Thierer, "Benefit-Cost Analysis."

114.   Sunstein, *Laws of Fear*, 46.

115.   Ibid., 45–46.

116.   Upon retirement, former Twitter CEO Dick Costolo noted: "I can't think of an example
where regulation didn't have unintended consequences, and I'm unable to conceive of
a regulatory body that will be swift enough to deal with the constantly evolving issues
of ethics, communication and technology. I just don't think it's possible." Quoted in
Alexei Oreskovic, "Twitter's CEO Signs off with a Warning: 'Regulation Is a Threat to
Free Speech,'" *Business Insider*, June 30, 2015, http://www.businessinsider.com
/twitter-ceo-dick-costolo-warns-about-free-speech-2015-6#ixzz3eeNDqyf6.

117.   See Dudley and Brito, *Regulation: A Primer*, 97–98. ("The cost of a regulation is the
opportunity cost—whatever desirable things society gives up in order to get the
good things the regulation produces. The opportunity cost of alternative approaches is the appropriate measure of costs. This measure should reflect the benefits
foregone when a particular action is selected and should include the change in consumer and producer surplus."); Ellig and McLaughlin, "Regulatory Analysis in 2008."

118.   See Richard B. Belzer, "Risk Assessment, Safety Assessment, and the Estimation of
Regulatory Benefits" (Mercatus Working Paper, Mercatus Center at George Mason
University, Arlington, VA, 2012), 5, http://mercatus.org/publication/risk-assessment
-safety-assessment-and-estimation-regulatory-benefits.

119.   White House, Office of Information and Regulatory Affairs, *Regulatory Impact
Analysis: A Primer* (Washington, DC, 2011), 2, http://www.whitehouse.gov/sites
/default/files/omb/inforeg/regpol/circular-a-4_regulatory-impact-analysis-a
-primer.pdf.

120.   Ibid.

121.   Ibid.

122.   Ibid.

123.   Ibid., 7.

124.   Ibid., 2, 5.

125.   White House, *Regulatory Impact Analysis*, 3.

126.   Ibid., 3–4.

CONCLUSION
IT'S ABOUT FREEDOM, PROGRESS, AND PROSPERITY

1.   Robert Nisbet, *History of the Idea of Progress* (New Brunswick, NJ: Transaction Publishers, 1994), 236.

2.   Hayek, *Constitution of Liberty*, 29.

3.   Karl Popper, *The Poverty of Historicism* (London: Routledge, 1957, 2002), 146–7.

4.   George Gilder, *Wealth & Poverty: A New Edition for the 21st Century* (Washington, DC: Regnery Publishing, 2012), 329.

5.   Gilder, *Wealth & Poverty*, 326.

6.   Clay Shirky, *Here Comes Everybody: The Power of Organizing without Organizations* (New York: Penguin Press, 2008), 298.

7.   Hayek, *Constitution of Liberty*, 41.

8.   Ridley, *Rational Optimist*, 276.

9.   Ibid.

10.   While "it is difficult to know exactly in which direction technological change will move and how significant it will be," Joel Mokyr reminds us that "something can be learned from the past, and it tells us that such pessimism is mistaken. The future of technology is likely to be bright." Joel Mokyr, "The Next Age of Invention," *City Journal* (Winter 2014), http://www.city-journal.org/2014/24_1_invention.html.

11.   It is what Postrel was referring to when she centered her dynamist vision on "the unpredictable, spontaneous, and ever shifting, a pattern created by millions of unco-ordinated, independent decisions." See Postrel, *Future and Its Enemies*, xv.

12.   See Adam Thierer, "Our Conflict of Cyber-Visions," *Cato Unbound*, May 14, 2009, http://www.cato-unbound.org/2009/05/14/adam-thierer/our-conflict-cyber -visions.

13.   See Ellig and Lin, "A Taxonomy of Dynamic Competition Theories," 19. ("Schumpeterian competition is a dynamic vision. Because change requires time, the benefits of competition may not arrive immediately. Market participants may have to tolerate short-run inefficiencies in order to gain long-run efficiencies.")

14.   Frederick Ferré, *Philosophy of Technology* (Athens, GA: University of Georgia Press, 1988, 1995), 26.

15.   Downes, "Take Note Republicans and Democrats." ("Republicans and Democrats regularly invoke the rhetoric of innovation, entrepreneurship, and the transforma-tive power of technology. But in reality neither party pursues policies that favor the disruptors. Instead, where lawmakers once took a largely hands-off approach

to Silicon Valley, as the Internet revolution enters a new stage of industry transformation, the temptation to intervene, to usurp, to micromanage, to circumscribe the future—becomes irresistible.")

16. Michael Sacasas, "Borg Complex: A Primer," *Frailest Thing*, March 1, 2013, http://thefrailestthing.com/2013/03/01/borg-complex-a-primer.

INDEX

ABOUT THE AUTHOR

Adam Thierer is a senior research fellow with the Technology Policy Program at the Mercatus Center at George Mason University. He specializes in technology, media, Internet, and free-speech policies, with a particular focus on online safety and digital privacy. His writings have appeared in the *Wall Street Journal*, the *Economist*, the *Washington Post*, the *Atlantic*, and *Forbes*, and he has appeared on national television and radio. He also contributes to the *Technology Liberation Front*, a leading tech policy blog.

Thierer has authored or edited eight books on topics ranging from media regulation and child safety issues to the role of federalism in high-technology markets. He has served on several distinguished online safety task forces, including Harvard University's Internet Safety Technical Task Force and the federal government's Online Safety Technology Working Group, and he has testified numerous times on Capitol Hill.

Previously, Thierer was president of the Progress and Freedom Foundation, director of telecommunications studies at the Cato Institute, and a senior fellow at the Heritage Foundation. He received his MA in international business management and trade theory from the University of Maryland and his BA in journalism and political philosophy from Indiana University.